LITERATURE, RELIGION, AND POSTSECULAR STUDIES
LORI BRANCH, SERIES EDITOR

CLASHING CONVICTIONS

SCIENCE AND RELIGION
IN AMERICAN FICTION

ALBERT H. TRICOMI

THE OHIO STATE UNIVERSITY PRESS · COLUMBUS

Copyright © 2016 by The Ohio State University.
All rights reserved.

Library of Congress Cataloging-in-Publication Data
Names: Tricomi, Albert H., 1942– author.
Title: Clashing convictions : science and religion in American fiction / Albert H. Tricomi.
Other titles: Literature, religion, and postsecular studies.
Description: Columbus : The Ohio State University Press, [2016] | "2016 | Series: Literature, religion, and postsecular studies | Includes bibliographical references and index.
Identifiers: LCCN 2016009680 | ISBN 9780814213063 (cloth ; alk. paper) | ISBN 0814213065 (cloth ; alk. paper)
Subjects: LCSH: American fiction—History and criticism. | Science in literature. | Religion in literature.
Classification: LCC PS374.S33 T75 2016 | DDC 813/.509382—dc23
LC record available at http://lccn.loc.gov/2016009680

Cover design by Martyn Schmoll
Text design by Juliet Williams
Type set in Palatino LT

♾ The paper used in this publication meets the minimum requirements of the American National Standard for Information Sciences—Permanence of Paper for Printed Library Materials. ANSI Z39.48–1992.

9 8 7 6 5 4 3 2 1

To our grandchildren,
Carter, Julia, Charlie, Anna, Miriam, Kate, and Sam

CONTENTS

	Acknowledgments	ix
INTRODUCTION	Terminology and Purpose	1

PART 1 INTERNAL STATES OF BELIEF AND UNBELIEF

CHAPTER 1	Emergent Formations of the Science-Religion Binary: Sara Orne Jewett's *A Country Doctor,* Edward Eggleston's *The Faith Doctor,* Milton Scott's *Henry Elwood,* and Henry Adams's *Esther*	31
CHAPTER 2	The New Biblical Criticism and Darwinism: Harold Frederic's *The Damnation of Theron Ware*	53
CHAPTER 3	An American Response to Darwinism: James Lane Allen's *The Reign of Law*	72
CHAPTER 4	An Enlightenment Critique of Religious Mania: W. D. Howells's *The Leatherwood God*	92

PART 2 SECULARISM RESURGENT

CHAPTER 5	A Research Scientist's Religion: Sinclair Lewis's *Arrowsmith*	115
CHAPTER 6	Satirizing Fundamentalist Education and Revivalist Preachers: Sinclair Lewis's *Elmer Gantry*	135
CHAPTER 7	Transhistorical Parable: Jerome Lawrence and Robert E. Lee's *Inherit the Wind*	156

PART 3	**A POSTSECULAR AGE?**	
CHAPTER 8	Contemporary Perspectives: James Scott Bell's *The Darwin Conspiracy* and the Soul of America	181
	Bibliography	199
	Index	219

ACKNOWLEDGMENTS

THE IMPETUS FOR my writing a book on this subject dates back to the later years of my academic career, in the 1990s, when I served as Binghamton University's vice provost for undergraduate studies. At that time the university undertook to reform its curriculum in general education by creating a more integrated undergraduate experience. As part of this initiative, I became the principal investigator for a large National Science Foundation grant, written mainly by my colleagues in science, Anna Tan Wilson and Wayne Jones, for "Science Across the Curriculum." In later years "SxC," as it was called, became "Evolution Across the Curriculum," led by nationally recognized biologist David Sloan Wilson.

From this period, I began to think seriously about ways a literary-historical scholar and teacher such as I could foster the values of science while also giving voice in my work to the religious convictions held by many people of faith, then as now. As the book has evolved, I have sought to direct attention not only to those for whom religious faith conflicts with the knowledge produced by science but also to those for whom religious faith and scientific knowledge are not in conflict and are, at times, mutually supportive.

This book is also the result of other converging scholarly interests, including my disciplinary training in English and American literature and engagement with a reformed version of new historicism, which I have come to call *cultural historicism*. In particular, I theorize and then practice the ways in which fictional literary texts are capable of contributing to historical knowledge. I call the endeavor "Fiction as History." My last book, *Missionary Positions: Evangelicalism and Empire in American Fiction*, provided a foundation for my present involvement with evangelicalism and fundamentalism in American literature and culture. Out of that study has come this present project in an unexplored area of American studies, the impact of scientific thought (and discovery) on religious faith as revealed in American historical fiction.

Binghamton University has been my scholarly and teaching home for over four decades. Throughout these years I have experienced its forward-looking character and its unfailing support, for which I am most grateful. I feel the same way about the steady, often generous, support I have enjoyed from the Department of English. I feel a special debt of gratitude to my departmental colleague Alvin Vos for his encouragement as well as his multiple readings of my work and his valuable perspectives as a Christian. My Americanist colleague now at the University of Wyoming, Scott Henkel, and I had many valuable discussions about our interdisciplinary work and the publishing process in America today. To Phil Kraft, a sociologist, and Conrad Krebs, a cardiologist, I owe a debt of thanks for their clear-sighted perceptions about the concepts in the book and, above all, their interest in my endeavors. I thank as well my longtime English department colleagues, Bernard Rosenthal and Michael Conlon, for their interest in and support of my work.

To John Weaver, a talented Binghamton PhD whose 2010 dissertation, "Jesus Freaks, Freakin' Jesus: Evangelicalism and American Literature," was published as an online resource in the Binghamton University library, I owe a debt of gratitude for alerting me to James Scott Bell's *The Darwinian Conspiracy*. My son-in-law, Michael Shiflett, and daughter, Elizabeth Tricomi, both neuroscientists at Rutgers University, Newark, contributed an important dimension to the making of this book by introducing me to Jonathan Weiner's *Time, Love, and Memory*, a biography that pays homage to Sinclair Lewis for his enduring influence on famed geneticist Seymour Benzer and his graduate students.

To my wife, Bet, I feel a special kind of gratitude. I thank her, once again, for her careful readings of the manuscript in its various stages and for all her patience in listening to and then discussing with me the various challenges this project has presented. The book has been a recurring subject of our dining room conversation for years.

I also wish to thank Sally Parry, editor of *The Sinclair Lewis Newsletter* at Illinois State University, for taking notice of my work in the *Newsletter* and subsequently for printing an essay of mine—"Modern Science and Biblical

Literalism in *Arrowsmith* and *Elmer Gantry*" (22:2, Spring 2014), 1, 4, 6, 8—which treats some of the material that appears in this book in my two chapters on Sinclair Lewis.

I particularly appreciate the suggestions and critique offered by my two outside readers. Their insights and suggestions made this a much better book. I am also happy to express my gratitude to the staff of The Ohio State University Press, most especially acquisitions editor Lindsay Martin for her wisdom and guidance, and Lori Branch, series editor of Literature, Religion, and Postsecular Studies, for her support of my project. All these people have made significant contributions in helping to shape the argument and sharpen my awareness of the variety of readers that this book is likely to attract. Responsibility for the final result, including errors and omissions, I recognize as my own.

INTRODUCTION

TERMINOLOGY AND PURPOSE

OUR UNDERSTANDING of the historical relationship between biblical and scientific conceptions of the world has been impeded by the shorthand terms we customarily use to define them—in a word, binaries. In common parlance, we speak of science as knowledge and religion as faith or belief. The trouble is, these terms are reductive in their disregard for the mutually constituted inter-relationships of each, and in their reification of science and religion, as if each stood for an unchanging, essential truth.[1] And yet the terms themselves are indispensable.

For instance, to most educated people, the term *scientific knowledge* seems unproblematically to refer to such activities as observation, experimentation, measurement, deduction, and replication, all of which are elements in the production of knowledge of the physical world. Historically, however, the term has sometimes meant little more than the formal study of an emergent area of human investigation whose object of inquiry has been defined and its procedures or methods systematized. This kind of disciplinary activity that took to itself the name of science appeared in the social

---

1. Derrida, "Faith and Knowledge," 1–6, 26–29.

scientific fields of paleontology, linguistics, and psychology from the latter half of the nineteenth century (except paleontology, which came earlier), and several novels of the period dramatize their findings. Thus the concept of scientific knowledge, as appears in this book, can and does refer to quite distinguishable activities. The one theoretical idea common to these varieties of scientific activity is that the findings they produce are, according to their own epistemology, provisional. This last stipulation means that *belief* in science signifies allegiance to its methods and its claims over time to produce knowledge of the physical world.

Similarly, the familiar phrase *Christian belief* has the limitation that it is used in conjunction with its binary, *knowledge*. For whereas knowledge is seen to belong to science (the world of the knowable), belief is seen to belong to the world of religion, the unseen and the transcendent, and thus relegated to the realm of the private or subjective. Inevitably, the question arises as to whether these two terms ought in fairness to be collapsed into one, as in *scientific and religious knowledge*. There are, after all, people of faith who attest to their experience of the divine, whether by way of inspiration or spiritual communication, as a form of knowledge. Thus in the body of my text, I do on several occasions speak of two ways of knowing, two epistemologies.

Moreover, the experience of the divine or, more simply, the spiritual world can be construed as knowledge, but knowledge of a different order from that provided by scientists, for the former is communicated directly as a personal experience and corroborated, not by experiment and replication, but by an inner conviction that rests ultimately on faith. By definition these experiences are intensely personal and difficult, if not impossible, to fully convey to others. We may call this *personal knowledge*, but since its truthfulness rests on a different foundation, I use the terms *belief* and *faith* analytically to identify the kind of knowing each term signifies.

In summoning these several considerations, it is not my intention to submerge the concept of knowing into the category of belief, or vice versa, as if the two are really interchangeable. Rather, my aim is to disrupt the reflexive associations attached to these binaries and, instead, to draw attention to the constructed nature of both. I should also point out that use of the term *faith* to describe the nature of religious knowing is by no means of my making, since it has been and continues to be widely employed in Bible-centered communities. One such community is an academic evangelical organization of scientists called the American Scientific Affiliation, which in the 1940s affirmed that "the whole Bible as originally given" is "the inspired word of

God, the only unerring guide of faith and conduct."[2] Similar asseverations appeared in the early twentieth century during the emergence of the fundamentalist movement, when a number of leading conservatives took the conciliatory position that Darwin's theory could at least partially be accommodated to Christian doctrine.[3] Given these self-descriptions, I employ the term *Bible-based belief* because it can apply, flexibly enough, to the beliefs of those who hold the Bible to be the foundation of Christian belief in the most general sense, scriptural literalists and, in a slightly more moderate sense, evangelicals who, although not literalists, revere the Bible as the *inerrant* or inspired word of God.[4]

Despite the diversity of the truth claims made by biblical literalists, all such claims rest on at least one of two very different foundations. The first is the faith-based concept of the Bible as the literal word of God transmitted directly to humankind, and the second, on the purportedly empirically based research produced by proponents of creation science, now morphed in intelligent design (ID). Their project is the material corroboration of research findings about the world that confirm the Bible's authority; claims contrary to biblical authority, it should not be forgotten, are false. Inasmuch as this research program makes empirical claims to scientific knowledge, it must compete for acceptance with mainline scientific methods and procedures. In the last chapter of this book, on the early twenty-first-century fundamentalist novel *The Darwin Conspiracy*, I describe the way that proponents of ID, as distinguished from scientists in paleontology, geology, and other evolutionary disciplines, have increasingly come into direct conflict, since the respective epistemologies of each group appear to be radically incompatible with one another.

The incompatibility of these belief systems raises the question of why I have chosen as my chief descriptive term *clash* or *clashing* instead of the often-used words *warfare* or *battle*. The reasons are several. As used in the title of this book, the phrase *Clashing Convictions* is an attempt to avoid the binary opposition between that which belongs to knowledge (science) and that which belongs to faith or belief (religion). Also, while clashing perspectives signify conflict, they are not polar binaries. Moreover, on balance, I think that the novelistic evidence on the relationship between science and religion comports better with the less dramatic word than with *warfare*.

---

2. Stephens and Giberson, *Anointed*, 47.
3. Ibid., 46.
4. Worthen, *Apostles of Reason*, 53–54.

Even more important, this *clash* has the virtue of flexibility because it offers a way of referencing both external conditions of debate and conflict as well as more cerebral and internal states, expressed in such usages as the *clash* of ideas, attitudes, and feelings. Certainly the novels that appeared prior to 1916 manifest this kind of subjectivity. In *The Reign of Law*, for example, David is the most inward of heroes; he internalizes the clash of competing worlds. Even in his dark months of religious doubt, his troubling feelings and ideas are best described as clashing.

Throughout this book, I have striven to employ a nomenclature appropriate to the descriptive and analytic needs of this study. I should also make clear that my orientation to the novels, play, and films I treat is that there is no single, overarching meta-narrative that governs all these works; in fact, just the opposite, as the last two chapters demonstrate. But I make the claim that they are all marked by ideology. By *ideology*, the primary meaning I intend, following Foucault, is that the practices and knowledge that constitute science and religion as discursive formations (unstable and shifting) are all implicated in a dynamic that Foucault called *power/knowledge*, for when knowledge is linked to power it becomes per force ideological.[5] In this context, "ideology is neither the opposite of truth nor the reflection of an infrastructure" (as in Marxist criticism), nor is ideology either bad or good; it is the inescapable consequence of knowledge being linked to, or accompanied by, power.[6] In this principal regard, the purposes of literary criticism are to uncover the embedded ideology in the work and to assess the efficacy of that work—here fiction—as it functions in culture. But ideology is not always concealed, as when people say that a work is ideological because it functions as propaganda. This charge, repeatedly lodged against *Elmer Gantry* by its detractors, was itself ideological because it sought to undermine the novel's authority, and is evaluated on just this ground.

Since the relationships between scientific and religious outlooks have long been understood in terms of binary oppositions and since I have wrestled with them, it seems appropriate to conclude this section with a theoretical-historical summary of the reasons lodged against their use. What follows after this is then a methodological account of my own practices in interpreting the works of fiction in this book.

From the eighteenth through the twentieth centuries, the history of the science-religion binary reveals that at one time it was not a binary at all, because religion in the Western world suffused all inquiries into the nature of

---

5. See Foucault, *Power/Knowledge*, and Lemert and Gillan, *Michel Foucault*, 59–60.
6. Lemert and Gillan, *Michel Foucault*, 112.

the world.[7] Only with the Enlightenment did the reformist philosophes, in an effort to curtail the domain of the clerics, whom they held in contempt, begin referring to the study of nature as separate from the study of God, or theology.[8] Ever since, this has meant that science defines itself in relation to religion or faith, each related to the other and bearing in some degree the religious qualities from which science originated, while religion in turn retained its theological investment in the study of God's created world.[9] Theorists today see this binary as a subset of a more comprehensive binary—the secular and the religious—in which the latter term, according to Talal Asad, is devalued and relegated of the category of "myth."[10] With equal bluntness, Charles Taylor states that from the seventeenth century to this day, "the secular was, in its new sense, opposed to any claim made in the name of something transcendent of this world."[11] The fact that we are aware of these alternatives signifies that we live in a reality constituted by the secular-religious binary. Helpfully, Lori Branch addresses the current situation comprehensively, stating,

> Contemporary theories of religion increasingly dissociate religious faith from the binaries rationality/irrationality and knowledge/superstition, understanding these as Enlightenment paradigms that confined religious experience either to "rational religion" (morality) or irrational "mysticism." Religion or religiousness is instead becoming associated with the realm of interpersonal relations, ethics, and faith that is both made possible and necessitated by the epistemological indeterminacy that has been the concern of much postmodern philosophy.[12]

For the reasons just stated, my own treatment of the novels, films, and play in this book strives to avoid such binaries. However, I find that it is not always possible, or even desirable, to ignore the cultural power of several

---

7. Calhoun, Juergensmeyer, and VanAntwerpen, introduction to *Rethinking Secularism*, 7, and Taylor, *Secular Age*, 3. On secularism in relation to the religious/secular binary, see Modern, *Secularism*, 8–10.

8. Calhoun, Juergensmeyer, and VanAntwerpen, introduction to *Rethinking Secularism*, 7.

9. On the effect that each pole of a binary has on the other and on the contingencies that make binary relationships dynamic—an important theoretical point for my own treatment of binaries depends—see Kaufmann, "The Religious, the Secular," 610–11.

10. Asad, *Formations of the Secular*, 23. On this page, Asad also lists other related binaries. See also Calhoun, Juergensmeyer, and VanAntwerpen, introduction to *Rethinking Secularism*, 8, 21.

11. Taylor, "Western Secularity," 32, 36.

12. Branch, *Rituals of Spontaneity*, 246n46.

novels that deliberately employ binary oppositions. From the late nineteenth century, when novelists began to juxtapose scientific and religious beliefs, most of them inherited the prejudicial assumptions that accompanied the binaries they treated. However, few employed them uncritically or let the binaries they used remain unquestioned or unaltered. These diverse conditions lead me to present several distinctive approaches according to the need.

In Henry Adams's *Esther*, in which binary oppositions are clearly in play, I call attention to the crucial places where such oppositions give way to more productive, nonpolar alternatives, as in the novel's conclusion, wherein the heroine rejects both an Episcopal minister's creed and that of a scientist, choosing instead a third path—spiritualism. Among the most partisan of novels, Lewis's *Arrowsmith* expresses a transparently secular ideology, but, I argue, that ideology draws much of its force through Lewis's appropriation of a religious imagery and rhetoric to express the exultant experiences of the scientific researcher. In this way, my method works to disrupt a straightforward reading and reveals the novel to be a more complex cultural product than would otherwise appear. Similarly, my examination of *Inherit the Wind* interrogates Drummond's courtroom peroration on freedom to think. In particular, it points out the striking contradiction that the speech is excessively emotional, even apocalyptic, and yet it is predicated on the lawyer's argument that identifies the secular with the rational and the religious with the irrational and the barbaric.

At least two of the novels reveal a scientific discipline or profession in the process of separating and distinguishing itself from formerly unquestioned spiritual or religious practices. *The Faith Doctor*, for instance, pits Christian Science healing practices against those of licensed physicians, based on the germ theory of infectious diseases. In this case, my strategy is to identify the empirical foundation of Eggleston's viewpoint while still calling attention to the novelist's prejudicial representation of the faith healer's character—her avarice and fraudulence, each of which undercuts the healer's philosophy and practice along with the person herself. A more sophisticated example of this process of translating putative miraculous events into secularizing terms is Howells's *The Leatherwood God*. I approach this novel by acknowledging that it is presented from a dominant, wholly secular standpoint but go on to argue that it deserves close study because the recontextualization of religious experiences is made visible. I therefore view the novel as making a valuable contribution to intellectual history as the reader discovers the process whereby a new academic discipline—psychology—emerges from Howells's appropriation of his historical sources.

On a cautionary note, I observe that these works do not manifest a high degree of technical scientific expertise. With the notable exception of *Arrowsmith*, on which Lewis collaborated with bacteriologist Paul de Kruif (who later became a renowned popular science writer),[13] these novels, along with *Inherit the Wind*, display a general, nonspecialist's command of scientific concepts and procedures. Their strengths, however, reside in their penetrating representation of the clash of ideas generated by the great controversies created by evolution, the higher biblical criticism, and the increasing authority of scientific methodologies.

FICTION AS HISTORICAL EVIDENCE

The general subject of this book has attracted large numbers of historians of science and of religion, whose work has shaped our way of understanding the history of the science-religion conflict in America. Yet one important kind of evidence has not been explored: the contributions that novelists and playwrights have made to this ongoing cultural transformation. By examining a select group of American novels, a play, and several films devoted to the clash between science and religion, I seek at the most basic level to serve the humanistic objective of bringing readers in many fields—literature, history, science, and religion—to a greater appreciation of the social issues and personal struggles that people of faith as well as converts to an empirical (rather than a God-centered) worldview have experienced.

More ambitiously, I wish to demonstrate that this body of literature offers access to a kind of historical understanding that would otherwise remain largely unexplored. Whereas most historians concern themselves, as well they should, with event-based occurrences as revealed in legislation, public statements, speeches, biographies, debates, personal testimony, and so forth, this book draws attention to a body of literature in its historical context. A second, complementary goal is to treat these works of fiction as occupying a public space and exhibiting from fresh perspectives various secular and theological ideologies intended to move public opinion. In this latter sense, these novels, plays, and screenplays also function rhetorically and persuasively in a wider historical context. Considered together, these works present themselves for interpretation and provide access to an affective kind of historical understanding, one that is distinct from traditional historiography but also part of our social history, and thus contributory to the whole.

---

13. Schorer, Afterword to *Arrowsmith*, 433–34.

Strangely, from the 1880s, when several American novels unapologetically introduced the topical subject of the opposition between science and religion, through the early twenty-first century, the total output of such novels appears to have been ten, not including the play *Inherit the Wind* and several film versions of this fiction. By contrast, from the early 1840s, Victorian England produced about fifty novels that treat the impact of science on faith. This English canon has been studied in two notable literary-historical books; American novels on this subject not at all. That is to say, the American novels have never before been gathered together for examination. This situation creates fresh opportunity and at the same time raises important questions about how these works are to be constituted into a body. Why has there been no study of these American novels before, and of what quality and cultural importance are they, particularly in comparison to the larger body of Victorian literature?

Over the course of this book, I strive to show that this body of American fiction comprises a dramatized narrative history of the highly fraught relationship between emergent scientific ideas and traditional religious ways of viewing the world. At the end of this chapter, I present an overview of this body of work and of its quality, but before doing so, readers will find helpful the subsections that follow, since they offer a further orientation to methodology and historical contexts. The first subsection, in which we are already placed, explains my use of a methodology I call cultural historicism, which treats this historical fiction as contributing to our historical understanding. The second subsection presents changing concepts of science and the theological responses to these changes from the late eighteenth century through to the mid-twentieth century (the time periods treated in these works of historical fiction). The third describes the character of the Victorian novels on faith and doubt, not only because these novels preceded, for the most part, the American ones, but because they help to establish, by contrast, the distinctive character of this American fiction. The final section of the introduction orients the reader to integrating themes that run across these works.

This body of American fiction is best examined, I believe, through an approach I have employed before, *cultural historicism*.[14] The method emphasizes the embeddedness of the work of literature in such disciplinary contexts as history, biology, linguistics, sociology, philosophy, and theology. The term denotes the practice of treating the literary work not merely as the

---

14. Cultural historicism has its roots in new historicism, as demonstrated below in the work of Greenblatt's *Shakespearean Negotiations*. On cultural historicist practice, see Tricomi, *Missionary Positions*, 14–15, and *Reading Tudor-Stuart Texts*, 1–17.

product of its historical circumstances, and surely not as a mere reflection of its historical context, but as a productive cultural phenomenon in itself. The literary work thus functions recursively; it participates in the making of culture even as it is produced by culture. As applied to this set of novels, my cultural-historicist practice considers each published work as already embedded in a discourse that generates, to borrow new historicist Stephen Greenblatt's terminology, an additional degree of "circulating social energy."[15] The extent of this social energy, itself a cultural product, may be gauged by the novel's *symbolic capital*, a term used to refer to the critical esteem the work generates.[16] Measures of this esteem include the novel's critical reception and comments in private letters, sermons, and notices in newspapers. This method reveals that many of these novels possess *cultural capital*, a form of energy that exceeds the strictly *symbolic* esteem that may accrue to them from literary critics.[17] In this case, the novel obeys mass-market forces, and its social energy may also be measured economically by appearances on best-seller lists and from sales figures. This energy dissipates over time, but if readers in later generations (including readers of this book) discover in these fictional works new social significance, this literature acquires renewed social energy and, like a set of heated electrons, over-leaps its original boundary, or field, to function in a new context.

Then too, all the novels treated in this book are embedded in a centuries-long contest between those educational institutions that promote scientific learning and those that were founded to promote Bible-based or, more broadly, religious learning. They thus offer a measure of continuity between past and present, providing perspectives on our present situation. In this way, the nineteenth- and twentieth-century novels treated in these chapters participate in a diachronic recreation of cultural history and are thus part of a *usable past*. As Lois Zamora has theorized it, a usable past is the process by which history becomes *valuable*, attains relevance, by virtue of its being available to constitute and give warrant for present needs.[18]

---

15. Greenblatt, *Shakespearean Negotiations*, 1–20. Sociological theorist Bourdieu employs the terms *social capital* and *social energy* in respect to literary and artistic value in *Cultural Production*, 54, 81. The link between Bourdieu's and Greenblatt's theoretical work is well recognized. See Randal Johnson, "Introduction: Pierre Bourdieu," 19.

16. Bourdieu, *Cultural Production*, 29–73.

17. The terms *cultural capital* and *symbolic capital* are drawn from Guillory, *Cultural Capital*, viii–xiii. Guillory's work depends upon and critiques Bourdieu's own. For example, Bourdieu does not make provision for aesthetic works that transcend their field by actively participating in the formation of social thought. See Guterman, "Field Tripping," 565.

18. Zamora, *Usable Past*, ix.

The novel as a genre also has the capacity to facilitate interdisciplinary understanding. Although it is a stylized, complex form of communication that may be studied as an autonomous artistic product, the novel also possesses special attributes useful to cultural historicists. As a form of historical evidence, the novel differs from the scientific treatise, the tract, and the sermon in that these latter forms are solely monologic or univocal forms of public pronouncement, useful to documentary historians but limited in respect to understanding the cultural processes that produce them. By contrast, the novel is a protean form that combines public discourse with the subjective thought that we associate with diaries and private letters. But insofar as it participates in public discourse, the novel enters the field of ideology as it seeks to influence public perception of controversial issues.

So it is with the works of this study. Further contributing to the function of these novels as historical texts is the fact that substantial portions of them are narrated, thereby affording readers the opportunity to examine the author's way of shaping his topical or historical materials. Then too, since a number of these novels are set in the not very distant past, they open a window both on the period that the novelist depicts as well as the novelist's own period—and thus on the interrelationships between these periods. In the well-expressed formulation of Philip Stevick, "The novel, also, more than any other genre, can give form to a set of attitudes regarding society, history, and the general culture of which the novel is a part."[19] Similar arguments may be made on behalf of plays and film, since they too present attitudes and affective states that bear on our understanding of contemporary issues. Even when the subject treated appears to be a creative construct, the work of fiction is important in disclosing a contemporary understanding of the past it represents. Fictional though they are, novel, play, and screenplay are embedded in the doings of the world and are material products of it.

From this vantage point, such fictional artifacts furnish a distinctive kind of historical evidence not always granted by historiographers. For example, in representing the process by which ideas about the natural world began to be perceived as incompatible with a number of religious convictions (such as those named above), novels and even plays or screenplays can register the private struggles of the self when confronted by ideas that challenge core beliefs. They can also show the individual attempting to negotiate dearly held personal beliefs in an ever-shifting public space, or that person in the process of being inwardly transformed.[20] In this way, the novel

---

19. Stevick, *Theory of the Novel*, 3.
20. See Tricomi, *Missionary Positions*, 15–17.

clearly partakes of the history of consciousness, which is a legitimate object of social-historical study, although it is largely ignored or dismissed by documentary historians focused on an empirical practice of history.[21]

It also participates in a larger process that religious studies scholars reference as *the secular*, a "central modern epistemic category" that José Casanova identifies as functioning "to construct, codify, grasp, and experience a realm or reality differentiated from 'the religious,'" such that "'the religious' and 'the secular' are always and everywhere mutually constituted."[22] In both these contexts, cultural historicism can enhance our understanding of the epistemic formations that emerged to distinguish science from religion,[23] for the novel, along with the play or screenplay, locates the field of conflict recursively, not merely in events but in the social setting where new ideas appear to challenge received beliefs and in the subjectivity of thought and feeling where belief is sustained or overthrown.

EVOLVING CONCEPTIONS OF SCIENCE AND THEOLOGY

The concepts of science employed in this book are neither static nor self-explanatory. Over time scientific methods and their objects of study have shifted in unexpected directions. Several notions of what constitutes scientific thinking belong to earlier periods and reference earlier conceptions of what knowledge is. For example, Matthew Braile, the skeptical lawyer in *The Leatherwood God*, is a historically situated model of early nineteenth-century Enlightenment rationality. He even carries around a copy of Thomas Paine's *Common Sense* (1776) and *The Age of Reason* (1794). As an advocate of Paine's radical Enlightenment views, he employs a mode of interpretation free of miracles or other transcendent explanation. By contrast, Allen's *The Reign of Law* locates its idea of science in an evolutionary worldview that is constituted both by Darwin's gradualism and Georges Cuvier's catastrophism as well as mechanistic notions of causation derived from Newtonian physics and Keplerian astronomy. This being so, it is important to distinguish one form of scientific inquiry from another.

---

21. For a fuller discussion of the limitations of documentary historicism, see Tricomi, *Reading Tudor-Stuart Texts*, 45–49.
22. Casanova, "The Secular," 54.
23. See Calhoun, "Secularism, Citizenship," 83, whose discussion of Jürgen Habermas affirms that both religious and secular orientations to the world "depend on strong epistemic and moral commitments."

The revolution in seventeenth-century astronomy altered the way people apprehended the world not only because it explained the heliocentric motions of the planets but, more precisely, because it did so through "celestial mechanics," revealing seemingly irrefutable laws that rested on mathematical, and especially geometrical, relationships. The precision of this mode of study, which depended upon exhaustive sets of data based on observation, vindicated a scientific ideal that yoked deductive principles (which Euclid's geometrical proofs illustrate) to experimental application.[24] This new model of investigation turned scientific inquiry of the natural world toward what Francis Bacon had called *natural history*. For Bacon science was not yet compartmentalized or professionalized as it is today. In what was in many ways a formative age of discovery in the seventeenth century, both amateurs and professionals, including theologians, scoured the earth for new information—"data," "facts"—which "natural philosophers" (but not Bacon) could interpret in terms of a teleology of providential design, whose object was to demonstrate God's great plan in filling the universe with organisms that were precisely created for the niche each filled.[25]

This providential teleology, which rested on a quite straightforward conception of facts, fostered an alliance between theology and science. The very terms that people used to signal the "union between natural history and natural theology" indicate that there was no inherent reason why their mutual investigations should be in conflict.[26] The cornerstone of this alliance was famously displayed by Cambridge clergyman William Paley, whose early nineteenth-century work, *Natural Theology,* presented a compendium of teleological illustrations showing how the capabilities of each species function to teach mankind moral habits and behaviors.[27] Paley's enduring argument that the human eye is in its complexity and perfection like a watch that only a benevolent designer, God, could have created, served many theologians and scientists well throughout the nineteenth century and beyond.[28]

---

24. Butterfield, *Origins of Modern Science*, 158.

25. On Bacon, natural history, and data collection, see Butterfield, *Modern Science*, 105, 127, and Bronowski, *Common Sense of Science*, 46–47.

26. Livingstone, *Darwin's Forgotten Defenders*, 111.

27. Paley, *Natural Theology* passim. See White, *Warfare of Science*, 1:42–43, for an account of the kind of moral and scientific arguments Paley and his predecessors employed.

28. On the eye's perfection, see Paley, *Natural Theology, with Illustrative Notes*, 2:253–57. For commentary on Paley's eye argument, see Ruse, *Evolution Wars*, 39, and Larson, *Evolution*, 91–92. John Greene, *American Science*, 15–16, points out that in nineteenth-century America, the difference between true and false science was one of attitude, not

This largely harmonious approach to the study of nature, in which an inchoate secularity still existed as part of Christian theology, was first threatened by a powerful Enlightenment movement in the eighteenth century that extended the methods of studying the natural world to burgeoning disciplines concerned in one way or another with human behavior. The French philosophes and particularly Voltaire spread the idea that where science marches ahead, superstition retreats. Science historian Peter Gay articulates this belief, stating that where dogma reigns, "dispute and mutual abomination" everywhere prevail, but where science advances, "an accumulation of knowledge is possible to which all reasonable men . . . [can] assent."[29] In practice, this method of investigation meant skepticism, along with data collection and rational analysis. These ideas, which reveal the emergence of scientific investigation as a nascent secular enterprise opposed to religious superstition and the ignorance that fed it, had as a point of origin opposition to the Catholic Church's largely unchecked temporal powers over affairs of state.[30]

Nowhere was this new scientific attitude applied more rigorously than in the study of the Bible. To it a completely naturalistic—not mythic, mystical, or miraculous—approach was applied. In philosophical terms, the proponents of naturalism rejected dualistic explanations of the physical world—that is, explanations that blended, joined, or presupposed metaphysical (e.g., spiritual) explanations to the operation of the physical world. Only naturalistic explanations were to be employed.[31] Thus when Friedrich Strauss composed his famous, methodologically revolutionary *Life of Jesus, Critically Examined* (1835), which George Eliot translated into English in 1846, readers discovered that the author rejected "religious and dogmatic presuppositions" as "unscientific"; instead he vowed to "keep aloof from bigotry and fanaticism."[32] When *A Primer on Assyriology* (1894) appeared, its author, A. H. Sayce (whose name Harold Frederic invokes in his novel), compiled a synchronous chronology of Assyrian and biblical events that put both historical accounts on an equal footing.[33] To these archaeological and

---

method: "The true scientist approached nature reverently," whereas "the false scientist" did not scruple to contradict "God's word."

29. Gay, *Enlightenment*, 163–64.

30. Unless otherwise noted, this account of the Enlightenment builds on Calhoun, Juergensmeyer, and VanAntwerpen, introduction to *Rethinking Secularism*, 7.

31. Drees, "Religious Naturalism and Science," 109–11.

32. Strauss, *Life of Jesus*, 1:4. The influence of Strauss's biography of Jesus in England and America dates from George Eliot's translation (1844–46). See Ashton, *German Idea*, 147–54. On the hermeneutics of Strauss's biography, see Frei, *Eclipse of Biblical Narrative*, 233–44.

33. Sayce, *Assyriology*, 125–26.

linguistic explorations Sayce applied the term *scientific*.[34] By the end of the nineteenth century, A. D. White, who was very much the product of Enlightenment thinking, could devote an entire section of his mammoth study of science's war with theology to the science of comparative philology, wherein he explained that the biblical account of how languages became dispersed—at the fall of the Tower of Babel—was at bottom no more than a national myth.[35] In the sense that all these endeavors subjected ancient literature and, most notably, the Bible, to the same methods of rational inquiry and social-scientific analysis as any other discipline, this form of investigation can be called *scientific*, an endeavor that in a larger sense is carried out in the service of the secular.

Among theologians, the strong tendency was to try to harmonize the new scientific evidence with scripture. Even among many educated evangelicals, the motivation to do away with myth and superstition and put biblical study on a firm scientific footing, in the sense just described, was and is strong.[36] For example, in the late nineteenth century, William Robertson Smith, a prominent American evangelical scholar, characterized his work as "progressive Biblical Science" and defended his results with the argument that "true Protestantism" has always stood against any effort "to limit the freedom of hermeneutic research or to determine beforehand what conclusions shall be drawn from the study of the sacred text."[37] Idealistic ministers such as Henry Ward Beecher were even more affirming. In scientific progress Beecher saw moral progress, both bringing humankind closer to God's kingdom.[38]

But as Lyell's geological and Darwin's biological studies gained influence in England and America, the former harmony between natural theology and natural science slowly began to turn into discord. In the mid-1870s Asa Gray, probably the most prominent American Darwinist along with geologist George Frederick Wright, later to be an eminent contributor to the interdenominational theological document called *The Fundamentals* (1910–15), made a valiant attempt to achieve concord.[39] But by the early 1880s a gaping rift appeared in many Protestant communities. When ordained

---

34. Ibid., 18.
35. White, *Warfare of Science*, 2:168–208.
36. Stephens and Giberson, *Anointed*, 49.
37. The quotations are from Smith, *Old Testament*, v, and his *Answer to the Form*, 63. For analysis, see Cameron, *Biblical Higher Criticism*, 232–33.
38. Marsden, *Fundamentalism*, 24.
39. James R. Moore, *Post-Darwinian Controversies*, 72, 269. On the content of the "fundamentals," see Livingstone, *Darwin's Forgotten Defenders*, 147–49.

Presbyterian minister and South Carolina College professor James Woodrow began to teach that Adam's body was probably created by evolutionary means though his soul was created by God, the rift attained national prominence. Despite Woodrow's insistence that nothing in his teaching contradicted scripture, he was subjected to a long trial by the Synod of South Carolina, which after years of litigation ended in his conviction for heresy and dismissal from his teaching position.[40]

The underlying basis of the increasingly contentious relationship between conservative theologians and Darwinian scientists issued from rival concepts of what constitutes scientific proof—indeed, of what science is. *The Origin of Species* radically expanded scientific methods by emphasizing the study of origins, histories, developments, and processes rather than mere classification.[41] Darwin also introduced novel concepts of investigation such as probability, chance, and uniqueness.[42] Furthermore, Darwin had also come to the conviction that good science invited hypothesis-making and often exhibited a rationalist component. That is, it need not offer direct empirical evidence of causes so long as the conclusions reached were *consilient*, which is to say, corroborated by different branches of knowledge. In defending his hypothesis of "Natural Selection," Darwin also adduced empirical evidence drawn from Robert Malthus, showing that just as human beings are in a struggle for existence, so are the whole animal and vegetable kingdoms.[43] By way of illustration, he argued that just as humans artificially breed animals for preferred traits, nature also operates by such a process of selection.[44] Darwin incorporated these empirical and rationalist arguments into his grand hypothesis that the underlying principle of evolution is natural selection and that this principle answers hitherto unexplained observations in embryology as well as biology, geology and paleontology. In brief, the argument showed consilience, inviting further experimentation in every scientific field.[45]

For scientists reared in the older tradition of naturalistic philosophy, in which data collection leading to teleological speculation was normal practice, Darwin's methods as well as his findings were, at the least, suspect. For

---

40. Numbers, *Darwinism*, 60–66, and Webb, *Evolution Controversy*, 34–35.

41. Russett, *Darwin in America*, 11.

42. Mayr, *One Long Argument*, 2. See also Mayr's sections on "Darwin's Scientific Method," 9–11, and "Darwinism as a New Methodology," 104–7.

43. Darwin, *Origin of Species*, 116–17.

44. Ibid., 148–49.

45. The accounts of "consilient conclusions" and, throughout this paragraph, of Darwin's empirical and rationalist arguments owe a great deal to Ruse, *Evolution-Creation Struggle*, 61, 72–75.

example, famed American naturalist Louis Agassiz alleged that Darwin's book, unable as it was to demonstrate intermediate fossil forms, violated the concept of science as "accumulated facts" organized into a descriptive body of knowledge.[46] In consequence, Agassiz's summary judgment was that *The Origin of Species* was "a scientific mistake, untrue in its facts, [and] unscientific in its method."[47] Treading this path as well, Seventh Day Adventists defined *true science* as based on *facts* that accord with the Bible.[48] Evaluating this reactionary orientation in 1925, James Simpson, a theologically oriented historian of science, felt obliged to write, "In their legitimate striving after purely inductive investigation, they forgot that the mere gathering of facts is not enough, that the drawing of conclusions is an essential part of the induction, and that a mass of bare facts, however enormous, does not constitute a science."[49]

By the early 1920s, conservative responses to the new science, bolstered by the waxing influence of the series of pamphlets called *The Fundamentals*, had hardened.[50] Aimed at shoring up the erosion of core principles of Christianity, these pamphlets reaffirmed the reality of God, the divinity of Christ, the Virgin birth, and the authority of the Bible. The list did not include the rejection of evolution and, as Stephens and Giberson observe, "nowhere was it presented as incompatible with the Christian faith," although it was not affirmed either.[51] Still, along with this retrenchment came a shift in the perception of the core challenge of Darwinism. In David Livingstone's words, "For the older generation the issue centered on the problem of [providential] design; for the younger it was the authority of the Bible" as the ultimate arbiter of truth.[52] Furthermore, defenders of scripture continued to resort to their older, factual understanding of scientific investigation. In the late twentieth century, creationist Henry Morris advocated just such a restricted understanding of what scientific knowledge is.[53] Countering Darwin's rationalist hypothesis-making, experiment-producing, evidence-corroborating methods, these thinkers denounced Darwinism along with other emerging sciences as speculative, hypothesis-weaving, unhistorical, unscientific, and

---

46. Agassiz, "On *The Origin of Species*," 13, 16. See Webb, *Evolution Controversy*, 11.
47. Agassiz, "On *The Origin of Species*," 17.
48. Numbers, *Darwinism*, 95.
49. Simpson, *Landmarks between Science and Religion*, 174.
50. Marsden, *Fundamentalism*, 118–23; Livingstone, *Darwin's Forgotten Defenders*, 147–51, and Webb, *Evolution Controversy*, 53.
51. Stephens and Giberson, *Anointed*, 46.
52. Livingstone, *Darwin's Forgotten Defenders*, 166.
53. Morris, *History of Modern Creationism*, 24–32.

tending toward atheism.⁵⁴ In this way the former alliance between natural theology and the natural sciences found itself in tatters. It was in this tense, unstable environment that the Victorian novels of faith and doubt and the somewhat later American novels on similar themes were composed.

A ROBUST VICTORIAN CANON

As I have indicated, this study strives to make its contribution to an interdisciplinary intellectual history through the lens of American fiction. Surprisingly, the subject of faith and doubt in its relationship to scientific ideas has received considerable attention among Victorian novelists from about 1840 and very little in American studies. Two extensive surveys of English novels have appeared on this topic: Robert Wolff's *Gains and Losses: Novels of Faith and Doubt in Victorian England* and Leo Henkin's *Darwinism in the English Novel*.⁵⁵ Excluding overlap, Henkin and Wolff together treat almost two hundred English novels on faith and doubt, of which about fifty are on the subject of science's impact on religion (a substantially smaller field than Wolff's purview of "faith and doubt"). By contrast, the number of American novels addressing this specific theme, as far as I have discovered, is ten.⁵⁶

The overview of the Victorian novels of faith and doubt that follows affords a basis of comparison with the American fiction writers as well as a historical context for such fiction. Nor should it be forgotten that without such a context, claims for the distinctiveness of American treatments of this subject would be compromised.

Following established practice, the term *Darwinism*, which Henkin employs and which I use throughout this study, refers to the large cluster of scientific findings and speculations from numerous fields in the natural sciences that include but are not restricted to Darwin's work on evolution. More narrowly, the term *Darwinian evolution* refers specifically to Darwin's hypotheses and scientific investigations.⁵⁷ The English public began responding to a fast-growing scholarship on the earth's antiquity and the evolutionary development of species in the 1840s, roughly two generations

---

54. Marsden, *Fundamentalism*, 120–21.
55. Wolff, *Novels of Faith and Doubt*, and Henkin, *Darwinism in the English Novel*.
56. A distinction is called for. The number of American novels treating various religious subjects is extensive—see O'Connor's *Protestant Sensibility*—but after 1960 I find no significant work of fiction on the specific subject of the impact of science on Christian faith in American fiction, except James Scott Bell's *The Darwin Conspiracy*.
57. See Russett, *Darwin in America*, 4–8, and Mayr, *One Long Argument*, 90–107.

before these issues found their way into popular American fiction. Although Darwin's *The Origin of Species* did not appear until 1859, Robert Chambers's 1844 monograph, *Vestiges of the Natural History of Creation*, made such a powerful impression on the public that it sold out edition after edition into the 1850s, after which Darwin's own work supplanted it.[58] Published anonymously and breathtaking in scope, *Vestiges* presented far-reaching arguments for the great age of the earth and the gradual development of life-forms, including humans. Challengingly, it plainly set forth its claim that a "Divine Governor" conducts the affairs of the world "by a fixed rule ... [of] natural law," and it rejected voguish appeals by geologists to "special miracles" and "interferences."[59] Composed by a Scottish journalist, publisher, and geologist by avocation, *Vestiges* popularized complex scientific issues and also introduced highly speculative (some use the term *pseudoscientific*)[60] claims that evolution is purposeful and that the races of humanity have followed their own evolution, with the white race at the top. However, none of these limitations prevented this controversial work from framing the scientific issues for the fiction to come for over a decade.

The early novelistic responses from political conservatives tried to dismiss through ridicule the growing body of scientific evidence. From just such a position of superiority did Benjamin Disraeli's *Tancred* (1847) mock *Vestiges* under the thin disguise of a new book called *"The Revelations of Chaos"* (148).[61] In subsequent years, this evolutionary hypothesis gained credence and then converts. For autodidact Eliza Lynn Linton, born in 1822, *Vestiges* was instrumental in bringing about her own process of conversion to a materialist understanding of how the world functions. Curiously, Linton's fictionalized life story, *The Autobiography of Christopher Kirkland* (1885), transposes the chief character into a young male protagonist whose religious upbringing does not prevent him from being troubled by theological doubts that his elders are unable to allay. These include such matters as whether the immaculate conception is a fact and whether Jesus was "the Divine Man from all eternity" (1:146).[62] These unresolved questions lead to brain fever and the gradual erosion of the importance of religious dogma, which takes concrete form when Kirkland abandons the path of his forefathers to join the Unitarian Church, which embraces Christ not as Divine, but as Man. Although he

---

58. Chambers, *Vestiges*; Henkin, *Darwinism*, 27.
59. Chambers, *Vestiges*, v–vi.
60. Ruse, *Evolution-Creation Struggle*, 48; Henkin, *Darwinism*, 39.
61. Disraeli, *Tancred*.
62. Linton, *Autobiography of Christopher Kirkland*. Page numbers to this and subsequent quotations in the paragraph appear in the text.

is gratified to find among the congregation the eminent geologist Sir Charles Lyell, Kirkland remains spiritually listless until he discovers the values of science. As the narrator looks back on these early days, he (that is, Eliza Linton) singles out *Vestiges,* not for realizing the truth of scientific discovery—the narrator calls Chambers's book "in a certain sense pre-scientific" (3:75–76)—but for having brought about a new dawn that Darwin's *The Origin of Species* later brought to full light. Under the influence of these two works, Kirkland, in a peroration lasting a full chapter, rejects revelation and adopts "science and free thought" because they hold out the prospect of emancipating humankind "across the abyss of ignorance and superstition" (3:76).

A still more disruptive influence in the 1840s and 1850s was the gradual infiltration into England from Germany of the higher biblical criticism, or simply, the higher criticism. This scholarly movement, an outgrowth, really, of German Protestantism, which exhorted the faithful to find the truth of God in the Bible itself, developed a revolutionary hermeneutic. Word by word, passage by passage, and text by text, its method was to interpret scripture not as miraculous revelation, but skeptically, as if it were a text composed solely in accordance with naturalistic laws. In particular, the method called for the linguistic analysis of the early versions of the Bible (provenance), the dating and contextualization of each book of the Bible, and the comparative study of ancient languages such as Hebrew, Greek, Latin, and Assyrian to corroborate or impugn the veracity of biblical history. All this scholarship proceeded under the aegis of German rationalism, and in response to it many among Britain's upper classes feared that the new criticism would undermine the theological justification for their privileged position in society.[63] But influential though it was, the movement did not gather much momentum in the United States until the 1880s, and it was not until World War I that a large number of scholars embraced the German university's model of skepticism, thinking of their scholarship as "*Wissenschaft,* 'pure learning,'" rather than as service to the church.[64]

In England an early, novelistic example of this new hermeneutic is James Froude's sensational novel of 1849, *The Nemesis of Faith,* which treats the spiritual anguish of a classically educated young man dissatisfied with the doctrines of "rigid Protestantism" (121), as well as those of Catholicism and the Church of England.[65] These sectarian tensions are instantiated in Markham Sutherland, whose study of the Bible has uncovered "critical"

---

63. See Cameron, *Biblical Higher Criticism,* passim, and Ashton, *German Idea,* 149–50.
64. Menand, *Metaphysical Club,* 256, and Worthen, *Apostles of Reason,* 23.
65. Froude, *Nemesis of Faith,* 121.

and "scientific difficulties,"[66] showing that the God of the Old Testament is not the supreme embodiment of mercy, justice, and goodness. Nor does the God of the New Testament satisfy because of the doctrine of eternal punishment. Having learned that the Bible's seemingly immutable truths actually change over time, Sutherland also rejects his religion's absolutist precepts. Unable to reconcile his freethinking with his position as minister or with the substance of his sermons, he resigns, falls in love with an unhappily married woman, becomes burdened with guilt, and retires to a monastery in Italy, where he lives out an arid life.

The process of assimilating the new biblical criticism was an extended one. Elizabeth Charles's *The Bertram Family* (1876) and W. H. Mallock's *The New Republic* (1877) each attempt to achieve a rational integration of the advanced biblical criticism with faith. But as the impact of Darwin's *Origin of Species* reverberated throughout England, the spiritual implications were received as devastating. For many, many believers, the challenge was how to stay spiritually alive. An outstanding illustration of this condition appears in *The Outcast* (1875) by Winwood Reade. Through a manuscript and a series of letters, the novel reveals the parallel life stories of Arthur Elliott, who later commits suicide, and Edward Mordaunt, father of Arthur's beloved, Ellen. Classically educated, intellectually formidable, and firm though his religious convictions are, Arthur reads two books, Malthus's *Essay on Population* (1798) and Darwin's *The Origin of Species*, that cause him to go mad and eventually to commit suicide. Mourning for the fate of humankind, Arthur calls the first work "The Book of Doubt," and the second "The Book of Despair" (8).[67] Before his suicide, he dreams that he has composed an essay for the *Quarterly Review* that poses painful theological questions, such as why the Creator so cruelly employs the law of evolution as the law of life. Ellen's father Mordaunt strives to provide a degree of balance by leaving behind his own autobiography, but his story too is full of suffering, for when Mordaunt enters the ministry he finds his religious convictions undermined by Charles Lyell's *Principles of Geology*. Further thought brings him to the insight, analogous to Arthur's, that the idea of God's benevolence is unjustifiable and an afterlife unknowable. Still, he foresees that "from discoveries in science" and the "Diffusion of Doubt" will come a quiet revolution of tolerance, and, he hopes, a new "Religion of Unselfishness" will gradually take hold in the world (199, 203).[68]

---

66. Ibid., 10.

67. Reade, *Outcast*. Page numbers to quotations in the paragraph appear in the text.

68. It may be observed that to this period also belong conversion novels that reverse the depictions of *The Outcast* and *The Nemesis of Faith* by showing how faith can

These novels of the 1870s provide dramatic evidence of scientific books profoundly affecting readers, not merely cognitively as abstract ideas, but viscerally and spiritually as well. Composed as they were before American novels on the subject began to appear in the 1880s, they may be viewed as table setters for the extraordinarily influential Victorian novel by Mary Augusta Ward (called Mrs. Humphry Ward), *Robert Elsmere* (1888), which in turn made a deep impression on both general American readers and American novelists. Defying convention, Ward, a formidable reform-minded Oxford intellectual, presented her title character as a sensitive, intelligent parson who gradually loses his orthodox faith through intense historical study, exposure in Oxford to a pervasive atmosphere of skepticism, and, finally, friendship with a cynical, Berlin-educated freethinker. Having become soul-sick over this loss, Elsmere nevertheless recovers and in imitation of Jesus' ministry affirms his life's purpose, not in Christian doctrine but in service to others. The way out of poverty, he understands after reading T. H. Huxley's *Lay Sermons*, is by teaching scientific knowledge and experiment, and so he establishes with his good wife, Catherine (who never does lose her faith), a "scientific Sunday school."[69]

Unfortunately, Elsmere's sincere beliefs do not meet minimal Christian doctrinal standards (such as belief in Jesus' divinity and the promise of everlasting life). Largely for this reason, the novel attracted the attention of England's prime minister William Gladstone, who wrote a review of it, with the result that the novel became an international success, selling 70,000 copies in Britain over a three-year period along with—unbelievably—sales of perhaps half a million in America (many pirated) in half that time.[70] The public's understanding of the nexus between Ward's own personal faith and that of her hero only enhanced the novel's controversial status. In the stirring words of Margaret Maison, "It was quoted in a thousand pulpits, . . . it was passionately denounced by [rival, conservative, Victorian novelist] Marie Corelli [for contributing to a loss of faith], it caused a *furore* in America and it was translated into dozens of foreign languages. . . . Few novels have ever attained so great a vogue."[71]

---

emerge from unbelief. An excellent example is Ada Ellen Bayly's "runaway best-seller," *Donovan: A Novel.* See Wolff, *Faith and Doubt*, 433.

69. Huxley, *Lay Sermons*; Ward, *Robert Elsmere*, 456.

70. Wolff, *Faith and Doubt*, 457. For more specific data, see Ashton, introduction to *Robert Elsmere*, xx. For a discussion of Gladstone's review and others, see Willey, "*Robert Elsmere*," 53–68.

71. Maison, *Victorian Vision*, 258. *Robert Elsmere* also stimulated other novelists to depict a loss of orthodox belief followed by a liberal affirmation of faith enacted through good works. See, for example, Hocking, *Jabez Easterbrook*.

This admittedly selective body of material invites comparisons. The number and variety of novels posing challenges to religious belief as a result of the higher criticism and biological evolution is striking. However, the quality of the subgenre is quite uneven, ranging from propaganda fiction to agonizing personal responses to religious doubts. Often the more polished novels record the process of becoming a skeptic or atheist through exposure to scientific books.

The role that the national Church of England played in this discourse deserves special notice. Historically that institution has had a way of shaping public debate on scientific and religious matters. Even a nonmember of the church such as a dissenting evangelicalist or a Unitarian would have a vested interest in the position the national church adopted on religious and scientific matters. By virtue of this church, the domains of scientific and religious belief are not as separated in the British nation as in the United States. Darwin's burial inside Westminster Abbey is a visual testament to Britain's ability to celebrate the achievements of its best, even if controversial, scientists, in a nationally recognized religious setting without troubling the corporate faith. The case is easily extended to English novelists, for when Ward wrote of the need to refashion church dogma to accommodate recent scientific discoveries, she was, in effect, arguing that the established church must preserve its relevance in changing times. The point is that these novels are embedded in a discourse about the public good and, particularly, about Britain's future prospects in a tumultuous world.

A corollary to this generalization emerges from the related observation that an unexpectedly high percentage of the principal characters in this kind of novel are clergymen, or clergymen in training. Many also want to practice their profession in the Church of England. These shared features suggest that English novelists viewed the lives of their clergy as the crucible in which the impact of the new science could be most effectively dramatized. Among this professional class, ethical issues could be exquisitely dramatized: Should the doubting pastor resign his living? How can he avoid despair? Moving outward from this narrow class, we notice an overrepresentation of intellectuals, of those who discuss or write books, or leave behind letters responding to the New Science. These features illustrate how emphatically this fiction is shaped to publicly articulate the crisis of faith in Victorian England. In any one novel, these features may appear unremarkable; taken together, they turn out to be hallmarks of the English novel of religious doubt. By contrast, American novels on this same theme are invested with national features all their own—as we shall now see.

A DISTINCTIVE AMERICAN CANON

Mary Augusta Ward's *Robert Elsmere* may justly be said to have inspired American novelists who first began writing about the volatile relationship between scientific findings and Christian faith in the 1880s. Following Ward's novel, Scott's *Henry Elwood: A Theological Novel* (1892) and Frederic's *The Damnation of Theron Ware* (1896), each took for their title the name of an otherwise unknown protagonist, a minister, whose faith is threatened by scientific findings. *Henry Elwood* thoughtfully redirects Ward's emphasis on the new learning to address issues pertaining to the reform of the Presbyterian Confession of Faith in a New York City seminary, and, more creatively, Frederic shaped his novel toward a thoroughly distinctive purpose. Instead of dramatizing the harmonious reconciliation of science with a reformed practice of Christianity (e.g., as social service, as Ward had), Frederic portrayed a poorly educated Methodist minister located in upstate New York, who becomes spiritually corrupted by the secularizing influences of the higher biblical criticism, Darwinian evolution, and aestheticism.

In addition to Ward's literary influence on American novels of faith and doubt, other cultural influences were also converging in the 1880s. Chief among these was the come-lately influence in America of German rationalism, with its concept of academic freedom and secularizing model of research for its own sake. Louis Menand identifies 1884—coincidentally, the same year that witnessed the first two American novels on science and faith—as the date that Johns Hopkins, having opened just four years earlier, could boast that almost all of its fifty-three professors had spent time studying in Germany.[72] From this period came the popular atheistic essays of Robert Ingersoll and the mediating efforts of leading American evolutionary theorist Asa Gray in his *Darwiniana* (1876) essays and *Natural Science and Religion* (1880).[73] Then, too, the disintegrating effects of the American Civil War, with over 600,000 casualties, continued to cast doubt on the assumptions and beliefs of an older age, including God's providence.[74] Howells's *A Modern Instance* (1882) shows this principle at work, since that novel takes as its theme "the absence of any sustaining belief in post–Civil War New England."[75]

---

72. Menand, *Metaphysical Club*, 256–57.
73. See Anderson, *Ingersoll*, the unpaginated chronology, and Samuels, *Henry Adams*, 228, who also discusses the English contributions to evolutionary theory from this period.
74. Menand, *Metaphysical Club*, x.
75. O'Connor, *Protestant Sensibility*, 46.

From this period of the 1880s, the first American novels on science and religion were composed. Fully half of the total number that examine this conflict were composed between 1884 and 1896. We can speculate as to why there were not more composed in later years. A plausible surmise issues from the fact that the market for novels on the subject of denominational conflicts and intradenominational rivalries was considerably greater than for those on the conflict between science and religion. Over the course of U.S. history to 1990, Leo O'Connor in his annotated bibliography identifies a whopping 214 such novels under the heading of "Portrait of Sects and Denominations," of which only two appear on the subject of science and religion (both treated in this book).[76] If few novels of this kind were produced, it seems clear that it was not for lack of interest in religion itself.

The American novels treating issues pertaining to science, faith, and doubt reveal a distinctly American set of concerns. Whereas British protagonists are drawn predominantly from the professional or privileged classes, the American novels feature protagonists from humble backgrounds, small towns, and rural areas. Whether it is Allen's David, who was raised on a poor Kentucky farm, or Elmer Gantry from the town of Paris, Kansas, or Theron Ware, who preaches in Octavius, New York, or Dylks in a backwoods Ohio settlement, each attempts to rise in his station, sometimes impelled by ambition and sometimes possessed by an intellectual ideal or a thirst for scientific knowledge. The democratic character of these representations is, in short, very much in evidence and leads to other, related themes, such as apprehensions about religious fanaticism or the vulnerability of an ill-educated citizenry that can fall prey to irrationalism.

These issues in turn lead to broader considerations about the future of the American republic. Howells's novel explicitly considers the prospects for democratic government in an undereducated frontier community, whose inhabitants are not trained in disciplined critical thinking. Frederic's *The Damnation of Theron Ware* presents the prospect of a secularizing modernity that is spiritually lethal to the novel's intellectually unprepared minister. Similarly, Bell's twenty-first-century fundamentalist novel, *The Darwin Conspiracy*, treats the atheistic followers of Darwin as betrayers of America and the true faith. These several novels clearly reveal that not all novelists embraced the paradigm of the scientific secular.

Another persistent, distinguishing feature of these novels is the American predilection for presenting characters who function outside the restraining norms of moderation and conformity. The town atheist or cynical

---

76. Ibid., 55–101.

nonbeliever is a prominent figure in this literature. Matthew Braile in *The Leatherwood God* is the novel's observant agnostic who furnishes the skeptical perspective through which the religious frenzy in Leatherwood is interpreted. So, too, in *Elmer Gantry* the atheists Jim Lefferts and his father, a medical doctor, offer a caustic counterpoint to the dogmatism rife in Elmer's Christian college. Martin Arrowsmith's iconoclastic mentor, Max Gottlieb, lays aside traditional religion, rejects the materialism of American culture, embraces Nietzsche as saint-like, and pursues a life so dedicated to scientific discovery that the well-being of humanity is subordinated to the quest. In *Inherit the Wind*, Hornbeck, the cynical intellectual modeled on H. L. Mencken, plays a choric role as a mocker of religion, while the Clarence Darrow figure (Drummond) relishes his identity as a celebrated agnostic and embodies the play's progressive values.

The high quality of this fiction, I emphasize, does not result from my having been selective (rather, I have been inclusive), but because the subject attracted nationally recognized writers of unusual ability. Among the four earliest novels, which are examined in the following chapter, three were composed by nationally acclaimed authors, Henry Adams and Sarah Orne Jewett, as well as the celebrated Midwesterner, Edward Eggleston, whose exposé of the faith healing practices of Mary Baker Eddy's Christian Science religion achieved national recognition. Among the works that followed, most achieved still greater national stature. Frederic's *The Damnation of Theron Ware* was declared to be "a minor classic," even a "masterpiece."[77] Allen's *The Reign of Law* racked up sales that put it fourth among American novels in 1900.[78] Howells's critically regarded *The Leatherwood God* (1916) has been largely forgotten until recent years, when it has been republished several times; as a penetrating psychological examination of a community's irrational religious behavior, it merits a special place in American letters.[79] Lewis's *Arrowsmith* was awarded a Pulitzer prize, though he refused it, while his *Elmer Gantry* became all at once a *succès fou*, a number one best seller, and a scandal.[80] Its 1960 film version starring Burt Lancaster won multiple awards, including best actor and best screenplay from

---

77. For twentieth-century critics judging *Theron Ware* to be a "minor classic," see Raleigh, "*Damnation of Theron Ware*," 210, and Wallace Evan Davies, "Religious Issues," 344; and as a "masterpiece," Garner, *Harold Frederic*, 38, and Donaldson, "Seduction of Theron Ware," 441.

78. Hackett, *60 Years of Best Sellers*, 100.

79. See the bibliography for examples of late twentieth-century and early twenty-first-century reprintings.

80. Schorer, *Sinclair Lewis*, 451–53, 474–75; and Hackett, *60 Years of Best Sellers*, 143.

another medium.[81] So, too, Lawrence and Lee's *Inherit the Wind* received ten Tony Award nominations, three wins, and a Variety Critics Poll Award—plus it inspired three television revivals led by the 1965 Hallmark Hall of Fame production.[82] The four Academy Award nominations the film version received in 1960 are further testaments to the influence and durability of its subject.[83]

Inasmuch as this is a chronologically sequenced study, readers will find it helpful to keep in mind their sequencing. Part 1, "Internal States of Belief and Unbelief," covers the period from 1884 to 1916 and focuses principally on subjective states. The first four novels of this canon, all published between 1884 and 1892, are gathered in one place to demonstrate from divergent points of view the emergence of a scientific discipline or profession from the formerly all-embracing category of religion. Distinctively, Milton Scott's *Henry Elwood* exemplifies through its title figure, a Presbyterian minister, the preservation of faith by accommodating the theory of evolution within the boundaries of received religion. Chapters 2, 3, and 4 in Part 1 are each devoted to a single novel that lends itself to the exploration of the emotional and spiritual consequences that issues from new scientific ideas.

Part 2, "Secularism Resurgent," is devoted to three major twentieth-century works of considerable complexity and influence: Lewis's *Arrowsmith* (1925), Lewis's *Elmer Gantry* (1927), and the play and film *Inherit the Wind* (1955, 1960). All of them exhibit a secularist ideology that promotes a progressive agenda affirming the values of scientific rationalism while holding up to various degrees of ridicule the religious beliefs of scriptural literalists. Yet *Arrowsmith* complicates a straightforward, secular interpretation by elevating scientific research to a level of spiritual awe. In contrast, the incendiary *Elmer Gantry* depicts the shady practices of evangelical preachers, controversially making preacher Gantry stand for the entire enterprise as a cynical, corrupt venture. Lawrence and Lee's rendering of the Scopes trial in *Inherit the Wind* has become the most influential creative work about the clash between William Jennings Bryan and Clarence Darrow—that is, between advocates of evolution and a generic form of scriptural literalism. But the play and film move toward a reassuring conciliation as Drummond/Darrow gathers together both *The Origin of Species* and the Bible and leaves the courtroom.

---

81. *Academy Awards Index*, 35, 95.
82. Guterman, "Field Tripping," 567.
83. *Academy Awards Index*, 35, 95, 118, 169.

Part 3, "A Postsecular Age?," consisting of a single chapter, attempts to identify the cultural forces at work over the last thirty years that have led to a resurgence of fundamentalist opposition to science and, concomitantly, the disappearance of nationally celebrated works of fiction on the relationship between science and religion. Crucially, the chapter observes the inability of moderating voices to make themselves heard when competing with more militant and colorful voices. The modern novel that illustrates such an alienated position is the antiscientific *The Darwinian Conspiracy*. At war with the secular world that has deprived conservative Christians of their former place, the novel mocks as a grand hoax the findings that support evolution and denounces as well the secularist philosophy that supports such research. The vigor of this challenge to scientific knowledge and the relative ineffectiveness of religious moderates prompts my closing question—whether the United States is headed toward a postsecular age.

PART 1

INTERNAL STATES OF BELIEF AND UNBELIEF

CHAPTER 1

EMERGENT FORMATIONS OF THE SCIENCE-RELIGION BINARY

Sara Orne Jewett's *A Country Doctor*,
Edward Eggleston's *The Faith Doctor*,
Milton Scott's *Henry Elwood*,
and Henry Adams's *Esther*

EACH OF THE four novels treated in this chapter are formative in two important senses: they were all published between 1884 and 1892, in that first decade that American novelists took up the subject of religious beliefs coming into dialogue with new scientific knowledge, and in diverse ways they also record and respond to the emergence of scientific disciplines from a series of spiritual practices. Whereas Sara Orne Jewett's novel laments the prospective loss of a holistic spirituality in the physician's practice of medicine, Edward Eggleston reveals the professionalization of modern medicine as it separates itself from faith-healing cures. In particular, Eggleston depicts the dangers to public health of nonscientific treatments of infectious diseases. A third novel, Milton Scott's *Henry Elwood*, portrays a Presbyterian minister whose intellectual and spiritual openness allow him to avert the otherwise splintering effects among his congregation of the new evidence of evolution by recommending a more accommodating interpretation of the Confession of Faith. The fourth, Henry Adams's *Esther*, the work of a novelist of rare analytic ability, explicitly treats the science-religion binary as a competition between two realms of knowledge—two epistemes, in Foucault's terms. One is personified by a professor of science and the other by an Episcopal minister who would like to wed Esther. But instead of choosing between them, she declines both and chooses her own path, spiritualism.[1]

SARA ORNE JEWETT'S *A COUNTRY DOCTOR*

A Country Doctor, 1884, has the distinction of representing a practice of medicine before the science-religion binary had fully emerged. That is to say, the two doctors featured in this novel are both aware of what they regard as a distasteful innovation: the introduction, notably, of thermometers and microscopes in family doctoring. To them, these innovations get in the way of the personal and spiritual relationship between doctor and patient, but they do not see that these developments are harbingers of a powerful epistemic formation in the treatment of disease. What they do see is a new fashion in the use of medical implements that does not comport with their own holistic practice, in which a patient's well-being was evaluated both physically and spiritually.

Surprisingly, this quiet novel portraying, as it does, the casual conversation of two country doctors in a small community in Maine captures the stirrings of what was soon to be a medical transformation.[2] Much of the novel's beguiling strength proceeds from Jewett's widely admired, understated style as well as her studious method of observation as a local colorist—qualities that made her famous in her time and highly regarded today.[3] The

---

1. Foucault theorized the episteme as the *a priori* metaphysical foundation of knowledge in any given time. Since the episteme is suffused throughout culture, it is invisible to those who live in its midst. In *The Order of Things*, 168, he specifically stipulated that at any one moment "there is always only one *episteme* that defines the conditions of possibility of all knowledge." Later, in *Power/Knowledge*, he expanded the application of the term, explaining that multiple epistemes can exist at one time as part of power/knowledge relationships in, for instance, discursive formations. There he defined the episteme as "the 'apparatus' which makes possible the separation, not of the true from the false, but of what may from what may not be characterised as scientific" (197). Unless otherwise noted, I employ the term in this second sense. It is worth observing that the episteme has affinities with Thomas Kuhn's concept of the "paradigm" in *Structure of Scientific Revolutions*, except that the episteme, because already embedded in the structure of discourse, is usually invisible. For a discussion of epistemes as applied to antebellum technological and spiritual developments in America, with several nods toward Foucault, see Modern, *Secularism*, 21–35. On the invisibility of ideology, which is often associated with the episteme, see Brannigan, *New Historicism*, 27–28.

2. These stylistic qualities were recognized at once in early reviews. See review of *A Country Doctor* in *Atlantic Monthly*, 418–20, and "Miss Jewett's First Novel," 15, 13.

3. Cary, *Jewett*, 18, 23, 52.

novel, Jewett's first, is heavily autobiographical. The model for Dr. Leslie, the book's original country doctor who is succeeded by his adopted daughter, was Sarah's own beloved father, Dr. Theodore Herman Jewett, a physician of no mean accomplishment who published in medical journals and thus successfully integrated theoretical and practical knowledge.[4]

Accompanying her father in horse and buggy as he made country house calls, the young Sarah Jewett acquired what she regarded as her real education.[5] From this knowledge, she was able to make her otherwise autobiographical heroine, Anne (Nan) Prince, a believable character who endeavors to follow her dedicated father in becoming a physician and who entertains her own spiritual ideas about service medicine. In pursuit of these goals, she forsakes all else, including the approval of her conformist neighbors and the opportunity to marry.

Given these autobiographical and semiautobiographical elements, it is easy to see why *A Country Doctor* is regarded as an early feminist work on professionalization, and for this reason it is still easier to understand why the long conversation between Dr. Leslie and his retired surgeon friend, Dr. Ferris, about the new fashion in ministering to patients is generally overlooked. In a chapter simply called "At Dr. Leslie's," the doctor affirms that we know two things, "love to God and love to man" (84).[6] The doctor feels keenly that many of his patients don't know that and live unfulfilled lives. Possessed of a false idea of duty, they work against nature instead of with it. But he hopes that Nan will follow her inclinations and pursue her dream of becoming a physician. These early remarks clearly reveal Dr. Leslie's belief that "nature" is a kind of living thing, a voice, perhaps from God, to which people ought to listen (84).

The virtues of this older practice of healing are memorialized throughout the novel. Dr. Ferris, for his part, adopts the view that medicine is an art. His ideas attain vitality in relation to the innovative medical technology then taking hold among family practitioners. Ferris describes these physicians as an "army of doctors who carry a great array of small weapons, and who find out what is the matter with their patients after all sorts of experiment and painstaking analysis, and comparing the results of their thermometers and microscopes with scientific books of reference" (85). The army metaphor suggests a mechanical conformity to a diagnostic norm as

---

4. Ibid., 20.
5. Donovan, *Jewett*, 3, 64–65.
6. Page numbers to quotations are from the 1999 reprint of *A Country Doctor*; all subsequent page numbers appear in the text. This edition may be distinguished from others by its introduction, written by Paula Blanchard.

presented in medical handbooks, while the description of the doctor's tools as "weapons" expresses an alienation from modern medical technology.

The chapter proceeds to elaborate the critical differences in what reveals itself to be two divergent medical practices emerging from what had formerly been one. In the new manner of treatment, doctors "don't even try to follow nature," meaning their own inclinations; rather, they mechanically apply what they have learned from their books (86). Thus book learning takes one "to more theory and scientific digest rather than to more skill" (86). "A man has no right to be a doctor if he doesn't simply make everything bend to his work of getting sick people well" (86). "The anatomists and the pathologists have their place," Dr. Ferris declares, "but we must look to the living to learn the laws of life, not to the dead" (86). This metaphoric insight works to undercut the modern anatomist, who examines dead bodies, not people. It also applies to the laboratory researcher who studies microscopic organisms. To doctor well, a physician must understand the circumstances of people's lives, their troubles, and their failures.

Remarkably, Dr. Ferris's complaints about the new medical practitioners captures a cultural phenomenon that science historian Paul Starr has described as a social transformation in American medicine. From the mid-1800s, he states, new diagnostic instruments such as the stethoscope came into favor among family physicians along with other diagnostic technologies that depended on use of the microscope. These enabled doctors to evaluate the patient's physiological condition by providing quantitative information regarding heart rate, pulse, and temperature that could not be gathered by simply consulting the patient.

In what we would now identify as an older practice of medicine, Starr states that physicians of the nineteenth century relied on their "patients' statement of symptoms and . . . the patient's subjective judgment."[7] This personalized manner of treatment is what Sarah Jewett's father practiced before his death in 1878 and what Dr. Leslie is seen to practice in the novel.[8] The price paid for diagnosing by means of mechanical instruments was a loss of intimacy and face-to-face interaction. Instead of valuing the information the patient could provide, the doctor listened to the internal sounds of the patient's body, distancing, detaching, if not isolating, one from another. But at the time that Sarah Jewett wrote, and earlier when her father practiced, this kind of doctoring was praised as the more effective, artful, comprehensive, and personally satisfying.

---

7. Starr, *Social Transformation*, 136–37. Medical information throughout the paragraph is from this text.

8. Cary, *Jewett*, 11.

Dr. Ferris tells Dr. Leslie that the latter possesses "the true gift for doctoring" because he listens to his intuition, which becomes "a wonderful second-sight' (85–86). Here intuition functions not by itself but in concert with medical study. By experience young doctors become good doctors. They learn to think for themselves, to, in fact, practice the art of medicine, instead of applying normative standards or succumbing to skepticism because the textbooks list as many as eight different treatments for pneumonia, for example.

These considerations lead Dr. Leslie to express in inspirational terms the spiritual convictions underlying his medical practice:

> When we let ourselves forget to educate our faith and our spiritual intellects, and lose sight of our relation and dependence upon the highest informing strength, we are trying to move our machinery by some inferior motive power. We worship our tools and beg success of them instead of remembering that we are all apprentices to the great Master of our own and every man's craft. (88)

In a view that appears repeatedly in several of these novels of science and faith, Dr. Leslie identifies fever and other signs of illness as the effects, "not the causes," of illness (89), which is why physicians ought to resist relying too heavily on mechanical tools. Rather, all of us should assess the state of the soul in the body, and of "our degree of receptivity" to the intimations of the divine in us. Articulating a belief not in reprobation but in transcendence, he exclaims with evangelical fervor that "the powers of Christ were but the higher powers of our common humanity" (88–89).

These powers are revealed through a finely attuned intuition, a sphere in which truth is directly apprehended and in which—following the progressive theories of contemporary historian T. H. Buckle—women particularly excel (88).[9] These beliefs lead, quite naturally, perhaps even transcendentally, to Nan's spiritual apprenticeship to her father. She begins to think independently and embraces the view that in addition to drill and experience, every medical student "should be fitted by nature with a power of insight," an "instinct" for recognizing disease and also its cure (145).

---

9. Buckle's *History of Civilization* is a proximate, explicitly named, source for Nan Prince's transcendentalist bent. His views include the need for a comprehensive general history that will transform religion, literature, and government into a science and that is capable of ascertaining "the whole of the laws which regulate the progress of civilization" (133). Nonetheless, critics associate Jewett's transcendentalism with that of Emerson. See Cary, *Jewett*, 158.

In Nan's elevated statements of belief, we hear the full voice of a physician who has achieved wholeness in herself and in her practice. She has overcome division and the threat of binary division by uniting soul and body and by bringing together the professions of minister and physician. In this spirit of harmonic integration, Jewett even allows her heroine an autobiographical moment that references the creative artist. In that moment, Nan perceives that just as "the great poet tells the truths of God, and makes other souls wiser and stronger and fitter for action, so the great doctor works for the body's health, and tries to keep human beings . . . ready to be the soul's instrument of action and service in this world" (145–46).

Having come to her profession as to a ministry, Nan, full of gladness, prays, "O God, . . . I thank thee for my future" (274). These last words of the novel recapitulate the author's view of a practice of medicine that values intuition and spirituality above technical skill and diagnostic instruments, while nevertheless acknowledging such skill. In the mid-nineteenth century, such a spiritually based practice of medicine, though threatened by the new secular practice, was still the prevalent one, especially in rural communities.

EDWARD EGGLESTON'S *THE FAITH DOCTOR*

Although *The Faith Doctor* was composed several years later than Henry Adams's *Esther*, its subject of spirituality in modern medicine is so irresistibly similar in subject and so divergent in point of view from *A Country Doctor* that I treat it next. If Jewett's novel treats the secularization of medicine as a come-lately fashion that threatens but fails to displace a more holistic, spiritualized practice, *The Faith Doctor* (1891) exposes notorious spiritual practices that if not restrained would threaten public health. To do this, the novel depicts the philosophy and secular practice of medicine, based on germ theory, that emerges to supplant the practices of faith healers.[10] Whereas both novels dramatize these not yet fully separated practices of medicine, Eggleston's alone demonstrates that only the biological approach to germ theory can safeguard the populace from the spread of communicable disease.

Eggleston composed his novel near the end of a long career as a successful novelist, historian, and children's writer. Having begun as a Methodist

---

10. The context in which I use the term *secular* should make clear that it refers to a modern practice of medicine, still dominant today, that has removed the spiritual element that the practice formerly possessed. For this and other critical usages, see Modern, *Secularism*, 2n1.

circuit rider in southeastern Indiana, he later became a preacher, and then an editor. However, in his later years, his theological orthodoxy evolved to the point that his final view was reflected in the planning papers left for a novel entitled *Agnostic*. This same skeptical orientation governs *The Faith Doctor*, whose plot derives from an unpublished short story called "An Irregular Practitioner" and whose rights Eggleston purchased from the author.[11]

Eggleston's preface to *The Faith Doctor* explains his subject, mind cure, faith cure, and Christian Science. His purpose, however, is "artistic, not polemical" (3).[12] In this effort he may have been influenced by his publisher, Richard Watson Gilder, who was apprehensive about the novel offending Christian Scientists, but the rest of the preface shows that as a modernist Eggleston stood tall. The novel, he avows, "was not written to depreciate anybody's valued delusions"; it is rather a study of human nature that shows the persistence of superstitious credulity. He still remembers "the religious fervor of millenarianism and the imitation science of curative mesmerism [which] gave way to spirit-rappings and clairvoyant medical treatment. Now spiritism in all its forms is passing into decay, only to leave the field free to mind-doctors and faith-healers. There is nothing for it but to wait for the middle ages to pass; when modern times arrive, there will be more criticism and less credulity, let us hope" (3–4).

Although it is an exposé of fraudulent faith cures, the novel avoids binary oppositions in its depiction of several sorts of faith healers, each revealing a degree of ethical commitment or blameworthiness. Eggleston's intelligent young heroine, Phillida Callender, is sensitive, loving, and sincere, but credulous, and that credulity leads to a temporary humiliation and a needlessly broken engagement to her wealthy suitor, Charley Millard. The daughter of a missionary, Phillida follows her father's footsteps in wanting to serve others, which she does in a New York City mission, where she thrives among the poor. Phillida's problems begin when she becomes drawn into a Bible-reading circle led by one Mrs. Frankland, who is no fraud but is nevertheless venal and gets carried away by her own gifted oratory. Highly susceptible to Mrs. Frankland's fervency, Phillida slides into a faith-curing mode herself. Out of loving sympathy for a poor, bedridden invalid of thirteen named Wilhelmina, Phillida urges the young girl to believe with all her heart that she can be cured, as Phillida herself believes. The two believe

---

11. The information in this paragraph is from Randel's 1963 critical study, *Eggleston*, 119–22, 190–91.

12. Page numbers to Eggleston, *The Faith Doctor*, appear in the text following quotations.

together, and, summoning every ounce of energy she possesses, Wilhelmina painfully rises from the bed. Hoping to get the invalid to walk, Phillida commands, "In the name of Jesus of Nazareth, rise up and walk!" (209), and when Wilhelmina again responds, Phillida believes she possesses the true faith-curing gift. As her reputation spreads, she is called a worker of miracles. Through this incremental process, Phillida, a devout Christian, becomes, in effect, converted anew to her own faith cures. The process functions homiletically to show how good but credulous people can be duped into a false belief in their special powers.

At this critical moment, with Phillida's reputation in doubt among the well-to-do class of conservative women, a professional faith healer appears. She brandishes a calling card, "Eleanor Arabella Bowyer, Christian Scientist and Metaphysical Practitioner" (283). Her curing practices are scientific, she declares, not blind like those of Miss Callender. The term *scientific* is her signature word; she applies it to her work at every turn. From a narrative standpoint, these depictions allow the novelist to contrast the amateur faith healer with the professional operator, and gradually to educate Eggleston's readership as to what *scientific* really means.

In a chapter called "Proof Positive," Charley Mallard, the novel's worldly skeptic, questions his own Uncle Martin, who is an advocate for Bowyer's philosophy. Their Socratic colloquy effectively functions to promote critical thinking among Eggleston's readers. Asked what proofs underlie Miss Bowyer's claim that spirit power will do away with sin, misery, and sickness, Uncle Martin blithely proclaims her cures to be wondrous. He also propounds the theological argument that since God is good, he cannot create evil. Therefore, there is no real evil, and since "sickness and sin are evil . . . they don't really exist at all" (220). Millard's response is to turn this metaphysical premise around and thus to introduce an empirical standard into this rationalist argument: if we know sin and sickness are evil, then there is no good God. The nub of the issue is whether Christian Science produces its miracles or whether they are the result of a philosophy. Told that their modern miracles are just like those in the Bible, Millard objects that belief in biblical miracles is part of received religion, but "Christian psychopathists" introduce the muddying term "science," such that the processes of magnetism, or mind cure, or psychopathy each become objects of scrutiny that fall far short of proof (221). This argument makes scripture an article of faith and exempts it from material corroboration. But the faith cures of Christian Science practitioners, by virtue of the fact that they claim their cures to be scientific, must be evaluated, the novel urges, according to scientific criteria.

Having offered a spirited evaluation of the questionable epistemology of Christian Science, Eggleston homes in on Eleanor Bowyer herself, whose character is made prejudicially shady. But contemporary reviewers delighted in the portrayal as true to experience. Partly comic, partly historical, she speaks in inflated propositions that sound like "burlesque," but that might, as one reviewer puts it, "in reality have been taken verbatim from the writings of . . . expounders of Christian science."[13] The ridicule of Miss Bowyer could also have worked as personal satire since Mary Baker Eddy, the charismatic founder of the Church of Christ, Scientist in 1879, was very much alive when Eggleston's novel was published.[14]

Melodramatically and reductively, Eggleston makes Miss Bowyer the polar opposite of Phillida, for whereas the latter is the innocent ingenue, Miss Bowyer is selfish and driven by the profit motive. On this binary the novel's outcome depends, for when Bowyer offers Phillida a partnership by using Christian Science to get rich, the young idealist turns away from both Miss Bowyer and her religion. Consequently, when the dying Wilhelmina asks for Dr. Beswick, a formally trained graduate of the College of Physicians and Surgeons, he and Phillida begin to work together, an event that brings about her reeducation.

When Phillida inquires whether the doctor believes that divine agency plays a role in treating disease, Beswick's skillful answer is that in Wilhelmina's case the starting point is that she has runaway consumption, now past cure, caused by rapidly reproducing bacilli, against which prayers alone will not suffice. Surprisingly, however, Dr. Beswick allots a limited place for mind cures. Acknowledging that the mind has extraordinary influence over the body, he recommends mind cure in cases of mental disturbance, but for diseases brought about by microorganisms, such as diphtheria, which presents as white spots on the throat, the invading bacillus must be defeated. The doctor's methodology is thoroughly empirical without being ideologically rigid, for even on strictly empirical grounds mind cures have a recognized utility. But in matters of infections by microorganisms, faith healing is a grave public concern, since lives will be lost, and even epidemics may result if medical doctors are not involved.

The final action of *The Faith Doctor* becomes an illustrative admonition. At issue is a case of severe illness visited upon "Tommy," the inner-city child of Mr. and Mrs. Phillip Martin. Over Tommy's treatment a battle goes

---

13. Review of *Faith Doctor*, *Critic*, 7, and review of *Faith Doctor*, *Literary World*, 373. See also Payne, review of *Faith Doctor*, 278.

14. *Cambridge Dictionary*, 214.

on unresolved between wife and husband. Whereas Mrs. Martin prepares to call on Dr. Beswick and Dr. Gunstone, her husband wants Tommy treated "on the spiritual plane" (342) and peremptorily summons Miss Bowyer. Phillida, having quite forsworn faith healing, remembers Dr. Beswick's lesson, looks in the patient's throat, sees the telltale signs of diphtheria, and urgently requests that Mrs. Martin summon Dr. Beswick. In this way, Phillida resolutely allies herself with the proponents of germ theory.

The object lesson is brought home by Miss Bowyer's resort to "occult therapeutic powers" (355) to practice her magnetic theory of energy by turning the patient toward the magnetic north. Absurd as this treatment appears today, it made apocalyptic sense to mid-nineteenth-century spiritualists. Surrounded as they were by technologies and networks such as the telegraph, high-voltage-use streetcars, and other examples of invisible action at a distance, such as magnetism, spiritualists sought to make further contact with the unseen world of spirit.[15] Although Miss Bowyer is not fully aware of the history of the spiritualism she practices, the possibilities for creating a science of spiritualism seemed limitless earlier in the century.[16]

That said, Eggleston's novel makes two powerful arguments to discredit her, one epistemological and one epidemiological. The first is that Miss Bowyer's claims that her faith cures are established science, when, in fact, they have not nearly established themselves in the public sphere as any such thing. The second is that the consequences of treating communicable disease as purely a spiritual matter can be disastrous to public health. These propositions are worked out in concert with the exposé of Miss Bowyer's opportunistic tactics. For instance, Bowyer's hyperbolic claim that Christian Science is "the science of sciences" (287) is put to the test. With Tommy's life at stake, and possibly others, Charley Millard takes action. In the face of Bowyer's claim that she is the designated practitioner in the case, he informs her that he will immediately report her to the County Medical Society and the Board of Health. He then asks whether she has reported this case of diphtheria as the law requires. When Millard learns that she has not, he abruptly escorts her out of the house. Her last words, "But you will not refuse me my fee" (362), remind us of the signature feature of her character.

Self-promoting and foxlike, Bowyer's character becomes enveloped in fraud. But, once again, reviewers cheered both her flamboyant characterization and the poetic justice of her fall. As *The Critic* wrote, "The enormous amount of fraud" in the present day "cannot be too rigorously exposed, nor

---

15. Modern, *Secularism*, 27–28, 31.
16. Ibid., 31.

can any amount of ridicule heaped upon it be deemed unjustifiable."[17] For these readers, the novel functioned as a sharp-eyed exposé of fraudulent cures. Unfortunately, the near-exclusive focus on Miss Bowyer deflected attention from Eggleston's more urgent didactic theme—that is, if faith healing replaces proven prophylactic health measures, contagious diseases may become epidemic. This threat is dramatically underscored by Phillida herself after she falls victim to diphtheria. At the same time, Eggleston makes the further medical point that in some circumstances the mind can cure the body. He shows this by depicting how Phillida fails to recover because she is depressed due to her shame over her credulity about faith healing and her consequent broken engagement to Millard. What her case requires is, indeed, a mind cure that arrives in the form of Millard's proposal of marriage. On this outcome rests the novel's restrictive view of the circumstances in which mind cure may legitimately function.

When contemporary reviewers seized on Miss Bowyer's extravagant medical vocabulary, with her "inflated dialect," her "'magnetisms,' 'odylic emanations,' and the like,"[18] as evidence of her fraudulent practices, they were celebrating the comedy of a made-up language that signified nothing real. But from a Foucauldian perspective, preoccupied as it with the power that expresses itself in unseen places—in fact, everywhere–a different perspective emerges.[19] What the faith healer's medical vocabulary points to, however, is a failed episteme, one associated with Christian Science but also current among other spiritualist groups. Like the technical vocabulary of modern medicine, "spiritism" (3) is invested with its own professionalized terminology, and at the time that *The Faith Doctor* was composed, this spiritism was vying for acceptance and respect among the public. The ridicule that Eggleston heaps upon Miss Bowyer as the fraudulent practitioner of Christian Science faith healing, accompanied as it was by the cheers of contemporary reviewers, provides substantive evidence that the Christian Science movement was losing its bid for acceptance. That is to say, Eggleston's satire of Bowyer and company signals to the novelist's audience that it is witnessing the rejection of a contending epistemology.[20] In another place

---

17. Review of *Faith Doctor*, Critic, 7.
18. Review of *Faith Doctor*, Literary World, 373.
19. On the proposition that power is everywhere, even when it seems to be invisible, I am thinking in a general way of Foucault's *The Order of Things*, and to a lesser extent *Power/Knowledge*.
20. Foucault, *Order of Things*, 365, is uncommonly clear about this theoretical point. There are practices, he states, "with scientific pretensions ... at the level of opinion ... that are not (or are no longer) part of a culture's epistemological network"—for example, "natural magic."

and time, Christian Science could conceivably have been accepted as a useful kind of knowledge.

The fact, moreover, that Miss Bowyer is driven from the New York City scene by Charley's threat of notifying "the Board of Health" (360) is a reminder that the board, as a secular medical authority, embodies a more concrete form of power. It regulates, licenses, and sanctions. That it may be called upon to resolve such jurisdictional disputes is a persuasive demonstration that in the era Eggleston composed *The Faith Doctor,* Christian Science healers were competing with trained physicians for clients. As their name denotes, they were striving for acceptance as legitimate practitioners of a legitimate science. With their own distinctive conception of disease, terminology, and protocol for cure, Christian Science healers possessed what amounts to their own rival episteme. Eggleston's novel is in some important sense a critique of that episteme. Presumably, this is why in his preface Eggleston expressed his hope that "modern times" will bring more critical thinking and "less credulity" (4) to the general public.

MILTON SCOTT'S *HENRY ELWOOD*

Henry Elwood: A Theological Novel is an obscure work by a little-known author. About a quarter of the novel appears in the antiquated epistolary format that became popular in England in the 1740s following the publication of Samuel Richardson's *Pamela* and *Clarissa.* Scott's handling of character is workmanlike and rather flat, and the plotting lurches from the conversational to the melodramatic, as when the novel is brought to an abrupt conclusion by a train wreck that ultimately takes the life of Elwood's wife, Alice. Despite these deficiencies, the novel is culturally important because it dramatizes the insinuation of religious doubts into a tight-knit Presbyterian community and the response of leading members of that community. Within this circumscribed world, Scott's novel explores a range of theological responses to the higher biblical criticism and Darwinian evolution.

Like Mary Augusta Ward's 1888 English novel, *Robert Elsmere,* Scott's title figure is a minister who faces the new doubt in an intensely academic environment. The singular differences are that Scott's novel explores the Presbyterian intellectual climate in New York City, in contrast to that of the more urbane Oxford, where debate is always measured relative to the position of the Church of England. Distinctively, Scott's novel champions Elwood's persistent efforts to bring about reconciliation and reform within the bounds of his own Presbyterian faith. The process of response and adaptation is the very heart of the novel, whose purpose is to repel insidious agnosticism and preserve faith. In this major respect, it is the only religious novel on the science-religion conflict in the 1880s and '90s to depict educated people of faith defending against the advance of the secular while affirming their own religious values.

The opening pages of the novel show faculty members of Beulah College commenting on Herbert Spencer's prescription that the curriculum should reflect the new reality that the physical sciences have "superior value" and that schools should offer scientific training (8).[21] To this claim the school's superintendent, Mr. Carroll, affirms that "all knowledge is noble, all knowledge is practical, and I had almost said, all knowledge is divine" (14). That is to say, the superintendent declines to accept the superiority of scientific learning over a holistic conception that refuses to treat science and religion or science and the arts as binary systems. Rather, he reasserts the traditional epistemology that unifies all learning under a divine power. Professor Ironsides, as his name suggests, adheres to the old ways. For him, William Paley's *Evidences of Christianity* (1802), which he teaches, are unassailable,[22] and the miracles of Christ are "the most conclusive proof of the truth and divine origin of Christianity" (36). Yet Ironsides reports that murmurings have entered his classroom that signal the entry of "that awful giant of Doubt" (50). Among Elwood's classmates, George Marvel, a Civil War veteran, has become so disillusioned that he wonders whether humans have been placed on this earth for any purpose.[23] Although plagued by a similar loss of faith, Homer Vernon, Elwood's roommate at Beulah and the son of strict Presbyterian parents, spends three years at the Union Theological Seminary, but because of theological doubts he withdraws to enter the College of Physicians and Surgeons, where he throws over most of the theology he learned.

Against this backdrop appears Henry Elwood, the rhetorically and intellectually gifted young man of impeccable character who is the valedictorian of his class. Yet when he is appointed minister of Beulah's First Presbyterian Church, he delivers inspirational sermons that Professor Ironsides warns are irregular because they do not fully endorse all the doctrines of the Presbyterian Confession of Faith. His teaching is irregular, he is told, and works to "undermine rather than build up, our Calvinistic system" (92). But rather than meekly conform, Elwood begins a long journey to bring

---

21. Page numbers to Scott, *Henry Elwood*, appear in the text following quotations.

22. Paley's *Evidences* was the popular name (used by Professor Ironsides) for the work whose formal title is *Natural Theology*.

23. Menand, *Metaphysical Club*, x–xi.

about the liberalization of Presbyterian doctrines. Never breaking faith with his Presbyterian heritage, Elwood seeks to reform from within. He is fortunate to find support from an Episcopal rector nearby, appropriately named Mr. Albion, who adopts the view that neither his church's creed nor Elwood's is likely to be the last theological word. Through her letters, Elwood's mother offers her own support, stating that no catechism or theological system ever solved all problems; to be effective, ministers must "Live and Learn!" (118). Theology must bend, in short, to real-life situations.

Despite Elwood's doubts, his star continues to rise because he is a loving pastor whose sermons are reputed to save many from skepticism and unbelief. Consequently, he receives a call, which he ultimately accepts, to lead the Excelsior Presbyterian Church, a much bigger church than his own, with a wider array of worshipers, rich and poor, young and old. This prospect of bringing the faith across class lines appeals to Elwood. Alice, the young woman he loves, and his young colleagues have become painfully aware of the need for social services among the poor. Vernon's girl friend Clara, a high-school teacher, starts a home for fallen women. A boy of ten named Harry Howard becomes Elwood's mission-school protégé; yet others from poor families, especially children, become sick or even die. Having absorbed such values of social service as these circumstances present, Elwood arrives at a crystalizing moment in which he writes that he has come to doubt the doctrines of "future punishment" and "total depravity" (176).

Experience is, however, heavily informed by theology. As a novelist and religious intellectual, Milton Scott shows himself to be deeply concerned about the challenges brought to faith by two major influences, modern medicine and scientific discovery. Through Elwood's conversations with Homer Vernon, the schoolmate who broke with his childhood faith in order to become a physician, and also with the arrogant scientist Professor Humboldt, Scott's major theological ideas emerge with particular force. Vernon's position, articulated with some nostalgia for his lost faith, is that "the practice of medicine ... doesn't tend to restore one's belief in miracles" (179–80). He further reasons that the biblical controversies over whether the tides are six thousand or six million years old are irrelevant to the crucial concept that "the laws of Nature are all unchanged and unchangeable" (180). In response to this naturalistic view, Elwood interjects a remark that shows the minister's faith to be quite intact: "Except by divine power" (180). Vernon's subsequent admission that he doubts medicine is "an exact science" (181) shows the physician's understanding of the limitations of science in building knowledge. Similarly, when Vernon explains the reality of the placebo effect, as it is called today, he acknowledges a realm of investigation beyond the physical boundaries of normative scientific investigation. This acknowledgment of unknown mind-body relationships lends some credence to the metaphysical foundation of Christian Science and faith cures, a point conceded in *The Faith Doctor*, as we have seen. On this ground, both Elwood and Vernon agree, the "GOSPEL OF HEALTH" should not be despised (183).

Elwood uses this platform of common belief to launch a synthesizing hypothesis, namely, that just as the physician must understand people's thinking and feelings in order to be effective, how much more does the preacher need to employ all of his faculties to aid his church members. Throughout this discussion, Elwood and Vernon find common ground. Thus Vernon explains that whereas he once believed that the preacher had only to relate the word of the Bible, he now takes a wider view, just as Elwood does by raising questions about the Trinity, the infallibility of the Bible, and even the Atonement effected by Christ's death for the redemption of humankind. Though specific practices or beliefs may be questioned, the doctor of medicine and the doctor of divinity work together toward the same curative ends. The novel, in effect, keeps saying that these two professions need not occupy antipodal positions in an ineluctable binary; they ought to function together.

The same strategy that gives ground to secular studies in order to preserve a more inclusive religious faith is clearly in play in the Union Seminary's handling of the advances of German rationalism. Vernon explains that others like him "are trying to reconcile Christianity with Reason, and Science and Philosophy, instead of proving its divine origin by miracles and prophecies" (184). This theological shift in emphasis, Scott indicates, could be transformative. From this reformist standpoint, it becomes possible to imagine that doctors of divinity may lose faith in a specific remedy, just as doctors do, but they would not lose their *"religiousness"* (185). The same logic would apply when divines read Charles Darwin, Thomas Huxley, and Herbert Spencer, along with Ernest Renan, whose *The Life of Jesus* treats its subject as a purely historical phenomenon. Adaptability and openness are essential to the survival of traditional Christianity.

Religion, Scott seems to say, need not always be on the defensive. Secularists too must be open and responsive to probing questions. In this spirit, Elwood is able to carry the argument to theological opponents who do not believe, as when he asks, "Why . . . [do] so many scientists and philosophers seem to ignore the religious instinct in man?" (224). Its presence, he argues, is as scientific as any fact. As a dramatic demonstration of the power of theology to hold its own against those who leave no place for religion, Scott introduces a Professor Humboldt. Clearly named for the German naturalist who put scientific investigation on a modern footing by insisting on exhaustive data collection and classification, Humboldt thinks of science as an accumulation of facts and then makes bold assertions about modern science that leaves him vulnerable to counterarguments.[24] Thus, when Humboldt declares, "There is no superstition about science" because "she stands upon fact and fact alone," Elwood's reply is that scientific knowledge is provisional, and as such "science can give us no *absolute* knowledge of anything" (269). He observes further that many scientific advances have been based on investigations carried out with incorrect premises or hypotheses.

Having mounted this critique of the basic *facts* that underlie the practice of modern science, Elwood goes on to defend major articles of the Christian faith. He does so by pointing out the inappropriateness of Humboldt's condemning, from his secular point of view, the mystery of the doctrine of vicarious atonement. Finally, Elwood discloses that his belief in miracles is based on the manifestation of a higher law. Given the limitations of human nature, he reasons that the case for miracles under a higher power more fittingly applies to the believer than to one who denies them. Continuing on his path of synthesis, Elwood holds that Christianity is both a divine revelation from heaven and a subject of evolution. "If evolution is the universal law or principle of the universe, why should not Christianity be brought within its scope and operation?" (268).

Elwood's flexible view of religious doctrine permits him to avoid theological improbabilities and trouble spots. When asked, for instance, whether the Bible is infallible, Elwood acknowledges that its composers were not above human error, but he also advances the proposition that preachers ought "to inspire our faculties, rather than to impress their authority upon us" (273). This orientation reflects in turn on Elwood's efforts to reform the Confession of Faith by persuading the Presbyterian Church to adopt a more latitudinarian position. Although these efforts enjoy only limited success (for while the assembly votes in favor of revision, it declines to change the Calvinist system of doctrine), Scott declines ever to portray Elwood working outside the boundaries of his church.

This is the wisdom of the novel, a wisdom that refuses binary oppositions and that seeks instead to enlarge the embrace of the Presbyterian Church. Repeatedly the novel strives to identify underlying commonality among various forms of Christian belief. This impulse of inclusion is consecrated by Elwood's dying wife, Alice, whose final act is to place her friend Clara's hand in Vernon's, uniting them both once more, despite Vernon's skepticism. Scott's last chapter, entitled "Mortality and Immortality," brings

---

24. Kelner, *Humboldt*, 233–34.

together the finite with the expectation of the infinite, a hope made vivid through Alice's final gesture, which shows her "serving and blessing to the last!" (324).

At Alice's funeral, the allegorically named Dr. Goodway delivers the funeral eulogy to an assemblage greater than any previously gathered in Elwood's church, whose proper name, we recall, is "Excelsior." This conclusion may be read as a reaffirmation of the vitality of Excelsior, despite the encroachments of science and secularism. Its religious identity not only survives but flourishes among the faithful, where the faithful are recognized less by their creedal convictions than by the spiritual unity engendered by communal acts of service.

HENRY ADAMS'S *ESTHER*

The luminous figure of Henry Adams, who possessed an uncommon artistic sensibility and whose philosophic orientation leaned heavily toward scientific determinism, is viewed by many as the most outstanding American historian of the last two centuries.[25] A non-Christian in the sense that he rejected supernatural explanations and embraced natural causation throughout the universe, he meditated throughout his life, like a speculative Greek philosopher, on the underlying unity of reality within multiplicity.[26] Declining to accept uncritically binary depictions as a reified reality, he sought for other ways to present foundational issues underlying the conflict between reason and faith. The idea he hit upon was to join this philosophical preoccupation to the contemporary issues of women's spirituality and self-realization. The form he chose for representing multiple voices was the novel, whose subject owed more than a little to the problem-play, or "drama of ideas," that Ibsen's *A Doll's House* (1879) had ushered in.[27] Privately published in 1884 under the pseudonym Francis Snow Compton, his novel, which he entitled *Esther*, made little impact in its day,[28] but the work, qua novel, is formidable in its philosophic analysis of disciplines and its probing portrayal of women's problematic place in the modern world.

The philosophic vision that informs *Esther* was most fully delineated in Adams's later years in *Mont-Saint-Michel and Chartres* (1904) and *The Education of Henry Adams* (1904). There, instead of depicting an epistemological

---

25. Bishop, *Henry Adams*, 132–33.
26. Deneen, "Mont-Saint-Michel," 175–81.
27. Gassner, introduction to *Four Great Plays by Ibsen*, xiv–xv.
28. Bergmann, "Henry Adams's *Esther*," 63.

conflict limited to a single period, as did other writers of this period, Adams boldly posited what might well be called (following Foucault's terminology in *The Order of Things*), the two governing epistemes of Western civilization. In the twenty-fifth chapter of *The Education*, Adams identified two kinds of "force" or "energy" bearers, the Virgin and the Dynamo. In the first, the Virgin of the twelfth century represented the inspiration and spiritual apogee of the medieval world, while in the second, in the late nineteenth and twentieth centuries, there emerged a worldview epitomized by that modern symbol of the mechanical and electrical power of the new age, the dynamo. To Adams, the Virgin stood for an idea or presence without which the world could not be conceived, just as the modern world cannot be conceived without the technological and mechanical forces that govern it. Unlike each of the disciplinary epistemes discussed previously, these master epistemes that Adams discerned fulfill Foucault's *a priori* criterion that at any one moment "there is always only one *episteme* that defines the conditions of possibility of all knowledge"[29] As Adams put it in *The Education*, he had crawled to a "knife-edge" that "divided two kingdoms of force which had nothing in common but attraction. They were as different as a magnet is from gravitation."[30]

In this early version of Adams's epistemic thought, *Esther* embodies in representative figures the clash of these two competing worldviews. On one side stands George Strong, a professor of paleontology and theological skeptic, who embodies a scientific view of the world. On another side stands the Rev. Stephen Hazard, the high-church Episcopal rector of St. John's Church on Fifth Avenue, and caught in the middle is a mediating third figure, the inexperienced young painter and aesthete Esther Dudley, who finds herself attracted to the self-assured rector. This primary attraction is complicated by Strong, Hazard's good friend, who plays the role of Esther's confidant, while also offering to marry her himself. In lesser hands, this formulaic marriage competition could lead to heavy-handed allegory; instead, this romantic formula is used to pose what becomes an insoluble problem that emerges out of Adams's tough-minded analysis of the fundamental nature of modern science and modern religion.[31]

---

29. Throughout the paragraph I draw from Foucault, *Order of Things*, 168. For the distinction between disciplinary and epochal epistemes, see note 1 of this chapter.

30. Throughout the paragraph, I refer to chapter 25 of Adams, *Education*, 317–26, 320–21.

31. Donoghue, "Henry Adams' Novels," 200–201, takes the view that Adams could not overcome his limitations as a novelist because he could only imitate the conventional

As the novel opens, Hazard is preaching an uplifting Emersonian vision of the divine unity that governs life. He takes for his text Descartes's rationalist discovery of the "I AM!" (8) experience, which he celebrates[32]—except that Hazard transfers the Cartesian discovery of the self to the recognition that God is the creator of all. "Science like religion kneels before this mystery" (8), he informs his worshipers. Symbolizing Hazard's confidence, predisposition to synthesis, and intellectual reach is his library, which is filled with Western classics of every kind, some examples of Eastern literature, novels, and art books depicting the achievements of every major civilization. But to Esther, this very power of assimilation bespeaks the imperial reach of Hazard's personality and his religion. To the intuitive Esther, all these achievements translate into a form of domination that could suppress her own personality in marriage.[33]

Esther struggles to find her own identity among three men—Hazard, who lives for his religion; Strong, who lives for science; and Wharton, who has been commissioned to create the murals for the new church and who lives for art.[34] Socialized into the triviality of her class and formerly not much of a reader, she strives to find her own self through her painting. Whereas Hazard and his church committee prefer the somber style of early Byzantine art, while Wharton wishes to work in the high medieval style around the Madonna, Esther is unsure of her beliefs and at first takes direction from Wharton. Soon, however, she discovers her intuitive preference for a style that captures the soul in a state of blessedness, peace, Nirvana. The theme of women discovering their identity is enriched by the appearance of the unsophisticated Catherine Brooke, an orphan from Colorado, who serves as a model for the painters, and whom Esther, despite Wharton's strictures, insists on painting "as she is," joyful and angelic (97). In this way, Esther's spiritual identity, her pagan "spontaneous religion of nature," as one critic puts it, signifies the emergence of a plausible third choice, filled as it is with its own iconography and discursive power.[35]

---

forms available to him, "melodrama, drawing-room comedy, the conversation piece." While I concur about Adams's limitations, I think his virtues as a novelist of ideas are substantial.

32. All quotations from Adams's *Esther* are from the 1938 facsimile reprint.

33. On these matters, see the well-thought-out argument of Millicent Bell, "Morality of Taste," 151–53.

34. The sentence is adapted from Samuels, *Henry Adams*, 237–38. Samuels's detailed, comprehensively contextualized reading of *Esther* is the best there is.

35. Colacurcio, "'Democracy' and 'Esther,'" 62.

Ernest Samuels points out that Esther's developing relationship with Hazard poses a far more difficult problem, for their prospective marriage presumes to unite not people of two different religions but a Christian and an agnostic.[36] Despite their strong mutual attraction, their diverging values produce a battle of wills. When the tension Esther feels reaches the point where she considers calling off their engagement, Strong intervenes on behalf of Hazard. Her problem, as Strong diagnoses it, is that she is seeking to secure her faith in Hazard's religion by rational demonstrations of its certainty. But this is not how faith works. She must take a leap of faith somewhere; she must understand that there are so absolutes in Hazard's church or in science. "Mystery for mystery science beats religion hollow," Strong declares, and, later, "There is no science which does not begin by requiring you to believe the incredible" (191, 199).

This idea that science is much like religion in the unproven assumptions upon which it rests was a crucial concept in Adams's thinking. He pointed out in an essay for the American Historical Association that there was no absolute way to determine the truth of scientific investigation due to the problem that two events may be correlated in time, but the first event cannot absolutely be determined to be the cause of the other.[37] In a letter written in 1910, he argued that because of its epistemological foundation, science cannot disprove revelation, and yet many scientists act as if it can.[38]

Adams further undermines the stereotypical binary relationships between science and religion by having Esther ask Strong, "Is religion true?" (198). Once Strong confesses that the question is beyond his scope and responds with an emphatic "No!" (198) to Esther's follow-up question on whether science is true, we realize that the novel refuses clichéd conceptions of both science and religion. Instead it portrays Strong as living with relative truths in existential indeterminacy. Indeed, his loyalty to science radiates an air of spirituality when he discloses that he remains loyal to science "because I want to help in making it truer" (198). The nature of his creed is further delineated when Ether asks whether Strong believes in God. His answer, "Not in a personal one," and certainly not in an afterlife with rewards and punishments, is the product of his materialist epistemology (269). What he believes in is "mind and matter," a doctrine that Esther

---

36. Samuels, *Henry Adams*, 237–38. Pertinent to this point is Spiller's observation in the introduction to *Esther*, x, that Hazard's hold over Esther will become dominance.

37. Samuelson, "Politics of Scientific History," 155–56.

38. Ibid., 164–65. But see Wasser, "Science and Religion," 5, who adduces evidence that Adams thought religious-based solutions to problems of knowledge were "inadmissible" because "religion discarded reason and postulated faith."

thinks "horrible" (270). But his response to this judgment is disarmingly honest. He doesn't want to convert anyone because he wouldn't expect anyone to choose to believe what he does. True to his beliefs—and in keeping with Adams's thought as well—Strong concludes their discussion by acknowledging that while he doesn't believe in an afterlife, he can't rule it out as a possibility. In this manner Strong sums up the gains and losses that accrue to a modern "belief" in science.

But if science does not answer Esther's needs, the question arises as to whether she would be happier marrying Hazard. Niagara Falls, with it magnificent natural spectacle, is the setting in which the novel answers this question. As numerous critics have observed, Hazard must "argue his case for supernatural religion, not from the pulpit but in competition with the thundering cataract," a setting in which religious dogma must be weighed against a different sort of worship based on a reverence for nature.[39] Hazard's core argument is that of Pascal, who wagered that in the absence of absolute certainty, one should place one's bet on the reality of an afterlife. The position of the atheists, he argues, is all loss and no gain. His second argument is that Esther should not worry about her lack of faith but should leave the problem to him. To this second argument, she flares, "Spare me! . . . Why should you . . . force me to take this leap? Are all men so tyrannical with women? You do not quarrel with a man because he cannot give you his whole life" (293). If he and his religious profession are one, she is certain that to be "half-married must be the worst torture" (293). This scene brings together many problem-drama issues in women's lives: the personal issue of preserving an independent point of view within the marriage bond, the smothering inequality that requires the woman's submission to her husband, the unfairness of the husband's entitlement to be "half-married" to his profession, to say nothing of the uncertain status of working women in the modern world.[40]

Of all these points, it is the first question about Pascal's wager that speaks most incisively to the objections Esther raises to Christianity. Instead of taking up the wager, Esther feels repelled by its crass appeal to self-interest. The same holds for the doctrines of punishment and reward for sins. The church is not spiritual at all, and its doctrines, she charges, in an allusion to the rite of transubstantiation, prompt her to think of Hazard as a priest at service in a pagan temple preparing to "bring out a goat or a

---

39. Samuels, *Henry Adams*, 255.
40. For discussion of these women's issues, see Bergmann, "Henry Adams's *Esther*," 66.

ram and sacrifice it on the high altar" (296). Oddly, the religious sentiments Esther expresses show the secularizing effect of comparative-historical criticism, which treated the Bible as if it were any other classical text.[41] Esther's litany of objections culminates in her rebuke to Hazard for attempting to assign her a maternal role by virtue of her "natural instincts"—"I ask for spiritual life and you send me back to my flesh and blood as though I were a tigress you were sending back to her cubs" (299). This last objection shows Esther answering the call of her inner self. Refusing to choose between either a rigorous, scientific materialism or the dogmatism and patriarchalism of Episcopal Christianity, Esther wants a spiritual life beyond self, a transcendence signified by Nirvana and the Niagara cataract.

This pronouncement bears directly on Esther's retort to Strong's belated offer to marry her: "But, George, I don't love you. I love him!" (302). These concluding words underscore the difficulty of matching compatibility of ideas with sexual attraction. In allegorical terms, Esther refuses to marry herself either to Strong's science, which is bleak and arid, or to Hazard's prescriptive, patriarchal Christian doctrines. Esther's spiritualism is an emerging but undeveloped third choice.[42] This choice is, however, filled with irony, for while Esther embraces spiritualism to lose her "self," her spiritualism is very much the product of her individuality, her will, which in turn reveals itself as the product of her highly developed sense of self, her secular identity.[43]

As must now be clear, each of the four novels discussed in this chapter exhibits its own distinctive orientation to the conflicts emerging between science and religion in the 1880s and early 1890s. Each also occupies a position along a continuum in an emergent, ideological discourse on the place of religion in an increasingly secular, science-oriented world. In the novels that follow in Part I, the cultural importance of this dynamic binary is even more pronounced—and compelling. All the novels were, in fact, well received; two of the three were best sellers, and all display high degrees of inwardness and complexity, which is why I devote a separate chapter to each.

---

41. A good example of such criticism, treated more extensively in the next chapter, is Sayce, *Primer of Assyriology*, 18, which speaks of archeological investigations that bear on biblical studies as "scientific" explorations.

42. On Esther as a divided person, see Wallace Evan Davies, "Religious Issues," 328–33. As discussed in the introduction to this book, many Victorian novels are constructed to highlight the personal conflicts created by the shock of Darwinism and the higher criticism, and *Esther* participates in this discourse.

43. Modern, *Secularism*, 119–20, does not treat *Esther*, but its discussion of spiritualism prompted several of the insights I have drawn.

CHAPTER 2

THE NEW BIBLICAL CRITICISM AND DARWINISM

Harold Frederic's *The Damnation of Theron Ware*

AS SEVERAL VICTORIAN novels of doubt show, the scandalous spectacle of ministers losing their faith was not new. Victorian novelist Mary Augusta Ward treated just this subject in *Robert Elsmere* in 1888, and American novelist Harold Frederic followed her in *The Damnation of Theron Ware* in 1896.[1] However, Frederic was the first to surround his protagonist minister with characters who embodied the major intellectual currents of late nineteenth-century America. Blending realism with typological representation, Frederic ascribed to each of his otherwise realistically drawn major characters a dominating idea that exerts a powerful influence upon Theron Ware, a likeable and aspiring but narrowly educated Methodist minister assigned

---

1. One of the few criticisms of Frederic's novel was its similarity to *Robert Elsmere*. See the summaries of Hutton's "Literary Notes," 3–4, and of the review in the *Manchester Guardian*, 10, appearing in O'Donnell, Garner, and Woodward, *A Bibliography*, 179–80 (F412) and 177 (F401), respectively (the parenthetical number references the item number in their bibliography). See also Peck, "Damnation of Theron Ware," 352. For a comprehensive comparison of Frederic's novel to *Robert Elsmere*, see Brumm, "Religious Crisis in *Robert Elsmere* and *The Damnation of Theron Ware*," 160–61. See also Bennett, *Damnation of Harold Frederic*, 182. On significant differences between Frederic's and Ward's novels, see Horton Davies, *Mirror of the Ministry*, 71–72.

to a provincial area of New York. Not only did Frederic situate his novel in Octavius, near Utica, New York, where he had been born and raised, but he constructed with meticulous care—as is evident from the notes he made—the intellectual and religious subcultures depicted in the novel.[2]

Theron's transformational journey begins after he makes the acquaintance of three characters who are to change his life. Father Forbes, a skeptical Roman Catholic priest, introduces Theron to the biblical higher criticism. Forbes's friend, Dr. Ledsmar, is a Darwinian research scientist and atheist who sends Theron learned books that shake his faith, and Celia Madden, the third of the triumvirate, is an unconventional young aesthete, rich, redheaded, and independent, for whom the married Theron falls hard. Later, Sister Soulsby, the novel's philosophizing pragmatist, appears to advise Theron to forego idealism and live expediently.

Unlike Ward, who used the religious novel to advocate progressive social causes, Frederic allied himself with no social cause or philosophical position. One might think that his bohemian lifestyle, in which he maintained two households with children and, in effect, had two wives,[3] would incline him toward unconventional opinions, but it did not. Instead, he maintained a clinical attitude of studied aloofness toward his material and made his novel a *fin de siècle* exploration, not of the material transformations of the century—automobiles, telegraphs, railroads, unions, strikes, and the like—but of the more advanced ideas of his time, which Frederic portrayed as leading to the disintegration of received beliefs.

For example, although the philosophic pragmatism of Charles Peirce and William James were not developed until each published a book on the subject in 1903 and 1907, respectively, a popular version of the new philosophy clearly made its way into Frederic's novel.[4] While pragmatism generally stresses that the value of all concepts is to be judged by their practical results, Sister Soulsby expounds the view that "pragmatism" allows people to believe anything they want. Similarly, aestheticism, or the art for art's sake movement, which was widespread among the privileged classes, is depicted in the person of Frederic's Celia, who defies community norms, especially

---

2. On the place where Frederic was raised, see Garner, "History of the Text," 354. On Frederic's notes, see Polk, *Literary Manuscripts of Harold Frederic*, 17–23. These notes include genealogies, backgrounds for the characters, and even the titles of books used by the learned characters.

3. O'Donnell and Franchere, *Harold Frederic*, 65–72, and Garner, *Harold Frederic*, 38–40.

4. Menand, *Metaphysical Club*, 351–58; Peirce, *Pragmatism as a Principle and Method*; James, *Pragmatism*.

moral norms, so as to live a life of the senses. The influence in America of the German model of pure research reached its apogee in 1900 and was widely imitated. But the model, as might be surmised from the depiction of Dr. Ledsmar, drew opposition because the solitary laboratory life was seen as turning professors "aside from the everyday world of society, politics, morality, and religion."[5] Amid all these forces of change, none was more threatening in America than the new biblical criticism, which, as Father Forbes's learning illustrates, subjected the Bible, especially Genesis, to a rigorous historical analysis that put its status as revealed Truth into question.[6]

On this foundation Frederic created the first novelistic deconstruction of the cultural forces then converging to create a secular age. Frederic's ironic method is well suited to his materials. All Frederic's major characters, including Theron in his wide-eyed parochialism, are marked by the suffusive taint of irony. Writing in reaction to the romantic and sentimental trends in the novel that were not yet spent, Frederic adopted the journalistic realism of William Dean Howells, which is closely associated with the fiction of Stephen Crane, Frederic's good friend and fellow journalist, both of whom unflinchingly depicted the world as they observed it.[7]

However, Frederic's pervasive irony helped fashion a new way of writing fiction, even as the technique presented major issues of interpretation and point of view. For much of the novel, the internal dialogue Theron has with himself makes readers feel that his acquaintanceship with Forbes, Ledsmar, and Celia are liberating influences, leading the young minister toward illumination of mind and spirit. Later, however, this appraisal is thoroughly undercut, for Theron's illumination, we are informed by the testimony of several characters, has actually been a degeneration marked by vanity, obtuseness, and lack of responsibility. Be this as it may, this turnabout is so sharp that it begs for a careful reexamination of the point of view that actually governs the representations of science, the biblical higher criticism, and aestheticism. An appropriate place to begin this exploration is the novel's reception, since that is where the salient interpretive issues first revealed themselves.

---

5. References throughout the paragraph to the German research model are from Veysey, *American University*, 132–33.

6. Especially fine for its review of nineteenth-century criticism of Genesis is Cameron, *Biblical Higher Criticism*, 290–318.

7. On the literary movements, see Carter, *Howells and the Age of Realism*, 24–25, 59–67, 239–45, and Garner, *Harold Frederic*, 5–40. In respect to Frederic's journalism, see Garner, "History of the Text," 404, who faults Pattee, *History of American Literature*, 401, for his influential, "unfounded statement" that Frederic's loose journalistic standards lowered the quality of his creative work. See also O'Donnell and Franchere, *Harold Frederic*, 31–56.

I

As soon as it was published, nineteenth-century reviewers hailed Frederic's novel for its psychological depth and intellectual substance. In the United States, where the novel outpaced *The Red Badge of Courage* and rose to fifth place on the best-seller list, distinguished reviewer Harry Thurston Peck declared it to be "distinctly a great novel."[8] England, if anything, was even more adulatory. Arthur Waugh of *The Critic* judged that except for "a few blemishes," it was "a masterpiece," and Gladstone's daughter reported that her father held the work to be "a masterpiece of character drawing."[9]

Although praise flowed freely, few reviewers faced up to the crucial issue of the nature of Theron Ware's damnation. Among the most penetrating of these was William Morton Payne, who called Frederic's novel one of "the subtlest studies of moral disintegration that have been made," and although Theron is "weak and contemptible[,] . . . he is the sport of fate. . . . The tree of knowledge is not for him the tree of life."[10] More comprehensively, a reviewer for *The Critic* spoke of "the great forces which lay hold" of Theron Ware's soul, as if he were "dragged by giants," and the *London Daily News* explicitly pointed to Celia, Forbes, and Ledsmar as the embodied cultural forces that cause Theron to lose "his spiritual foothold."[11] In so saying, these reviewers identified Theron's downfall as tragic and as proceeding naturalistically from (somewhat unspecified) inexorable external forces.

There are other possibilities as well. One is that Theron's downfall proceeds from the suffocating, narrow worldview of his religious upbringing. In this case the issue is whether we are to assign Theron personal responsibility for the choices he makes. Alternatively, several reviewers interpreted the novel as a topical satire on "primitive Methodism" (175), predicting that there would be repercussions in religious communities around the nation.[12] Frederic's "attack [on religion] is certainly a bold one," declared one American newspaper, "and it will be strange if he does not bring down the unanimous maledictions of the cloth on his devoted head."[13] Howells too

---

8. Hackett, *60 Years of Best Sellers*, 96, and Peck, "Damnation of Theron Ware," 351.

9. Waugh, "London Letter," 316, and "Notes," 302, both excerpted in O'Donnell, Garner, and Woodward, *A Bibliography*, 176 (F395), 175 (F393), respectively.

10. Payne, "Recent Fiction," 336.

11. "Literature," 309–10, and review in *London Daily News*, 8, excerpted in O'Donnell, Garner, and Woodward, *A Bibliography*, 176 (F394), 179 (F409).

12. The phrase is from Frederic, *Damnation of Theron Ware*. Page numbers to quotations from the novel appear in the text.

13. *Chicago Evening Post* (n.d.), in O'Donnell, Garner, and Woodward, *A Bibliography*, 175 (F390).

opined that he did "not think the book would please either Catholics or Protestants," adding with reference to Theron's career that "it is a book of great power, and . . . a very moral book."[14] Other reviewers expressed sympathy for Theron. Frederic's is "a pitiless illumination," lamented the *Atlantic*, and even though Theron "damns himself," "his three accusers seem to get off scot-free."[15] These responses demonstrate that critics desired to read Frederic's novel as a didactic work but were unable to agree on its morality. Numerous reviewers saw Theron's faith and ministerial role as undermined by the secularizing influences of his mentors, but failed to identify precisely what attitude toward them the novel establishes.[16]

The ground on which Frederic measures the intellectual currents of his day begins with the careful presentation in the opening chapters of the generational varieties of belief within the Methodist Episcopal (M. E.) community, to which denomination Theron belongs. Using an indirect method of description to characterize the assemblage of the First M. E. Church of Tecumseh, Frederic delineates a pattern of decline, from the venerable set of former preachers, valorized as the "reverend survivors of the heroic times"; to the "imperturbable self-complacency" of its middle-aged men; to the younger set, including Theron, that is unaware of its preachers' failing dedication and is caught up in a fierce competition with its wealthier rivals, the Presbyterians (3). But once Theron learns that he is to be appointed to the provincial, far less prosperous, M. E. Church of Octavius, he finds himself exposed to the harsh, uncompromising beliefs of a subset of his denomination that he had not previously encountered.[17]

These internal tensions induce assessment on both sides. The critical scene, spiced with satire, is Theron's first meeting with three trustees of his new church. Brother Pierce establishes the tone with his no-nonsense, Old Testament authoritarianism. He demands that Theron's wife, Alice, had "better take them flowers out of her bunnit" (27), a behest that appears to carry the weight of the congregation with it. The incidental detail underscores this church's unforgiving Puritan hostility to the softening effects of beauty, an orientation that also suggests, correctly enough, an alienation

---

14. Howells, "My Favorite Novelist," 24.
15. "Four New Novels," 272.
16. In its review of *Theron Ware*, the *London Daily News*, 8 (F409), pointed only to Forbes, Ledsmar, and Celia, while the writer of "Recent Novels," in the *London Morning Post*, 4 (F411) held that Forbes and Ledsmar drained Theron's idealism and Celia played pagan temptress.
17. On the heroic generation of founders, see Davies, *Mirror of the Ministry*, 71–72, and on the pattern of decline ending in the worship of Mammon, see Donaldson, introduction to *The Damnation of Theron Ware*, xxii–xxvi.

from modern secular culture. Pierce's blunt assertion that what this congregation wants is "straight-out, flat-footed hell—the burnin' lake o' fire an' brimstone" (27), leaves no doubt that Theron will have little latitude in his preaching. This depiction of Pierce may seem like a stereotype, but the appropriateness of the depiction is corroborated by modern religious scholars Stephens and Giberson, who, after describing fundamentalism as "by nature ... aggressive and polemical—'evangelicalism with an attitude,'" explain that for this reason "it is easy for its leaders to shout loudly and be heard."[18]

Having established the style of worship prevalent in Octavius's Methodist Episcopal Church, Frederic uses Pierce to sound the bugle call of engagement in countering the paleontological discoveries then threatening the Methodist-Episcopal Church and other denominations:

> And then, too, our folks don't take no stock in all that pact o' nonsense about science, such as tellin' the age of the earth by crackin' up stones. I've b'en in the quarry line all my life, an' I know it's all humbug! Why, they say some folks are goin' round now preachin' that our grandfathers were all monkeys. That comes from departin' from the ways of our forefathers, an' puttin' in organs an' choirs, an' deckin' our women-folks out with gewgaws, an' apin' the fashions of the worldly. I shouldn't wonder if them kind did have some monkey blood in 'em. (28)

Pierce's rhetoric draws upon a set of religious beliefs and attitudes characteristic of his class, but the very rhetoric that defends faith against the findings of scientific paleology is itself encased in authorial ridicule. A childlike conception of paleontology, characterized as "crackin' up stones," is made to stand for the entire enterprise. Pierce presents as "common-sense" a preposterous understanding of geological evolution (with its challenge to young earth creation). All this is based on the laborer's experience in a quarry. The absence of any conception of how dates are derived from stratified geological formations is so complete as to suggest an unbridgeable chasm between the production of scientific knowledge and the sacred, received knowledge this hard-nosed laborer has imbibed his whole life.

Pierce's jeering allusion to monkeys as grandfathers, with its echo of the famous 1860 debate in England between Archbishop Samuel Wilberforce and his Darwinian opponent, T. H. Huxley, is also laden with comic irony that turns in upon the speaker. Surprisingly, Pierce's attitudes are

---

18. Stephens and Giberson, *Anointed*, 49.

reminiscent of Theron's own because the echo of the Wilberforce-Huxley debate recalls Theron's earlier attempt to read "Paley's Evidences" (14), the edifying theory of God's guiding hand in nature.[19] Theron's wish to read Paley's book ties the young minister's knowledge base to a worn-out theology that Darwin, and through him Huxley, exposed as inadequate to meet the challenge of evolutionary theory.[20]

Frederic's satiric presentation of Brother Pierce predisposes the reader to prefer the progressive ideas of those whom Theron soon encounters.[21] First among these is the iconoclastic skeptic, Father Forbes, whom Theron observes performing last rites for a dying Irish workman. Moved as well by the kindness of the priest's friend, the beautiful Celia, Theron begins to rethink his long-held prejudice that the Irish are "dynamiters and Molly Maguires" who make "a bonfire of the Bible in the public schools" (49). Instead, he perceives that Celia's organ-playing and the Irish love of music prove just how cultivated the Irish are.

By most measures, Theron's realization ought to constitute a genuine form of illumination, as would his subsequent reflection on his extreme ignorance. But just at this moment, Theron's reflections take a reprehensible turn. He begins to take on airs and to denigrate the people in his own Methodist Conference. Whereas he considers himself to be full of glowing promise, he judges his own congregants to be ignorant and "doomed by native incapacity" (59). The imagery he uses suggests that he is undergoing a process of illumination, while his brethren belong to the benighted and the damned. Significantly, his categorical thinking remains theological—redemption for himself as one of God's elect and damnation for everyone else in his conference. Salvation is now figured as the acquisition of high culture, and high culture in turn as the acquisition of a secularized form of knowledge. The latter completely replaces Christian salvation in Theron's mind, signifying that the temporal has crowded out the eternal, or as Charles Taylor frames this trend in modern society, the secular has replaced the transcendent.[22]

This turn invites a new line of interpretation. Far from appearing to be enlightened, Theron's vain presumption now suggests that he is the author

---

19. "Paley's Evidences" is the informal title of Paley's famous argument in *Natural Theology*.

20. On the "monkey debate" in Oxford, England, and Darwin's objections to Paley's methods, see Larson, *Evolution*, 91–96, and Ruse, *Evolution Wars*, 39, 59–61.

21. A shrewd point treated in Lyons, "Hebraism, Hellenism, and Frederic's *Theron Ware*," 8–9.

22. Taylor, *Secular Age*, 15–16.

of his own damnation. An adjacent passage indicates that Frederic really intends to create a mixed response to Theron. Aroused by the sudden opening up to him of new possibilities, Theron again takes up his idea of writing a book on Abraham as the founder of Israel, except that this time he sees his subject from a totally new point of view:

> The people he read about [in Genesis] were altered to his vision. Heretofore a poetic light had shone about them, where indeed they had not glowed in a halo of sanctification. Now, by some chance, this light was gone, and he saw them instead as untutored and unwashed barbarians, filled with animal lusts and ferocities, struggling by violence and foul chicanery to secure a foothold in a country which did not belong to them—all rude tramps and robbers of the uncivilized plain. (60)

This passage reads as if had been conceived by a practitioner of the new biblical criticism. It strips the Bible of its holy status and opens the way for a naturalistic examination of life. However, Theron has not yet learned about the existence of a higher criticism; rather, his attitude anticipates it, but with the signal difference that his new thoughts about Genesis are tinged with repulsion. His pejorative reading replaces a sanctified one. In short, Theron's judgmental thinking designates as barbaric not just his Methodist Church but the biblical tradition itself.

These two examples notwithstanding, Theron's "damnation" cannot wholly be attributed to his own ratiocinations since so much of the evidence, as we have seen, points to external influences. Theron, moreover, knows that he is comparatively ignorant; that is why he is intimidated by Father Forbes's ceiling-high bookshelves and by the erudition that Forbes and his friend, Dr. Ledsmar, display. After explaining his incipient Abraham project to them, he submits to Forbes's judgment that his approach is too literalist. From this subordinate position, Theron then learns about the results of the new historical research that reinterprets biblical events, including Abraham's career, in accordance with the latest archaeological and linguistic scholarship of the day.[23]

Thus Forbes instructs his pupil, saying, "Modern research, you know, quite wipes him [Abraham] out of existence as an individual. The word, 'Abram' is merely an eponym—it means 'exalted father.' . . . Abram is not a person at all; he is a tribe, a sept, a clan" (69). This assessment of the generic nature of key names in Genesis is now firmly established among

---

23. For example, Forbes's exegesis on Abraham as eponym follows Laing, *Human Origins*, 238.

modern biblical scholars.[24] When in bewilderment Theron asks why everybody does not know these things, Forbes replies superciliously by asking why everybody should be expected to know anything. The truth is still the truth, he affirms, even if "ten hundred thousand numbskulls" disclaim it (70). Thus, at the same time that Theron takes a lesson in the new biblical scholarship, he also finds in Forbes a model for his own budding elitism.

These disclosures demonstrate that Theron's new learning crucially depends upon the influence of his new intellectual acquaintances. Modern scholarship has been shaped by the finding that Father Forbes's character is modeled on Frederic's close friend from the 1870s, the brilliant Father Edward Terry, whose heterodox views prompted his being transferred from Utica, New York, to Albany.[25] Perhaps this is the reason why few critics, if any, see Forbes's character as being subjected to irony. But it is. A good number of Forbes's opinions are accompanied by a comic "purring chuckle" (70, 72), suggesting smugness. This quirk of personality combines with Forbes's haughtiness, creating critical distance between him and the reader. Furthermore, Forbes's seemingly impartial contempt for common humanity does not extend to the Irish Americans as a people, for whom he expresses an ethnic partiality, improbably predicting that the Catholic Church will eventually overcome all the other Protestant denominations.

There is also a snobbish condescension in Forbes's responses to Theron, as when the priest exclaims, "Bless you, no! My dear sir, there is nothing new. Epicurus and Lucretius outlined the whole Darwinian theory more than two thousand years ago" (69). This aperçu is flashily expressed but far from cogent. Despite the rough parallel that both natural philosophies affirm the law-bound nature of the world, denying that the gods intervene in human affairs, the Epicureans and the followers of Darwin addressed totally dissimilar philosophic problems.[26] Epicurus and Lucretius addressed the question of the essential physical nature of the universe (atoms); Darwin addressed the processes governing survival in biological nature.[27] Forbes may also enjoy a degree of pleasure in so casually undermining Theron's

---

24. Forbes's account of the characters in Genesis being generic types is correct. See the account of religious scholars Stephens and Giberson, *Anointed*, 49.

25. Donaldson, introduction to *The Damnation of Theron Ware*, xiv, and O'Donnell and Franchere, *Harold Frederic*, 110.

26. On the Epicurean view of the noninterventionist nature of the gods, see Epicurus, "Letter to Pythocles," 43–60, and for discussion see Howard Jones, *The Epicurean Tradition*, 38–40. On religion, the gods, and the avoidance of superstition, see Godwin, *Lucretius*, 28–30, and Strodach, *Philosophy of Epicurus*, 50–71.

27. Epicurus's atomic speculations address the question of the physical nature of the universe. See Epicurus, *Essential Epicurus*, 27–31, and Strodach, *Philosophy of Epicurus*, 13–25.

beliefs, as when he explains that the Chaldean name "Marmaduke" is a prototype of our "divine intermediary"—a prototype of this "Christ-myth of ours" (71). This last phrase brings home to Theron the secularizing implications of the higher criticism. Whatever readers may think of Theron's failings, his dignified reply, "All I have done is to try to preserve an open mind, and to maintain my faith that the more we know, the nearer we shall approach the Throne" (72), invites sympathy and approbation for the authenticity of Theron's religious values.

These several turns suggest two generalizations—that the novel's assessment of Theron's character is mixed and that Father Forbes's point of view should not be mistaken for Frederic's. Not just Theron, but Forbes too, along with Theron's other iconoclastic mentors, are subjected to a degree of irony such that we as readers are not totally sure of our moral bearings. By this definition, Frederic's novel functions much like the social problem plays of Shaw and Ibsen and consequently merits the label "problem novel."

II

Dr. Ledsmar has the distinction of furnishing Theron with the books that bring about the young minister's counterconversion. Chief among them is an English translation of Ernest Renan's *Recollections of my Youth*, a famous autobiographical account of how the author came "no longer [to] believe at all in revealed religion" (125). Having become immersed in *Recollections*, he tells his bewildered wife that he is "merely reading scientific works" pertinent to his Abraham project (126). This descriptive term, which Frederic reinforces in a second allusion to Theron's "scientific" reading (127), far from being hyperbolic, is consonant with the terminology contemporaries gave to the secularized methodology of the new biblical criticism.[28] Theron's use of the term also has the effect of underscoring the high esteem in which he holds these *scientific* works, for he feels that he has been mired in "the slough of ignorance" (131). However, a counter-irony undercuts Theron's enthralled embrace of Renan's autobiography:

---

28. In "Some Sources for *The Damnation of Theron Ware*," 49, Robert H. Woodward states that one of Frederic's prime sources for the European books Ledsmar references on Assyriology is Ragozin, *Story of Chaldea*. In it Ragozin references an Oxford professor who has written a book entitled "The Science of Language" (332). Similarly, another of Frederic's sources, Sayce, *Primer of Assyriology*, 18, speaks of archeological investigations that bear on biblical studies as "scientific" explorations. The concept of the new biblical study as "scientific" is ubiquitous. See, for example, Smith, *Old Testament*, v, who speaks of "progressive Biblical Science."

> The book he had been reading—this gentle, tender, lovable book, which had as much true piety in it as any devotional book he had ever read, and yet, unlike all devotional books, put its foot firmly upon everything which could not be proved in human reason to be true—must be merely one of a thousand which men like Father Forbes and Dr. Ledsmar knew by heart. The very thought that he was on the way now to know them, too, made Theron tremble. The prospect wooed him, and he thrilled in response, with the wistful and delicate eagerness of a young lover. (131)

The entire passage is built on the ironic transformation of this famous atheistic text into a devotional one.[29] Theron's loss of faith is made to be a function of his *illumination*. But far from recoiling at this prospect, he welcomes his coming to the light in a manner similar to Dr. Faustus in his pursuit of Helen of Troy. The passage also reintroduces the central methodological principle of the higher criticism, which is that "human reason" is to be the sole criterion of truth (131). From this point on, Theron acts as if he is becoming "a citizen of this world," and as such asks himself "not 'Is your soul saved?' but 'Is your mind well furnished?'" (132).

This internal monologue suggestively identifies Theron's "illumination" with his seduction. As initiated by Forbes and Ledsmar, the seduction is intellectual and spiritual, for Theron explicitly attributes his "meeting with the priest and the Doctor" as the "turning point in his career" (131). These seductions in turn anticipate the young minister's sexual fall, not through adultery per se, but through his intimacy with Celia, and insofar as the novel works allegorically, this sequence of events makes Theron's obsession with Celia and subsequent physical deterioration the direct consequence of the prior seductions he suffers from the learned priest and the doctor.

In his allegorical function, Dr. Ledsmar embodies the values of research under the paradigm of Darwinism. We know this from an interview Frederic gave describing one of his professional characters as "a biologist, who, among many other things, is experimenting on Lubbock's and Darwin's lines," and from Frederic's manuscript notes that include a newspaper clipping entitled "The Origin of Species By Hybridisation."[30] Darwinism also eats its way into the text, as when Ledsmar shows to Theron that in one of his laboratory

---

29. Contemporary readers of Renan, *Recollections of My Youth*, would not have found it to be a "gentle, tender, lovable book." Rather, Renan's intellect and the process of his interrogation of his Catholic faith are the book's outstanding features.

30. Donaldson, introduction *to The Damnation of Theron Ware*, xiii; Polk, *Literary Manuscripts*, 16 (item A7C.1). Frederic's invocation of Lubbock's *Ants, Bees, and Wasps* is odd in that the brand of science Lubbock practices is closer to the older practice of

experiments he is testing "the probabilities for or against Darwin's theory," specifically, that hermaphroditism is a late evolutionary phenomenon (222). However, the entire disordered laboratory becomes a commentary not so much on Darwinism as on Ledsmar's mind. Little that goes on in the laboratory appears to be productive, beginning with Ledsmar's disclosure that he does not expect to know the results of the evolution of plant hermaphroditism for hundreds of years, since no one has ever come to understand human females for many thousands of years. As a misogynist and ascetic whose sole friend is the celibate Father Forbes, Ledsmar resents "superstitious" females such as Celia with her "lascivious mysticism" and emotional enchantment with religious ritual and music (219–20). This misogyny attaches itself not just to Ledsmar the man but to Frederic's representation of the profession of the research scientist and, by extension, to Darwinism itself.

Insistently, Frederic further delineates Ledsmar's repellent character through diabolical symbolism. Despite holding a medical degree, the doctor is heavily involved in a narcotics experiment on his personal servant, a "Chinaman," whom he is injecting with increasingly high doses of opium in order to record his subject's tolerance for it. When Theron first observes the servant, he appears as if dead, but Theron quickly learns that the Chinese man has taken in enough opium to kill both the minister and the doctor and yet remains "strong as an ox" (223). This episode is a touchstone. Ledsmar's cruel, potentially lethal, experiment clarifies the meaning of the doctor's earlier declaration to Theron that it is incorrect to "imply a connection between Science and Medicine! . . . My dear sir, they are not even on speaking terms" (67).

This declaration revisits the concept of the science/faith binary and shows the potential fracturing of the science component. In Ledsmar's view, science is a domain to be restricted to primary research, not to the practice of improving people's health. In other words, for the German-trained Ledsmar, the scientific quest to discover nature's secrets does not include humane care and service, values that the medical doctor ideally embodies. Ledsmar's atheism and pursuit of scientific knowledge for its own sake are qualities that run counter to the American preference for the practical application of knowledge and, in Frederic's rendering, show Ledsmar's scientific practices to lie quite outside the American mainstream and, indeed, outside the bonds of common humanity.[31]

---

observational science, which the experimental sciences superseded. A number of Ledsmar's experiments also appear to be interminably observational.

31. Carter, introduction to *The Damnation of Theron Ware*, xx, usefully observes that Ledsmar's character signals a break in the literary treatment of practitioners of science,

As a literary type, Dr. Ledsmar is much less the product of American realism than he is of the allegorical and symbolic traditions exemplified in Nathaniel Hawthorne's *The Scarlet Letter*.[32] From this vantage, Dr. Ledsmar's progenitor is Roger Chillingworth, "the misshapen scholar" and physician with features like a writhing snake, who practices strange medicine acquired in the wilderness, well beyond civilization.[33] Coldly analytical and lacking in human sympathy, Chillingworth, though a medical advisor to the Reverend Dimmesdale, has a malevolent soul. Many of these qualities reappear in Celia's identification of Ledsmar as "that doctor and his heartless, bloodless science" (97).

Other images amplify the doctor's diabolical identity. Ledsmar is repeatedly associated with things reptilian and satanic—adders, lizards, snakes. An expert on Assyriology, he has written a learned book on serpent worship. Yet Theron completely fails to perceive Ledsmar's inimical nature. When he comes upon the drugged Chinaman in Ledsmar's symbolic garden, his first thought is "The Doctor *was* a beast!" (223)—but this idea remains only a thought because Theron does not pursue it.

The allegorical significance of Ledsmar's interactions with Theron come together when Ledsmar reappears with his right arm hanging limply by his side—an iconographic representation of the doctor as satanic. At that point, Ledsmar extracts from one of his tanks a "yellowish-green lizard, with a coiling, sinuous tail and a pointed, evil head" (226). With melodramatic emphasis, he addresses the lizard, saying, "You are the type," and with a grim, curled smile declares its name to be "the Rev. Theron Ware" (226). This revelatory scene ends by associating *both* the doctor and Theron with the satanic lizard. The episode redefines Theron as diabolically transformed. He has become Ledsmar's newest subject for experimental observation. From this perspective, the event portrayed prompts us to reinterpret Ledsmar's earlier gift of Renan's autobiography to Theron as a malevolent act aimed at precipitating Theron's descent into unbelief.

Frederic's rendering of Dr. Ledsmar as a diabolical scientist belongs typologically to the literary tradition of the daring scientist, from Dr. Faustus and Frankenstein to Chillingworth, whose research violates human laws and restraints. But as a contemporary depiction of a modern research scientist, and particularly the Darwinian researcher, it is a caricature. Just as

---

away from the dedicated scientist and back to Hawthorne's depiction of the cold, heartless scientist.

32. Bennett, *Damnation*, 186–87, treats fully Frederic's connections to Hawthorne's fiction.

33. Hawthorne, *The Scarlet Letter*, 43.

importantly, it displays next to no understanding of Darwinism, either as a concept or a practice, and no assimilation of the major findings of Darwinism or the theological implications of its evolutionary hypotheses.

As we have seen, late nineteenth-century Darwinism threatened to displace the former scientific paradigm that the investigations of nature also revealed that the universe was made and guided by a just and loving God. In one of its main expressions, Darwinian evolution also insisted upon the inexorable operation of the natural laws of chance variation and the struggle for existence, which applies to all living things, including man.[34] Also some explanations of evolution left no place for the transcendence of God or, at the personal level, the efficacy of prayer. Yet none of these contemporary anxieties surfaces in Frederic's novel. How this fiendish depiction of Ledsmar pertains to Darwinism or the cultural anxieties it produced is not addressed.

III

Celia's visceral antipathy for Dr. Ledsmar's scientific research proceeds from her own identification with aestheticism, which includes things unconventional, beautiful, and emotionally satisfying. In the symbolism of the novel, Celia's dislike of Ledsmar reenacts the traditional hostility between the arts and the sciences.[35] As a proponent of Greek culture, Celia celebrates what she calls "the Greek theology of the beautiful and the strong, the Greek philosophy of life and all that" (99), yet her understanding of that civilization is romantic and shallow. Greek theology was not a matter of surfaces, as Celia declares; it was concerned with modesty and piety before the gods, observing the mean, keeping the balance, comprehending the whole of life, and, as Greek tragedy illustrates, avoiding hubris by recognizing one's place in the universe.[36] Celia also declares her preference for Plato's philosophy over Saint Peter's but shows little of the depth that might lead a reader to take her views seriously.[37] A show-off as well, Celia appears to

---

34. Mayr, *One Long Argument*, 97–104.

35. See the learned discussion on this topic in Lyons, "Hebraism, Hellenism, and Frederic's *Theron Ware*."

36. Among those who describe foundational Greek beliefs, see Kitto's chapter, "The Greek Mind," in *The Greeks*, 169–94, and William Chase Greene, *Moira*, 3–9, 47–49.

37. Robert H. Woodward, "Some Sources," 49, shows that Frederic's limited knowledge of Plato was probably drawn from Draper, *History of the Intellectual Development of Europe*, 1:154. But pages 1:151–54 treat Plato's philosophy with appropriate *gravitas*, which is absent in Celia's remarks.

appropriate her own version of Greek culture and to use it to facilitate her rebellion against the misogynistic patriarchs of the early Catholic Church. Thus, despite Celia's telling critique of Ledsmar's character, she is herself subject to Frederic's pervasive irony.

The incongruous statuary adorning Celia's apartment, into which she daringly invites Theron, theatrically corroborates this impression. Surrounding Theron are Greek statues of females in various states of nudity along with serene, haloed pictures of the Madonna in full-length drapery. In Celia's narcissistic imagination, the integrating principle of both forms of art is that the female becomes the object of adoration, even though the two civilizations clash, both artistically and philosophically.[38] Similarly, when Celia plays for Theron the music of Chopin, she absurdly exalts the sensual composer as "the Greekiest of the Greeks," adding that all the Greeks were artists, "where everybody was an intellectual aristocrat" (194). These jejune proclamations are soon accompanied by narcissistic behavior bordering on cruelty. In the charged atmosphere she has fostered, she leaves Theron to wonder while she changes her clothes. When she reappears, she is wearing clingingly soft nightclothes, her red hair luxuriant and free. Without ever making an overtly sexual overture, she sways suggestively to the music and bids the sensually intoxicated Theron to smoke and enjoy a glass of Benedictine. Her only explanation to the enthralled minister is that all this is part of her idea about the Greeks—"absolute freedom from moral bugbears" (202)—and then she informs her bewildered guest that it is time for him to leave. As a figure who stands for the allure of the aesthetic and the sensual, Celia's behavior suggests that her influence upon Theron is detrimental to his well-being and his soul.

Obsessed with Celia, Theron neglects his good wife and even imagines her to have accepted an illicit relationship with the trustee Levi Gorringe. In these imaginings, Theron appears to be the author of his own degeneration. But Celia, too, through her sensual overtures, plays a role in Theron's enthrallment, or as Suderman puts it, his "counterconversion."[39] This again induces the reader to sympathize with Theron, notwithstanding his subsequent craven pursuit of Celia in New York City. Furthermore, Celia's romanticized—and sexualized—conception of Greek civilization, along with her self-absorption, undercuts her, just as Father Forbes and Dr. Ledsmar are undercut.

---

38. For a psychoanalytic discussion of these incongruities, see Crowley, "The Nude and the Madonna."

39. Suderman, "*Theron Ware* as a Criticism of American Religious Thought," 67.

Incongruously, Celia casts herself in the role of Theron's physician. Just before she invites the minister to her apartment, she informs Theron, who is recovering from a near nervous breakdown, "I don't believe in illnesses myself" (186). With these words, Celia adopts a concept of disease that recalls the contemporary teachings of Christian Science founder Mary Baker Eddy, who held that all illness is the result of a failure of faith rather than microbial disease. As shown in the previous chapter, Eggleston's *The Faith Doctor* had thrown light on the very real threat to the public health that could accrue from disregarding the microbial basis of many diseases. Irrespective of the growing awareness of how infectious diseases are communicated, Frederic has Celia, like Mary Baker Eddy, deny their reality. It is, perhaps, a mark of Celia's hostility to science and love of the role of iconoclast that prompts her to tout her own curative skills, saying, "I'm your doctor. I'm to make you well again" (187). Unfortunately, she exercises her powers in the role of a seductress, and the effect is to hurl Theron toward further degeneration.

In sum, each of Theron's three comforters, with their advanced scientific or humanistic allegiances, plays a part in bringing about Theron's mental, spiritual, and physical collapse. A fourth comforter, Sister Soulsby, along with her husband, is a Methodist debt-raiser who embodies the commonsense philosophy of pragmatism. An exuberant but shady type, Soulsby teaches a doctrine replete with allegorical imagery that recalls Ledsmar. "You simply *can't* get along without some of the wisdom of the serpent," she explains (140). As an example, she discloses that she takes tunes composed by the infidel George Sand and turns them into hymns. "It's a fraud—yes, but it's a good fraud" (179), she rationalizes. Her commonsense outlook, otherwise called "expediency," has a certain surface appeal, but her interventions are almost always accompanied by burlesque humor and thus subject, once again, to irony.[40]

Like Celia, she assumes the role of a physician. To her way of seeing, no one is all bad and no final judgments ought to be made until the Last Judgment. Attractively, she tends to the broken-spirited Theron, rescuing him from despair, but the strong medicine she administers is her teaching that life is a game and success to be achieved by play-acting. Unstated but clear is that her advice has nothing to do with integrity, authenticity, or self-knowledge. Under her influence Theron resigns his ministry, prepares to

---

40. But Briggs, *Novels of Harold Frederic*, 136, argues that the Soulsbys, unlike the three tempters, possess "the comic sense of knowledge." Thus, for him, there is no irony in the portrayal of Soulsby.

move with Alice to Seattle, and redirects his life toward the pipedream that he will employ his rhetorical skills to rise in the West, perhaps even to become a U.S. Senator.

From this mixed evidence, readers may reasonably wish to split the difference and conclude, as do Franchere and O'Donnell, that the Soulsbys are "'half-charlatans, half angels.'"[41] If, however, interpreters weigh more heavily Sister Soulsby's manipulativeness, as does Scott Donaldson, and the amorality of her doctrine of expediency, Stanton Garner's conclusion that Sister Solsby is "the true Mephistopheles of the morality" may seem more accurate.[42] It will not do, however, to account the Soulsbys "good doctors," by positing that their world view adds, as the other three tempters do not, a realistic "comic sense to knowledge."[43] To do this would be to discount the intrinsically mixed assessment of all the major characters in Frederic's novel.

IV

If any *éclaircissement* is to be found in the novel's point of view, it is usually attributed to Celia in her revelatory speech to Theron. Delivered after the young minister has ignominiously been discovered spying on Celia and Forbes in New York City, Celia's judgment is that whereas she and Father Forbes once thought him a promising acquaintance, unsophisticated but natural, they have instead discovered that he has assumed airs, behaved like a prurient boy, and deluded himself about her relationship with him. "'Your whole mind,'" she informs him, "'became an unpleasant thing to contemplate'" (322). Complementing this assessment is the judgment of the dying Michael, Celia's brother, who informs Theron that he has entirely deceived himself about the world he has entered, and his face has changed from that of a saint to a barkeeper. Michael's grave advice is, "'Keep among your own people, Mr. Ware! . . . There can be nothing better for you than to go and strive to be a good husband, and to set a good example to the people of your church'" (298–99).

Critically situated near the end of the novel, the two speeches share the common message that Theron's degeneration is his own doing, and numerous readers have taken this view to be Frederic's clarifying final judgment. Yet the ambiguities of the novel cannot wholly be shifted to one person.

---

41. O'Donnell and Franchere, *Harold Frederic*, 117.
42. Donaldson, "Seduction of Theron Ware," 445–46, and Garner, *Harold Frederic*, 34–35. See also Luedtke, "Harold Frederic's Satanic Soulsby."
43. Briggs, *Harnold Frederic*, 135–36.

If Celia's dying brother really functions as a choral figure, then we must accept the stern moral he draws—that Theron ought to keep to himself and the people he knows. In other words, if you are a religious conservative, don't attempt to learn more from other ethnic groups or religious communities; don't try to be part of the greater world or to integrate yourself in it; wrap yourself up in the safety blanket of the life you know. If spoken by alienated religious conservatives, this would be good advice, but one wonders whether this is actually the final word of the novel, especially coming from an author who was a foreign correspondent for the New York Times and lived for many years in a country not his own.[44] Michael's warning is also fully compatible with the more limited perspective of an Irish Catholic brother who has come face to face with the young Protestant minister who has tried to secure a liaison with his sister.

Nor can we unequivocally accept Celia's version of the affair. As George Johnson forcefully argues, she is "sadistic, and coldly superior"; Ledsmar, for his part, is "a misogynous advocate of scientism," and Forbes "a cynical defeatist."[45] In the subtle formulation of Edmund Wilson, "The three tempters, though Celia and the priest are presented not without sympathy, do behave rather badly."[46] They are all given to performance. This being so, we are left with the conviction that Theron is, at least in part, an agent; he makes choices, albeit in ignorance and vanity. But he is a seeker of *illumination* and, as such, subjects himself to the compelling scientific and philosophic forces that break his faith and ruin his life.

If this outcome does not affirm very much, it is because Frederic is a thorough-going skeptic and ironist. Frederic's papers reveal that he had, in fact, originally planned to have Theron Ware commit suicide.[47] Such an ending would have been melodramatic, though it might have drawn sympathy to Theron as a victim beguiled by the secular forces surrounding him—that is, by his tempters. Instead, Frederic settled on a more plausible, satiric conclusion that has Theron giving up his ministry and indulging himself in a narcissistic fantasy of a rosy future that will never be. This ending, too, supports the notion that Theron's damnation is his own doing, yet it does not erase the realization that Theron's suffering comes from a series of secular illuminations that prove to be spiritual death. This complex set

---

44. See chapters 3 and 5 in Myers, *Reluctant Expatriate*, 43–65, 91–113.
45. George W. Johnson, "Harold Frederic's Young Goodman Ware," 366.
46. Edmund Wilson, *The Devils and Canon Barham*, 63.
47. Frederic, *Correspondence*, 397, records that Frederic's notes indicate that in the original version Theron Ware died. Vanderbeets, "The Ending of *The Damnation of Theron Ware*," 358–59, explains that the death was to be a suicide.

of considerations amounts to just this: in his assessment of the new secular world just rising and an older religious world hanging on, Frederic cast a cold, analytic eye on both, and in so doing, he fashioned a prescient novel, modern in its pervasive irony and skepticism.

Frederic's dark vision of an increasingly secularized American society was not, however, to dominate the novelistic landscape. James Laine Allen, Frederic's contemporary and nationally recognized local colorist, treated with riveting intensity the impact of the Darwinian revolution on faith and found redemption in the new scientific learning. Drawing heavily on his own autobiographical experience, Allen composed a novel of great strength, defending his young hero's awakening to "Sacred, sacred Doubt of Man," for which heresy the author became swept up in bitter controversy.[48]

---

48. Allen, *The Reign of Law*, 137 (Kessinger Publishing reprint).

CHAPTER 3

AN AMERICAN RESPONSE TO DARWINISM

James Lane Allen's *The Reign of Law*

FOUR YEARS AFTER *The Damnation of Theron Ware* appeared, James Lane Allen composed *The Reign of Law* (1900), the most penetrating study an American novelist has produced on the transformative effect of Darwinism on a single person. In Allen's novel, that person is named David, a rural, Bible-believing, teenage farm boy in Kentucky. The novel's appeal flows gracefully from the fervency of its hero's search for truth. These circumstances mirror the author's own experiences, for he too was a poor Kentucky farm boy who attended the University of Kentucky, experienced the meanness of sectarian rivalry, and like his young protagonist fell into religious doubt.[1] But reviewers at first did not recognize these features of the novel so much as Allen's loving depictions of the Kentucky landscape, which reinforced the author's well-deserved reputation—based on *A Kentucky Cardinal* (1894) and *The Choir Invisible* (1897), both best sellers—as a local colorist.[2]

---

1. These matters were established in 1935 by Allen's biographer, Grant C. Knight, *James Lane Allen*, 135–36.
2. Hackett, *60 Years of Best Sellers*, 97; Grant C. Knight, *James Lane Allen*, 97; Bottorff, *Allen*, 48–49. Spiller, *Cycle of American Literature*, 96, 167, labels Allen as a Southern romance writer.

In England, where the work was published as *The Increasing Purpose,* one reviewer incanted, "The day of the American novel... is at hand," while another, from America, praised Allen as "easily the master-stylist of his time."[3] These converging circumstances help to explain why seventy thousand copies of Allen's novel "were at once sold on faith" and why it was reprinted six times, becoming a number-four best seller in American fiction.[4]

At home the celebrations turned to vituperative religious controversy. For using his novel to deny a personal God and for affirming through David that "the universe—it is the expression of Law" and that "all we know of Him whom we call Creator, God, our Father... is [through] the Reign of Law" (294–95), Allen was roundly denounced from the pulpits and in the religious press alike.[5] Fame slipped into notoriety when the president of the Bible College of the University of Kentucky (the college Allen's David attends), John W. McGarvey, defended his college's reputation and attacked Allen personally as an *infidel* whose purpose was to "degrade Christianity."[6]

This unfortunate confrontation did have the effect of turning attention to the novel's substantive engagement with social and religious issues. These shape the novel's dramatic presentation of social change as a manifestation of evolutionary principles—the Civil War, women entering the workforce, and the decline of small-town farming accompanied by a flight to the cities. Given the appalling human waste of the Civil War—623,000,000 dead and well over 1 million dead or wounded on both sides in a country of 30 million—the question of the moral significance of the war became a metaphysical one, often answered with profound skepticism. For Allen, the war had a significance found not among the battlefield dead but in the social revolution that followed, especially in the South, where freed blacks and displaced, declassé white women struggled to realize their talents in a transformed social environment. In 1850, 500,000 women worked outside

---

3. The quotations are from "The Increasing Vogue," 524, and Giltner, "A Study," 352. Examples of praise of Allen's natural depictions are "James Lane Allen's New Novel," n.p.; "The Increasing Purpose," 53; and "James Lane Allen, An Inquiry," 36.

4. Grant C. Knight, *James Lane Allen*, 137; Allen, *Reign of Law*, Kessinger Publishing edition, original copyright page; Hackett, *60 Years of Best Sellers*, 100; "Increasing Vogue," 524. On the eagerness of readers to purchase *The Reign of Law* even before its publication, see Maurice, "James Lane Allen's Country," 156.

5. All citations to Allen's *Reign of Law* are to the edition cited in footnote 4 and appear in the text. For an account of the denunciations Allen endured, see Grant C. Knight, *James Lane Allen*, 137–40.

6. "Is Mr. Allen's 'Reign of Law' an Infidel Work?," 198. Allen, however, was never expelled (unlike the fictional David). See Joseph Z. Tyler, "Historical Background of *Reign of Law*," 354.

the home; by 1900, that many were working in office jobs alone, and women teachers (such as Allen's Gabriella) began to organize to protect their interests. Of small farmers Allen knew firsthand. In the novel, David's father is that farmer; he cultivates a modest, slowly failing farm business producing hemp. Though not directly expressed in the novel, the economic fact was that by 1900 vastly more efficient (and expensive) heavy machinery was displacing small farm owners, like David's father.[7]

Allen's novel, it should be emphasized, does not belong to the genre of social realism; it is not like *The Grapes of Wrath*, but it uses the transformations it depicts to probe the metaphysical meaning of post–Civil War life for a great nation laboring under the new paradigm of evolutionary change. This new way of framing experience is most fully captured in Allen's treatment of the life cycle of the hemp. His lyrical depiction of the cycle of hemp production in Kentucky—from the sowing of inert seeds, to their sudden ten- to twelve-foot thrusting through the earth, to their cutting down and final bundling by strong African American laborers—has been celebrated by many readers for the several levels on which it functions.[8] The life history of the hemp poignantly obeys the same universal natural laws that govern humankind and every other living thing. Thus, as Allen suggests with reference to evolutionary biology, the hemp is "grown and finished" in a planetary year, having originally come forth from its "birthplace" in some "extinct river-bottom" where life reemerges after eons of decomposition (22, 8, 9).

Interspersed with this detailed evocation of the biological process of creation and extinction are Allen's observations of the hemp as a crop produced in Kentucky, whose importance recapitulates the history of the American nation and of the South in particular. As the product of "Anglo-Saxon farmers" (7), this hemp, Allen records, outfitted half the rigging on the frigate *Constitution* (the other half being Russian-made in a contest for superiority). Meanwhile, the same product was used extensively to bale cotton. Its dwindling use in the post–Civil War period—the period in which the novel is set—foretold a not "far distant [time] when the industry there will have become extinct" (7–8).

Immersed as the novel is in the turbulence and displacement brought about after the Civil War, its account of the history of the hemp crop in Kentucky embodies the novel's preoccupation with the ubiquity of change, a process that also governs the intellectual and spiritual quickening of its

---

7. Throughout the paragraph, I cite from Zinn, *People's History,* 232 (Civil War casualties), 223, 330 (women working), and 247–48 (agriculture transformations).

8. "James Lane Allen's New Novel," n.p.

obscure farm-boy protagonist as he struggles with religious doubt. From this vantage, Allen reaches outward to explore the cultural transformation implied by the establishment of Kentucky's premier public institution of higher learning. Even more comprehensively, Allen employs Kentucky's central geographical position as a "unique border state" (34) to explore the profound implications of the late Civil War as a process of social evolution for the South and the nation as a whole.

Just as Allen uses Kentucky's hemp crop to frame the larger evolutionary process of natural growth, decay, destruction, and recreation, so too does he frame the story of David (the only name by which he is identified) through an account of the educational vision of David's great-grandfather. This old Indian fighter held ample lands but was expelled from his church in 1790 for "the liberality of his religious opinions" (25) after he repeatedly entertained preachers of widely divergent theological beliefs. In response, the crusty landowner vowed to build a church and a schoolhouse where men and women would be free to learn and to worship. By the end of the Civil War, that institution with its many colleges, including its Bible College, became the University of Kentucky at Lexington, where the humanities again burgeoned as a "pledge of the new times, plea for the peace and amity of learning, fresh chance for study of the revelation of the Lord of Hosts" (34). From such genealogical seeds as these, Allen relates, did David's own unlikely process of intellectual development evolve.

I

Allen's title, *The Reign of Law,* resonates with interpretive possibilities. Bible readers who emphasize the term *reign* are likely to envision, in the manner of traditional Christian iconography, God the Father, who *reigns* as supreme King and law-giver over the universe. However, those who prioritize the term *law* are likely to interpret the title as referring to the scientific discovery of the regular operation of the laws of nature. Allen himself appears to have drawn the title phrase for his novel from Andrew D. White's *A History of the Warfare of Science with Theology in Christendom,* one of the most influential works of Allen's era. White's history, published in 1896, explicitly describes *modern science,* just as Allen does, as substituting "the reign of law for the reign of caprice, and the idea of evolution for that of creation."[9]

---

9. White, *History of the Warfare of Science,* 1:23. The idea of a "reign of law" was not entirely new. An earlier work by academic luminary John Draper, *History of the Conflict*

Despite this provenance, the novelist treats the notion of a reign of law as a kind of floating signifier intriguingly awaiting settled definition. In the novel, the full term, *reign of law,* first appears and is fully defined only in the last quarter of the work. Before that, the reader must follow the personal journey of Allen's protagonist as he struggles to discover to what *law* exactly he is bound. As a child of the heartland, David begins his intellectual and spiritual journey with his Bible, in the "cradle of faith in the morning of civilization" (56). Like his forebears, he believes that the cause of all things befalling humankind, whether welcome or dreaded, reach him through "the laws of nature," always working to "some benevolent [albeit often unknown] purpose of the Ruler" (61). In this dispensation, in which human beings are placed at the center of the universe, everything is made for "Man, Man, Man, nothing but Man!" (57). But once David enters the University of Kentucky, as did Allen, this innocent faith falls into confusion as the young man hears his pastor denounce all other Christian sects because each fails to pledge itself precisely to the same dogmas as his own. Acting upon a spirit of open-mindedness, David listens to the sermons delivered by preachers in other denominations, including those of the Presbyterians, Baptists, Methodists, and Episcopalians, only to learn that they are internally divided, each arrogating to itself sole possession of the inerrant truth of scripture.

Knowing that these Christian churches cannot all be right, David experiences the first of many dark nights of the soul as he begins to lose his faith, as Allen himself did.[10] The spiritual guidance he seeks from his pastor, an unnamed professor of the Bible College, leads to what arguably becomes the most compelling, emotionally taut scene in the entire novel. From a thematic standpoint, Allen uses the scene to call attention to the truth-claims made by old-school dogmatists. As the conversation unfolds, the pastor's intransigence functions as a hortatory demonstration of the parochialism and inhumanity into which the actual practice of Christianity has fallen. The nonsectarian point of view from which Allen's critique is launched may be gleaned from David's opening observation that his great-grandfather "built a church simply to God, not to any man's opinions of Him" (90)—an ecumenical orientation that David's professor summarily dismisses as a heresy endorsed by Voltaire and the Devil. From both artistic and historical points of view, this snide invocation of the French philosopher (named three

---

between Religion and Science, 228, employs the term to distinguish between two kinds of government: one upheld by the priesthood (providential law), the other by the law of science.

10. Grant C. Knight, *James Lane Allen,* 135–36.

times) is apt not only because of Voltaire's fame in America and Europe as an anti-Christian and a skeptic but also because his name became a byword for new learning, particularly investigations into the laws of nature. For instance, Charles Lyell in his renowned *Principles of Geology* explicitly highlights Voltaire's geological essays debunking contemporary clerical attempts to square geology with Genesis.[11] As the scene develops, the rigid doctrinal positions that the professor holds to be inviolate are revealed. Many of the dogmas the professor defends, it should be remembered, would in Allen's own generation come to be formally identified as Fundamentalist:[12]

> So bidden, the lad began:—
> "Is it Apostolic Christianity to declare that infants should not be baptized?"
> "It is!" The reply came like a flash of lightning.
> [...]
> "Is it Apostolic Christianity to affirm that only immersion is Christian baptism?"
> "It is!"
> "And those who use any other form violate the word of God?"
> "They do!"
> [...]
> "Is it Apostolic Christianity to make every congregation, no matter how small or influenced by passion, an absolute court of trial and punishment of his members?"
> "It is!"
> [...]
> "Is it Apostolic Christianity to require that the believer in it shall likewise believe everything in the old Bible?"
> "It is."
> "Did Christ and the Apostles themselves teach that everything contained in what we call the old Bible must be believed?"
> "They did!" (96–98)

David's repeated use of the phrase "Is it Apostolic Christianity" functions as an accusatory thrust aimed at uncovering the pastor's absolute allegiance to

---

11. On Voltaire's reputation in America, see May, *Enlightenment*, 105, 110, 121. Lyell, *Principles of Geology*, 65–66.

12. For a review of the origins of these "fundamentals" of Christian faith, as they were called, see Sandeen, *Origins of Fundamentalism*, 17–22, and Evans and Berent, *Fundamentalism*, xvii–xviii, 1–4.

the most uncertain of theological dogmas, dogmas that purport to stand as the one and only Christian truth. The Bible professor's explosive ripostes to David's pointed questions dramatize his authoritarianism and the narrowness of unloving beliefs that claim to be universal. As Allen shapes the confrontation, the pastor's angry affirmations compel the reader to behold what a theologically suspect set of Christian dogmas really looks like. Despite the narrator's remarks that the pastor is "a good man," "God-fearing and God-serving," Allen's depiction verges on caricature, as when the professor is described as a "logician" given to "stroking his beard with syllogistic self-respect," or when zealotry contorts his face, making it "livid with sacred rage" (90–92, 99). These satirical observations function as a stylistic complement to the argument that Allen has been making all along—the arrogance of those in the faction-riven Protestant churches of the United States who pretend to know the Law of God.

Given this rendering of the angry absolutist pastor, the real issue becomes whether this treatment is fair in the sense of true-to-life. Helpful in this respect is Scott Appleby's historicized account in "Rethinking Fundamentalism in a Secular Age" of the sensibilities of those committed to fundamentalist doctrine. Fundamentalist movements, Appleby says, are "both *reactive* and *selective*." They "react primarily to *the marginalization of religion*— that is, to the displacement of 'true religion' by nationalist political leaders, [and] scientific and cultural elites," and they are also "selective" in pointing to those elements of their faith that are "most resistant to relativism, pluralism, and other concomitants of secular modernity." Seeking to protect the holy book and cherished doctrines from "the depredations of historical, literary, and scientific criticism," they "embrace *absolutism* and *dualism* as tactics of resistance and as justification for extremism in the service of a sacred cause."[13] Given the reactivity to secularism and the degree of defensiveness that Appleby finds in the fundamentalist personality, Allen's rendering of the absolutist pastor appears to be both extreme and just.

One feature that Appleby does not cite but that is critical to Allen's narrative is that doctrinal absolutists, such as this pastor, must fend off not only the incursions of agnostics, atheists, and secularists in general, but they must also defend their creed against rival denominations. Hence Allen's emphasis in the confrontation scene on such precise points as immersion in baptism and infant damnation. For Allen's David, the turning point away

---

13. Throughout the paragraph, I cite from Appleby's "Rethinking Fundamentalism," 230–31. Branch, *Rituals of Spontaneity*, 222, makes the point that fundamentalist personalities are not restricted to one set of believers. They can be found, she implies, in any group, even in secular settings. Hence the term *fundamentalisms*.

from his received faith proceeds from his realization that the contradictory teachings of denominational Protestantism manifestly do not teach universal Christian doctrine.

This sequence of thought leads to the momentous question of what law exactly does govern the universe. An answer is urgent. As David himself reasons, "If I cannot believe what I formerly believed, let me determine quickly what I *can* believe. The Truth, the Law—I must find these and quickly!" (112). After hearing his pastor deliver a sermon denouncing by name scientific books that lead young people astray, David, in a decision that marks his integrity as a truth-seeker, resolves to read and judge them for himself. In these books he discovers "a mighty chain of truths" that organize themselves around the central idea of evolution (120). Through these riveting findings and a growing appreciation of the reach of scientific methods, David realizes that all fields of human knowledge, social and scientific, will need to be rethought. Much of the remainder of the novel is given over to exploring the implications and felt significance of this "New Science" in people's lives (124).

So transformational are these ideas that they constitute a new law governing life. Through science-focused similes and metaphors, Allen seeks to find fresh ways of explaining how the universe works. He is especially adept in rendering ordinary events and thought processes through images drawn from the natural world, particularly geology—that original evolutionary field in which such figures as Georges Cuvier and Charles Lyell established the great antiquity of the earth.[14] Except for Darwin, whose *Origin of Species* (1859) and *The Descent of Man* (1872) are explicitly cited (the latter anachronistically by a few years) as part of David's reading, Allen avoids specifically naming any of the "illustrious group of scientific investigators and thinkers" he hails (115). Instead, he prefers to foreground the

---

14. Cuvier's most influential, summative findings were published as *Recherches sur les ossemens fossiles* (Paris, 1812), and its preface republished separately as *Essay on the Theory of the Earth* (Edinburgh, 1813). Lastingly associated with "catastrophist geology," as contrasted with Darwin's gradualism, Cuvier was held in high esteem in the nineteenth century for his rigorous empirical methods in the field of geology. His was a historically important scientific practice, as Gould argued in *Structure of Evolutionary Theory*, 483–92, even though Cuvier's conclusions were adopted by believers in the biblical Deluge. For further discussion, see Gillispie, *Genesis and Geology*, 98–99, and Larson, *Evolution*, 7–8, 47–51, who explains that Cuvier's catastrophism "stood as a bulwark for creationism in the life sciences" (50). On Lyell's rejection of a young earth based on Noah's flood, see *Principles of Geology*, 24, and on his compelling arguments for the earth's antiquity, see 312–98. Rudwick's textual study, *Georges Cuvier*, 165–71, maps out Cuvier's meticulous comparative study of mammoth bones and molars, demonstrating that ancient animals are not the same species as those now existing.

impact of the evolutionary findings themselves, such as the extinction of species, cycles of death and recreation (championed by Cuvier), and the processes underlying the activity of volcanoes (examined in detail by Lyell).[15] Employing an epic simile, Allen compares this new law of life to a "volcanic upheaval under mid-ocean" that "rock[s] the tiny boat of a sailor boy in some little sheltered bay on the other side of the planet" (116). In just this way does this "sublime disturbance in the thought of the civilized world" reach the solitary David in Kentucky in the latter half of the nineteenth century (116). The new learning itself is like this; it comes like an irresistible storm sending "waves of influence rushing away to every shore," including the United States (116).

In an act of elegant transposition, Allen invests David's scientific learning with a spiritual aura betokening enlightenment. Quite unlike Frederic's ironic method of undercutting his protagonist's learning in *The Damnation of Theron Ware*, Allen's metaphors work to elevate his hero. Thus, the young scholar's "laboratory" of learning is represented as emitting a "sunlike radiance" and "his lamp" as a "vast purification of the world by the fire of truth!" (121). Self and world become reflections of one another. The earth, in its processes of decay and rebirth, elicits this sense of awe, as do the processes of social transformation, such that Allen is able to declare with Darwinian emphasis, "Old structures of knowledge and faith, dangerous, tottering, unfit to be inhabited longer, must be shaken to their foundations" (123).

Allen instantiates this theme of transformation in David himself, whose intellectual development involves casting aside narrow, worn-out ideas as he embraces broader, more enlightened ones. For example, as a direct consequence of his newly acquired scientific learning, David declines to sing in the choir, attend the Bible students' prayer meeting, or partake of "the Lord's Supper" (125). Subsequently tried for heresy and found guilty by the professors of the Bible College, he is dismissed. The event, we are reminded, is made to echo in a minor key other trials of great ones in the history of science. Again, we are not told specifically of Galileo's own trial by the Inquisition, or Giordano Bruno's, for that matter, because, one presumes, Allen wishes to be more delicate by modestly suggesting a distant kinship between David's personal travail and the greater agony of those followers of science who have gone before him. And there is this further

---

15. Allen's notion of cycles of destruction and creation seems to originate in the first instance, not in Darwin's work but Cuvier's. See Zimmer, *Evolution*, 143, who states that "Cuvier ... argued that catastrophes had punctuated life's history, each one clearing the world for a new set of creatures to take its place." See also Young, *Discovery of Evolution*, 71–73, and Ruse, *Evolution Wars*, 22–23.

consideration: had Allen wished to pursue this historical analogue, he could easily have made David's sentencing and expulsion from the church and the Bible College the theatrical climax of this section of the novel. The fact that the novelist refuses this opportunity demonstrates that Allen's purpose was not to sensationalize David's story, nor to elicit outrage at injustice, but to foreground the inwardness of David's journey as he strives to find his place in the world, despite believing in a natural rather than a supernatural reign of law.

II

Without question, Allen's multichaptered depiction of the great winter ice storm that brings ruin to David's father's farm is the novel's pivotal symbolic event. The storm, whose phases are well observed, detailed, and somberly convincing, also functions as a naturalistic piece of Americana. The depiction begins with the unusual observation of rising winds and falling temperatures, moves to a description of the raindrops that turn to ice as soon as they touch the earth, and then to the crackling sound of boughs breaking from the trees, to the "fragile sounds" of the "rotten, weakest, most overburdened twigs," to the falling of the fruit trees, and, finally, to the periodic, "deep boom" of the great forest trees as they come crashing down from the weight of the ice (206–7). Calamitous though it is, the storm leaves behind an awesome stillness and the terrible beauty of its "argent icicles" (210). For such craftsmanship as this in representing the beauty of American (and specifically, Kentuckian) landscapes, Allen won the acclaim of critics both at home and in England.[16]

Yet Allen attained something still rarer: he used the storm as a template or paradigm for revealing old-versus-new ways of interpreting such natural disasters. David says that before his conversion to a scientific outlook, he would have interpreted the ice storm in the manner of his judgment-driven father, as God's chastisement of man, or members of the community, for having offended Him. This would be to interpret awe-inspiring natural events from the point of view of Genesis, that man is the center of God's creation and the primary reason for the beneficence or punishments that befall humankind. But in the light of the physical sciences, the storm is but

---

16. Among American reviews praising Allen's stylistic qualities, see Payne, "Recent Fiction," 21, and for a comparable English review citing Allen's admirable feeling for nature, see "James Lane Allen, An Inquiry," 35.

a force of nature, a product of "natural laws, operating without regard to man" (224). Through this lens, farm animals are no longer seen as made to serve man—no more than man is made for predators to eat. That is, inexorable physical laws supersede a theological interpretation of natural events. "The law of storm" (206), as Allen puts it, operates irrespective of man's virtue or sinfulness. But if, indeed, that law works impartially, it also appears to function without discernible purpose, without plan, its "law being turned with seeming blindness, and in the spirit of sheer wastage, upon what it has itself achieved" (205). This perspective explains Allen's oxymoronic rendering of the storm's terrible beauty: the storm is "one of those vast appalling catastrophes in Nature" and yet "sublime" in its inscrutable awesomeness (205, 207).

The foregoing discussion may suggest that Allen's novel leads straightforwardly to the resolution of David's religious doubts on the side of science. But this is not quite the case, for David's groping toward a naturalistic worldview also lays bare the spiritual anguish he feels for his lost faith. Although the "New Science" overthrows the "Old Faith," the former brings about the "New Doubt" (124), since David no longer knows the purpose of his life, his Maker, or his destiny. Nowhere is this spiritual torment more evident than in David's meditation on a poor sheep, bloodied and killed by a dog-wolf during the storm. What killed the sheep? Was it the storm, the dog, the man who took it from its natural state, or nature itself? With eloquent bewilderment, David poses the teleological question, which the new light of Darwinism cannot answer, "Where and with what purpose began on this planet the taking of life that there might be life? Poor questions that never troubled you, poor sheep!" (350).

Such passages as these demonstrate that Allen's novel is not materialist at its core, despite its embrace of the New Science. Out of the anguish that makes David sick appears a young woman who nurses him back to health. Although somewhat muted and late-developing in *The Reign of Law*, this romantic turn functions as a complement to the novel's strong empirical and scientific commitments.[17] Thus, David, finding his father hostile to him and his stepmother, like nature itself, indifferent and unresponsive to his needs,[18] must seek out a more receptive home. Furthermore, since he is unable to continue believing in the Christian God of his childhood, David must redirect his spiritual yearnings toward a more temporal object,

---

17. For a statement of Allen's aesthetic, see Allen, "Realism and Romance," 283–86. The essay argues that the realm of romance is part of human experience and therefore consonant with realism.

18. Bottorff, *Allen*, 75, makes the point.

a young woman named Gabriella. Even so, Gabriella still functions as David's spiritual salvation, as Allen makes explicit in the metaphors that David applies to her. True to her name, she is his "archangel," a "divine presence," and though he has ceased to believe in miracles, she remains his "miracle" (228, 226). The comfort she offers, earthly and spiritual, is expressed in her nursing David back to health after he falls dangerously ill as a consequence of the ice storm, whose spiritual effect on him is implied by its brute power as a mute testament to nature's mystifying purpose.

Of still greater symbolic importance is that Gabriella's life's history is a parable of the social transformation of America. Her story complements David's. While David's is an inner drama of changing beliefs pertaining to deity, Gabriella's reproduces the momentous social events brought about by the recent Civil War and its aftermath. That is to say, David's life is progressively rendered as that of an enlightened Everyman for a new scientific age, Gabriella's by the momentous social transformation in which she is swept up. True to her allegorical name, Gabriella, again like the Archangel Gabriel, announces a new birth, a new birth of freedom for women and former slaves. These two novelistic movements are organically tied, for both record transformational processes that issue from the intellectual revolution that evolution has brought about. Allen's transitional metaphor shows this linkage: the meaning of Gabriella's life story, we are told, can be explained as an imagined four-volume book, perceived "as a slender seam of gold ... through the geology of the earth" (245), which means, in effect, that the lens of scientific explanation of evolution, having been applied to nature, is to be turned to the mid-century revolutionary social history of the United States.

Allen manages each of the imagined four volumes of Gabriella's life in such a way that the welter of mid-century events is reduced to essentials. Their crafted simplicity recalls parable and, in places, archetypal myth. Following the lead of Hawthorne, who reinterprets the Garden of Eden myth in *The Scarlet Letter* to reveal a new concept of salvation in Puritan New England, Allen presents Gabriella's life story as an incarnation of the moral history of the American nation. The first volume reveals Gabriella as a child of the slave-holding South who has known only entitlement her whole life. Central to her pleasure in Allen's archetypal rendering of her plantation life is a picture-perfect garden all her own. In this fairy-tale-like setting, Gabriella used to sit beneath the shade of an apple tree with a real switch, accompanied by her young slave, Milly, whom she rapped from time to time on her bare legs because "that was expected" (249). Routinely during the full summers there came to her home relatives from plantations all over the South, celebrating their own aristocratic virtues and "false ideals," sowing over many years the "fateful fruits" until "everything was ripe, sweet, mellow, dropping, turning rotten" (255). Such is Allen's poignant but clear-eyed appraisal of Southern high culture. The second volume treats Gabriella's history during the Civil War, which brought about the "downfall of the child princess" (256). Allen renders this historic national "struggle"—the signature Darwinian word, to which the novelist repeatedly adverts (260, 271, 273)—as the battle for the supremacy of four principles. On the one side stood "the idea of the right of self-government," along with the idea that men have a right to do as they please with their own property; on the other, the idea of a "nation-building race" that the "Union" cannot be compromised and that the "social evolution of the race" calls for the "overthrow of slavery" (256, 257, 259).

For Gabriella, the triumph of these latter two values provides the subject of the third volume, the post–Civil War period that was supposed to bring peace and brought instead a "sad, sublime history" (257). Having been dethroned and bereft of her plantation and her family, Gabriella is thrown on her own resources. This last event provides the theme for the fourth volume. As a "child of the Revolution" (258) that had cost her almost everything but had also freed the slaves and made them citizens, Gabriella comes to embody the promise of a new South. Imitating the processes of nature, she, like the freed slaves, is impelled to new strivings, fresh growth, renewal. Along with many of her contemporaries, she achieves independence, works for a salary, and actively contributes to the new society by becoming a teacher.

The issue of this paradigmatic life history is that through years of struggle, the young Gabriella is regenerated. Possessed of her new identity, she finds in the intellectually uprooted David her life's partner. Nevertheless, struggle and striving are part of life. David's new ideas about nature's law have separated him from his received Christian faith. There thus exists a necessary tension between the lovers, for Gabriella, as an Episcopalian, retains *her* belief in a providential Christian God and strives to bring David back to the fold. The novel never refutes or attempts to undermine this faith.

However, Allen affords David space to press his view that the Creator is no more knowable through Christianity than through any of the other great religions. The "great Law of Evolution" (297), David explains, governs all history—from that of humankind to the history of the earth, the solar system, and the universe itself. Thus, the Creator is known, though only distantly, through the laws that proceed from him: "His reign is the Reign of Law" (295). In this way, the development of humanity, especially in its moral and intellectual growth, is also an unfolding and a "revelation of Him!" (299). In order to pursue this greater understanding, David determines to leave behind the hemp field of his father, where "the trees must be deadened and cut down" (379), and to dedicate his professional life to the New Science.

With Gabriella by his side, David decides he will move to the more intellectually receptive environment of a university in the North.[19] There, Allen tells us, "two children of vast and distant revolutions" will face together a more promising, "wider" future (383).

III

Despite this sensitive, multisided depiction of evolution in action in *The Reign of Law*, showing it to be a process of individual transformation, a social process, a biological process, and a methodological process, Allen's reputation has suffered from his most widely read twentieth-century critic, William Bottorff, who makes several unfair claims that warrant review. Prominent among these are that in matters evolutionary and scientific, the author is "lacking depth of understanding" and that *The Reign of Law* is "unconvincing in its presentation of the modern temperament or of the modern dilemma."[20]

At the turn of the twentieth century, when Allen composed his novel, many American intellectuals were still getting over the loss, through Darwinism, of traditional belief while trying to retain faith in a higher power. Allen's contemporary, the scientist and philosopher Joseph LeConte, summarized this outlook in words that might have been used to describe David's progress in Allen's novel. LeConte wrote, "Every step in the advance of the science of geology has tended to sap, and finally to overthrow, our faith in certain dogmas concerning the antiquity of the earth and the introduction of death."[21] LeConte went on to describe the contemporary situation with the poignant irony that "the light of science is indeed

---

19. David's decision to go north comports with the sociological findings of Numbers, *Darwinism*, 25–26, that in the late nineteenth century members of the National Academy of Sciences were clustered in far greater numbers in New England and the Middle Atlantic states.

20. Bottorff, *Allen*, 73, 78. In a related observation, Grant C. Knight, *James Lane Allen*, 140, points out that Allen erred in having his hero read Darwin's *The Descent of Man* three years before its actual publication.

21. LeConte, "Relation of Theology to Science," 112.

a glorious light" but "unbelief is spiritual death."[22] In so saying, he was in effect identifying the danger that Allen has David confront as well. Similarly, LeConte recognized, as did Allen, that the law of evolution affects "every department of thought, changing our whole view of Nature and modifying our whole philosophy.... [So] the question presses upon us, 'What will be its effect on religious belief, and therefore on moral conduct?'"[23] This depiction of the problem of the age shows that Allen was very much in tune with the modern temper, and this despite Bottorff's stricture and that of the reviewer for *The Dial* that Allen's novel exhibits a paucity of "dramatic action."[24] Their criticism, in fact, devalued just the kind of inward suffering that spoke to the anxieties of the age and is one of the novel's singular strengths.

Similarly, the reputation Darwinism had for being an atheistic philosophy seriously underestimates the response of most intellectuals who grappled with evolution's theoretical implications and struggled to find a place for faith, or at least the religious impulse. Examples of this trend are numerous. Thus, when historian of science Paul Carus described science as "a revelation of God," stipulating that "through science God communicates with us,"[25] he was identifying a crux that Allen also wrestled with in composing *The Reign of Law*. Furthermore, in framing the view that "when a faithful Christian turns infidel, the world in which he lived breaks down,"[26] Carus could have been describing David's life at the point of his apostasy. So, too, when in 1897 Lyman Abbott proposed in *The Theology of an Evolutionist* that "evolution is, broadly speaking, the doctrine of growth applied to life; the doctrine that life is a growth," [27] he was articulating a progressive vision that has its counterpart in Allen's own idea about the evolution of social justice in the United States. The entire trend was epitomized by famed lecturer and philosopher-historian John Fiske when he avowed that science provided "a new road to God, not through the supernatural, but *via* nature herself." [28]

These several citations illustrate how fully Allen captured the spirit of his era—not that all scientific-religious leaders in America conceived of the

---

22. Ibid., 113.
23. LeConte, *Evolution*, 276.
24. Bottorff, *Allen*, 73; Payne, "Recent Fiction," 21c.
25. The quotations are from Carus's 1893 lecture, "Science a Religious Revelation," 77.
26. Ibid., 83.
27. Abbott, "Summary of Conclusions," 153.
28. The quotation is from Guthrie's review of "Fiske's 'Through Nature to God,'" 12. See also the statement of Fiske, *Through Nature to God*, xii.

modern condition as Carus, LeConte, Abbott, Fiske, and Allen did, but that their writings exhibit the combination of exhilaration and angst the new scientific age had engendered. So when Bottorff reproves Allen for his "failure to qualify as a sympathetic Defender of the Faith of Evolution," he seems to want Allen to be more like a twentieth-century activist.[29] But Allen was truer to his age in being a reflective thinker, especially one who was able to depict the crisis of belief as experienced from within.

These observations allow us to weigh Allen's effectiveness in capturing that spirit in the novel's closing peroration:

> O Mystery Immortal! which is in the hemp and in our souls, in its bloom and in our passions; by which our poor brief lives are led upward out of the earth for a season, then cut down, rotted and broken—for Thy long service! (385)

Bottorff's judgment of this passage is that *The Reign of Law* "concludes without resolution; it only points with optimism."[30] The critic thus demands closure when there is no closure. More importantly, the apostrophe expresses not so much a facile optimism as a fervent spiritual yearning for connection to a creator so distant that humanity has no clear idea how to serve that higher power, a power known only by the physical laws of nature it has set forth. The entire passage is built on the moving irony that even as the human spirit reaches upward, like the hemp, toward its unknown creator in an anguished gesture of service, the body is in a short time cut down and broken. This incomprehensible movement of growth and decay may be read as a plea for enlightenment; it is a spiritual urge that no longer knows the object of its worship. Still, the invocation of the "Mystery Immortal!" *does* recollect the novel's repeated proposition that humanity's intellectual growth is an unfolding of the Divine Power, which places David and all the other spiritual seekers in "Thy long service!"

These concluding words, charged with emotion, are both forward-looking and anguished. They bring to mind the pertinence of theorist Amy Hungerford's feeling insight that to live in a state of nonbelief and to struggle even to name what a person does believe is still "undoubtedly to live religiously."[31] To apply Hungerford's insight to Allen's novel, *The Reign*

---

29. Bottorff, *Allen*, 73.
30. Ibid., 77–78.
31. Hungerford, *Postmodern Belief*, xv.

of Law, is not a thorough-going example of the opposition between the scientific and the spiritual, for it ends with the affirmation of both.

Nevertheless, the area in which the novel became associated with the clashing of cymbals is in the conflict between the religious (narrowly construed as sectarianism) and the secular (defined as the pursuit of scientific knowledge). The interplay between this binary became self-evident, not in the novel per se, but in the topical controversy in which Allen became embroiled. On February 16, 1901, *The Literary Digest* reported, "Allen's latest novel has created a somewhat extraordinary amount of controversy in the religious world." The magazine went on to cite specific denunciations that Allen's book had provoked among leaders of Christian institutions and in the conservative press, although mainstream newspapers and magazine critics stood behind it.[32] To demonstrate that the novel also drew liberal supporters to its side, *The Literary Digest* recalled the statement by Unitarian minister Dr. Chadwick, who judged the novel to have "done more for the liberal cause than all the sermons preached in liberal pulpits during the past year." These circumstances show that Allen's novel was not a passive reflection of the historical reality surrounding it; to the contrary, it had become an integral part of a reality of conflict that it also helped to generate.[33]

Following the publication of *The Reign of Law,* President John McGarvey of the University of Kentucky's Bible College stepped forward to denounce Allen's novel as "essentially an infidel work," whose "chief purpose . . . is to degrade Christianity to the level of the great heathen religions of Asia." He took particular umbrage at Allen's naturalistic philosophy, whose "prejudice against miracles," as he called it, "has no reason to sustain it; and but for this prejudice such books as the 'The Reign of Law' and such lectures as those of the recent unlamented Ingersoll would never be written."[34] By invoking the renowned atheist lecturer Robert Ingersoll in this way,[35] McGarvey showed that he saw himself defending Christianity against the nonbeliever Allen had proven to be. If Allen's statements in *The Reign of Law* about the universe were true, McGarvey reasoned, "then our Bible is false . . . [and] it follows not only that the most important records of the

---

32. The dramatic story of the mixed reception of *The Reign of Law* appears in Grant C. Knight, *James Lane Allen,* 137–41.

33. Unless otherwise noted, quotations throughout the paragraph are from "Is Mr. Allen's 'Reign of Law' an Infidel Work?," 198.

34. McGarvey is referencing with repulsion the scientific method identified with naturalism or, more precisely, methodological naturalism, defined by Larson in *Evolution,* 51.

35. On Ingersoll's life and work, see Anderson, *Robert Ingersoll.* For examples of Ingersoll's heterodox and atheistic essays, see Ingersoll, *Superstition and Other Essays.*

Old Testament are false, but that Jesus is not the Son of God." Stung by the attack, Allen could not resist responding, and in so doing revealed the growing chasm separating the two men. He wrote, "But let the president beware! He must have in his classes many quick-witted boys of common sense and the rudiments of a public-school education. Any such lad will be able to tell him that all his cited illustrations of how natural laws reverse their action only prove that such laws do not reverse their action." Allen drove on to the bitter conclusion, "that such theology as the president has shown . . . , coupled with such ignorance of the intellectual condition of his age, helps to drive young men out of the church. In all probability it would have helped to make David an infidel. It would certainly make me one."[36]

Beneath the public acrimony there lay two radically different—and, as McGarvey framed it, irreconcilable—epistemological positions, one based on the truth as revealed in the Bible and the other on principles of observation and experimentation pertaining to natural phenomena only. Theirs was a foundational opposition. Less obviously, McGarvey and Allen were battling over the cultural authority that their respective worldviews would occupy in the life of the nation. As a Christian college president, McGarvey strove to maintain the place of orthodox Christian belief in higher education, while Allen, a former professor and advocate for college students, championed a concept of public higher education in which students would have unrestricted access to scientific methods and results.[37] The public dimensions of this struggle were just beginning to be felt in 1900, and we who live now in the first quarter of the twenty-first century well know that the issue is not only unresolved but as divisive as ever.

Since Allen's novel has this modern feel, it is hard to account for the obscurity into which it has fallen. Ironically, an explanation can be found in the novel's rare integrative impulse. The joining of spirituality to science may well have struck a responsive chord among a contemporary readership used to oppositional ways of representing the relationship between science and religion. Quite likely, the first generation to ignore the novel came to maturity in the 1920s, when the fundamentalist movement gained national visibility at the Scopes trial and secularists met their opposition with ridicule. On both sides, a long-lasting contretemps replaced compromise. In such circumstances, Allen's poetic local-colorist style may well

---

36. Quotations throughout the paragraph are from "Is Mr. Allen's 'Reign of Law' an Infidel Work?," 198–99.

37. In 1880 Allen became professor of Latin language and literature at Bethany College, West Virginia. See Bottorff, *Allen*, 15.

have appeared too provincial and the romance of the novel too sanguine to remain popular.

What is thoroughly clear, however, is that Allen's novel was attuned to his own times, and it did a good deal more than recirculate the energy swirling around the evolution-religion debate. Employing not just the abstract arguments as his contemporary essayists, philosophers, theologians, and scientists had done, Allen did dramatize to a wide general audience the stultifying effects of religious fanaticism. At the same time, he demonstrated how a young man's spiritual aspirations could actually be elevated by knowledge of the New Science. Similarly, by tying David's spiritual struggles to the life of Gabriella in the aftermath of the Civil War, Allen showed how both could be seen from evolutionary perspectives. In so doing, he modeled how American readers could view the larger meaning of their own turbulent social history. Furthermore, by having David take Gabriella for his life partner, the novelist intimated that those who believe in a Creator known only through the laws of nature need not live apart from those who retain a traditional faith. Promisingly, Allen concluded his novel by linking the lives of both Gabriella and David to America's unfolding destiny.

When Allen's novel first appeared, *The Dial* had predicted that it would appeal only to those whose experience could match the intellectual struggles of the hero. "That it should become widely popular we do not deem probable," the reviewer reasoned.[38] As subsequent events revealed, *The Reign of Law* became all at once both controversial *and* "widely popular." Thirty-five years later, Allen's biographer, Grant Knight, could claim that *The Reign of Law* had earned a historically significant place as "the first notable anti-fundamentalist novel to come from the pen of a southerner."[39] For this historical reason alone, the novel deserves to be rediscovered. This process may already have begun, since a number of modern reprints are now available. There are other reasons as well for rediscovering this fine work. The novel's controversial subject matter, intrinsic quality, and tumultuous reception give it a special place in American letters. So does its spiritual striving in the face of seeming unbelief. Simply put, *The Reign of Law* is the best American novel we have on the struggle for the acceptance of evolutionary ideas in a framework of spirituality. As Amy Hungerford might well have said, Allen's literary practice is best understood as a species of religious thought.[40]

---

38. Payne, "Recent Fiction," 22.
39. Grant C. Knight, *James Lane Allen*, 134.
40. Hungerford, *Postmodern Belief*, xv.

The novel that follows this, *The Leatherwood God,* also examines the beliefs of a Bible-believing community, but its center lies very much elsewhere. For whereas Allen and Frederic treat the inward effects of a young man's awakening to doubt, Howells depicts an elderly gentleman who is already a confirmed skeptic and who uses his powers to make rational sense of a mass frenzy that overcomes a small frontier community when a stranger walks into their midst claiming to be God.

CHAPTER 4

AN ENLIGHTENMENT CRITIQUE OF RELIGIOUS MANIA

W. D. Howells's *The Leatherwood God*

WHEN H. L. MENCKEN ridiculed *The Leatherwood God* (1916) for its failure to enter the mind of its Ohio impostor John Dylks, who claimed to be God,[1] he was in effect demanding the kind of exposé of religious chicanery that Sinclair Lewis later produced in *Elmer Gantry* in 1925.

But Howells did not write that kind of novel. Instead he composed a reflective, historically based work that functions much like a case study. Constructed, it must be acknowledged, from a wholly secular point of view, the novel takes a series of strange, seemingly miraculous events that transported—and divided—a small frontier community in 1828, when the historical Dylks suddenly appeared in Leatherwood, Ohio, and transmutes them into a secular domain of rational skepticism. Whatever one may think of this strong, secularizing orientation, Howells's novel richly rewards careful study because it makes visible the process of secularization, wherein formerly spiritual events are explained in terms of a newly emergent discipline that would come to be known as psychology.

---

1. Mencken, "The Dean," 261.

The distinctiveness, and importance, of Howells's novel may be further appreciated by comparing it to *The Damnation of Theron Ware* or *The Reign of Law*, in which the novelist enters the mind of the lead character, who loses his faith. By contrast, Howells's title figure is a mysterious person whose motives must be deduced by outside observers. Furthermore, the crucial character who tries to make rational sense of the stranger's behavior is not a young man discovering doubt but an elderly town justice of the peace, Matthew Braile, who is already a confirmed skeptic. Braile is Howells's strategic creation because he furnishes the skeptical lens through which the reader attempts to interpret Dylks's motives and the bizarre behaviors that might be called ecstatic by his devotees.[2]

Through Braile, Howells presents an Enlightenment approach to his subject—that is to say, a hypothesis-driven, evidence-gathering, empirical method of interpreting the revival of religious fervor in Leatherwood. This dedication to what science historian Edward Larson identifies as "methodological naturalism," in contrast to supernatural explanations of events, is a hallmark of French *philosophes*, who were precursors of and contributors to a secular method of scientific investigation stripped of its religious associations.[3] Profoundly influenced by the deistic leaders of the French Enlightenment were Thomas Jefferson and Thomas Paine,[4] the latter of whom Howells presents as a guiding influence on Braile himself. Although the novel does not quite make it explicit, Paine's empiricism, commonsense logic, and denial of the miracles of scripture are themselves features instantiated in Braile's approach to Leatherwood's religious troubles. But far from delivering a satiric assault on Dylks and his followers in the manner of *Elmer Gantry*, Howells's novel, like Braile himself, is deliberative and draws attention to the difficulty in comprehending the underlying causes of the religious mania that gripped the Leatherwood community in 1828.

As an early twentieth-century work, the novel also draws from and in its way contributes to the developing field of psychology, particularly the mass psychology generated by charismatic leaders. From this standpoint, the novel functions as ideology, wherein it seeks to replace an inspirational,

---

2. Similar points are made in Follett and Follett, "Contemporary Novelists," 256; Cady, *Realist at War*, 266; and Springer, "The Leatherwood God," 192.

3. Larson, *Evolution*, 51, defines *methodological naturalism* as the commitment to explaining "causes of physical phenomena" in terms of "natural (as opposed to supernatural or other non-natural) causes." In this usage, the term has nothing to do with the literary naturalism most closely associated with Emile Zola's manner of writing fiction.

4. On the French Enlightenment in relation to Jefferson and Paine, see Commager, *Jefferson, Nationalism, and the Enlightenment*, xi–xx.

miraculous narrative with a rationalized, secular one. I use the term *ideology*, not in its general usage as *biased* presentations of information, but, following Raymond Williams, in the sense articulated by John Brannigan, that "ideology is always the invisible, invidious force which unconsciously determines the limits and norms of thought and action through its material institutions, penetrating society and culture to the extent that it operates as unexamined common sense."[5] Through this latter view, Matthew Braile's project, which ends in an effort to delineate the psychology of the charismatic leader, reveals itself as ideology.

I

Strikingly, the empiricism that guides Howells's novel is also embedded in his primary source, Richard H. Taneyhill's *The Leatherwood God* (1870), a scrupulously recorded historical study of "The Appearance and Pretensions of Joseph C. Dylks."[6] Taneyhill's account is notable for its dispassionate tone and sincere effort to achieve objectivity by labeling the point of view (believer or unbeliever) of every eyewitness interviewed.[7] Taneyhill's method of collecting, organizing, and presenting all the known evidence on an otherwise unstudied, out-of-the-way subject is essentially that of an antiquarian. Such antiquarianism brought to historical scholarship much of the proto-scientific energy and methodology that initiated the rise of curiosity cabinets in England and Europe during the Age of Discovery. For example, Sir Hans Sloane's exotic, encyclopedic collection provided the core holdings for the British Museum. The procedures of collecting, observing, organizing, and systematizing hitherto unknown natural phenomena (whether they be species of shells, butterflies, or mastodons) were also the very ones that enabled Carl Linnaeus to develop his scientifically comprehensive botanical classification system.[8] In the nineteenth and twentieth centuries, similar systems began to be applied to all kinds of human behavior and provided the basis for scientific study in the social sciences, including history and social psychology—the realms into which Taneyhill and Howells entered in their examination of the Leatherwood God.[9]

---

5. Williams, *Marxism and Literature*, 64; Williams, *Problems*, 37; Brannigan, *New Historicism*, 27–28.

6. Taneyhill, *Leatherwood God*, facsimile title page.

7. Kummer, introduction to *The Leatherwood God*, xiv.

8. On Linnaeus see Fara, *Sex, Botany and Empire*, 19–46.

9. Unless otherwise noted, the account of scientific development in this paragraph is from Bronowski, *Common Sense of Science*, 47–49.

Undertaking to write his first historical novel, Howells honored his source materials in all major respects but one: he introduced an original domestic subplot consisting of Dylks's abandoned wife, Nancy, who believes Dylks long dead; their child, Joey, who does not know his father; and Nancy's gentle new husband, Laban, whom she loves. These characters, albeit fictive, furnish perspectives on Dylks consonant with Howells's source. Also, by resisting the impulse to tidily provide all the answers to what he called "the dreadfulness and the mystery of the [Dylks] imposture," Howells remained true to his source.[10]

Howells's creation of Matthew Braile is a different matter, since that character clearly originates in Taneyhill's account of James Frame, who, like Braile, was an early Leatherwood settler, a landowner bearing the courtesy title of "Squire," and the town justice.[11] However, whereas Frame was a practicing Methodist and a minor figure in Taneyhill's work, Squire Braile, in Howells's invention, is an unbeliever and the prime figure through whom the story of the Leatherwood god unfolds. These departures are substantial but still consistent with the goals of responsible historical fiction. As Joel Jones helpfully explains, the "historical novel" is a "literary form which projects *both* the thing that has been and the kind of thing that might have been and, in so doing, reveals universals of past, present, and future by depicting singulars of the past."[12] Both Braile and the characters in the Nancy plot satisfy the criterion Jones adduces of "thing[s] that might have been." Their depictions are also true to the spirit of historical investigation that Taneyhill established, even as they provide structure to the novel, heighten dramatic tension, and sharpen the core conflict between human reason and the persistence of belief in Dylks's miracles, despite contrary evidence.

Despite the scrupulous regard for precise terminology, the analysis is not neutral in that it is clearly undertaken from a secularist perspective. Howells, in fact, underscored the foundational difference between Braile's belief system and those of the community through the inspired idea of making Braile an inveterate reader of the heterodox Thomas Paine. Through this device, Howells delineates the philosophic divide between Braile and the two religious leaders who proclaim Dylks's divinity, Richard Enraghty and Peter Hingston.

10. Howells, *Selected Letters*, 57.
11. Taneyhill, *Leatherwood God*, 35.
12. Joel Jones, "Howells's *The Leatherwood God*," 98. My quibble with Jones's definition is that I would prefer the term *transhistorical truths* to the overreaching one of *universal truths*.

> Matthew Braile alone had the courage to disable their judgment which he liked to say was no more infallible than so much scripture, but the hardy infidel who knew so much law, and was inexpugnable in his office, owned that he could not make head against their gospel. He could darken their counsel with citations from *Common Sense* and *The Age of Reason*, but the piety of the community remained safe from his mockery. (40)

This passage firmly establishes that the basis of Braile's disagreement with Enraghty and Hingston is not personal but epistemological; it proceeds from the lawyer's skepticism regarding the inerrancy of scripture. Also clear is that Braile's identity is civic, since he is "inexpugnable" in office.[13] This fact seems to function straightforwardly, but it is actually saturated with ideology. The squire's insistence that Leatherwood has two temples, one for worship, the other for justice—the "Temple of Justice—Justice of the Peace" (11)—is a reminder that in America the two temples are distinct, and sometimes opposed, sources of authority. As a community lawyer and judge, Braile's primary duties turn out to be those of an arbiter, keeper of the peace, and intellectual leader, all roles that clothe him in a secular identity. Thus, though he is introduced as an observer and analyst of events, he is also a pivotal actor whose decisions have the effect of elevating the civic function and regulating—that is, curtailing—the excesses of Dylks's enthralled followers. This unacknowledged function of restraining religious enthusiasm comports with the evolving position of religion in American society, which over time finds its voice regulated in the public sphere, marginalized, and subsequently privatized.[14]

Braile's function as a proponent of the Enlightenment is seldom explored and weakly understood. For example, his celebrated "common sense" is often explained as a contrast to what one critic describes as the emotionalism or "false emotion" of the Leatherwood denizens.[15] Although this rendering is helpful, the term begs for interpretation in the context of Paine's explosive pamphlet, *Common Sense* (1776). This treatise, which sold 120,000 copies in its first three months and went through nineteen editions in the colonies, became America's most popular philosophic expression of

---

13. Braile's civic identity and deism, like Paine's, are expressions of his secular ideology. As observed by Asad, *Formations of the Secular*, 23, the term *secularist* was introduced into English in the mid-nineteenth century to avoid the labels *atheist* or *infidel*.

14. Asad, *Formations of the Secular*, 181–83; Pecora, *Secularization*, 2–5; Calhoun, Juergensmeyer, and VanAntwerpen, introduction to *Rethinking Secularism*, 7.

15. Joel Jones, "Howells's *The Leatherwood God*," 101.

republican ideals.[16] Fundamentally, it proclaimed the equality of all men in nature and set forth its rationale for a new nation free from the tyrannies of England and the other old-world monarchies of Europe.[17] In particular, *Common Sense* articulated two doctrines that are integral to Braile's value system. The first, which bears on Braile's disapprobation of Dylks's followers driving out of the common temple all other worshipers, was Paine's belief that there should be no established (national) church to enforce one particular form of worship. This self-evident secular value takes the reader back to the origins of the American ideology of separating church and state by privatizing the former.

The second value—the one that applies with special force to Howells's creation of Braile—is that in *Common Sense* Paine proffers an account of reason and experience that underwrites an empirical (and from a modern standpoint) proto-scientific manner of knowing: "In the following pages I offer nothing more than simple facts, plain arguments, and common sense; and have no other preliminaries to settle with the reader, than that he will divest himself of prejudice and prepossession, and suffer his reason and his feelings to determine for themselves; that he will put on, or rather that he will not put off, the true character of a man, and generously enlarge his views beyond the present day."[18]

Even more pertinent to the critique of religious beliefs in *The Leatherwood God* is Paine's later-written *The Age of Reason*, since it spells out in greater detail than does *Common Sense* Paine's epistemology, along with a jeering appraisal of traditional Christianity. Although initially a sensational success, *The Age of Reason* seriously damaged Paine's reputation because of its attack on religion, but following the author's death in 1809, the work regained its place at the forefront of American thought.[19] Given that the events depicted in Leatherwood occurred in the 1820s, Howells's making Braile a devotee of

---

16. Wilson and Ricketson, *Thomas Paine*, 14–15, estimate the number of copies sold. On the need for verification of this data, see Adkins, introduction to *Paine*, xxiii. Craig Nelson, *Thomas Paine*, 92, records that *Common Sense* sold between 150,000 and 250,000 copies in 1776 alone.

17. The most sustained study on the subject of nature, natural rights, and the religion of nature is Fruchtman, *Thomas Paine and the Religion of Nature*.

18. Paine, *Common Sense*, 16.

19. On Paine's controversial ability to democratize radical Enlightenment ideas in his *The Age of Reason*, see Kaye, *Thomas Paine and the Promise of America*, 84. Craig Nelson, *Thomas Paine*, 267–69, 335. Nelson highlights the durability of *The Age of Reason*, observing that Abe Lincoln took up "a life of deism" after reading it (335). On the determination of many post-revolutionary Americans to "tame" the radical Enlightenment, see Meyer, "The Uniqueness of the American Enlightenment," 172. On Paine's relationship to the radical Enlightenment, see May, *The Enlightenment in America*, 172–76.

Paine's *The Age of Reason* is a historically appropriate interpolation.[20] Paine's work also speaks to Braile's own iconoclasm, for it presents a sharp-edged account of the absurdities and wickedness recorded as divine revelation in scripture. Paine's tenacious, "common sense" empiricism reduces the Old Testament to a series of human transactions, which "needs no revelation" to explain it (217).[21] In particular, Paine the iconoclast holds that Jesus Christ of the New Testament may honestly be viewed only in his "historical relations strictly within the limits of probability" (212). This means that for Paine, God is truly known—that is, reveals himself clearly—solely through the natural laws of creation. These laws are known, he stipulates, through science, in whose study humankind's collective learning increases. In Paine's own words, "We see our own earth filled with abundance; but we forget to consider how much of that abundance is owing to the scientific knowledge the vast machinery of the earth has unfolded" (248).[22] Paine's argument may be regarded as exhibiting one of the first American attempts to show the peeling back of the religious elements that customarily accompanied scientific knowledge. The empirical orientation of Braile's own pronouncements, mocking but genial, are grounded in this same Enlightenment practice.

In sum, when Paine argues that Christianity, along with the religions of the Hebrews and the Muslims, keeps humankind in bondage through three sham devices, "Mystery, Miracle, and Prophecy" (250), he speaks as the most influential disseminator in the United States of an Enlightenment critique of religion. This Enlightenment mode of thinking can be seen to wend its way from Taneyhill to Howells. It appears most clearly when Taneyhill makes the exceptional generalization that "novelty, mystery, and miracle constitute the vital principles of every 'new faith,'"[23] and it resonates again in *The Leatherwood God* when Braile is asked whether he believes in "the Bible God," and he responds, "As much as the Bible'll let me" (76). In like manner, when asked about miracles, the squire makes problematic the very meaning of the term: "Does it prove that the person who does it is of God, or just that faith is stronger than reason in those who think it's happened?" (76–77).

Despite Braile's affinity for Paine, the squire does not fully share Paine's conception of deity, for whereas Paine's God is the proverbial grand

---

20. For the historical appropriateness of Paine's deism, see Curti, *Growth of American Thought*, 150–55.

21. Page numbers to Paine's *The Age of Reason* appear in the text.

22. The best study of Paine's attitudes toward scripture and authority as stated in *The Age of Reason* is Davidson and Scheick, *Paine, Scripture, and Authority*.

23. Taneyhill, *Leatherwood God*, 43.

watchmaker, benevolent and omnipotent, Braile's is more obscure, more problematic. In response to a question about how it is possible for an "all-wise and all-powerful God" to allow Joseph Dylks to play God, Braile raises ontological questions of his own: "What makes you say all-powerful? Haven't you seen time and time again when good didn't prevail against evil, and don't you suppose He'd have helped it if He could? And why do you call Him all-wise? Is it because men are no-wise? That wouldn't prove it, would it?" (76). This excursion opens the way for a consideration of pluralistic deities governing the universe and for Braile's idea of a less than omnipotent godhead. Such an ontological consideration may also account more readily for a seemingly amoral universe than a monotheistic one might.[24]

The place where Howells most plausibly acquired this concept was from his own contemporary, the renowned empiricist philosopher William James, who argued in *Some Problems of Philosophy*, published while Howells was writing *The Leatherwood God*, that a pluralistic conception of deity has several advantages over monism, including that pluralism removes the philosophical issue of how evil or even imperfection can arise from an all-perfect creator.[25] This link to James is not a matter of conjecture; rather, it is corroborated by external evidence provided in Howells's letter to William James's son, Henry, who had his father's unfinished *Some Problems of Philosophy* published in 1911. In this letter of August 15, 1913, Howells states that he is reading "your father's book" and adds, "If I do not find the meaning and the moral of The Leatherwood God amidst its wonderful common sense psychology, it will be my fault."[26]

Howells's concern to find the moral of his novel in the psychology of James's book demonstrates straightforwardly that Howells thinks psychology is central to "the meaning and the moral" of *The Leatherwood God*. Less obviously, Howells's observation illustrates that the novel was not written to present easy answers to the psychological and ontological issues it raises. Stepping back a bit from the specific language of Howells's letter, we should observe that James viewed the emergent scientific disciplines, including psychology, as proceeding from empirical attempts to answer questions that

---

24. On Howells's inability to believe in God as well as his distrust of irrationalism, see Goodman and Dawson, *William Dean Howells*, 418–19.

25. James, *Some Problems of Philosophy*, 72.

26. Howells, *Selected Letters*, 40. Howells's editor notes that the novelist's reference in the letter to "your father's book" is "presumably" to *Some Problems of Philosophy*, based on the facts that the son saw his father's book through to publication and wrote the prefatory note to it.

formerly belonged solely to philosophy.[27] Howells's novel follows a similar pattern by continually posing ontological questions about the nature of deity. But insofar as it strives to make sense of Dylks's parading evangelism and that of his converts, it does so by offering psychological explanations that may be tested against other historical examples as well as the events in Leatherwood itself.[28]

In this manner, a historical pattern is revealed from Paine to Taneyhill, to Howells, to James, each of them mapping out a secular domain, and the last, James, revealing the emergence of the new discipline of psychology, where secular explanations replace miraculous ones.

II

The novel's depiction of the conflict between a faith guaranteed by miracle and a skepticism about all events said to break or suspend the physical laws of nature is instructive. The emphasis repeatedly falls on the difficulty of knowing. From Dylks's first appearance, he is presented as a mysterious being, a purported stranger without name who heralds his presence with a horse-like snort and the loud shout, "Salvation!" (8). Braile's query, "And what was it?," and the reply of Abel Reverdy, who relates the event, "What was it? A man!" (8), announces the difficulty of knowing the most basic things about Dylks. This air of mystery continues to spread as the stranger encourages the temple worshipers to "Call me Dylks—for the present" (20), but then on the second night, exhibiting a magnetic presence and flawless command of scripture, suggests that he is sent by God. Those prepared to believe in him do.

A colloquy begins on the question of whether the stranger is *"sent"* (42). Sally Reverdy, whom Dylks has inspired, just knows that "he's *sent*"

---

27. James, *Some Problems of Philosophy*, 12. The entire first chapter (9–20) examines the close relationship between the problems posed in philosophy and those in the sciences.

28. In describing Braile's epistemology as empirical, I do not mean to suggest that empiricism is itself without problems as an approach to knowing the world. Modern critiques of empiricism have exposed inadequacies in empiricism's philosophical assumptions, including the problems that no observational system is free from error and that the logical principles required by empiricism are not themselves observational. On these matters, see Alex Rosenberg, *Philosophy of Science*, 237–42. My intention throughout this chapter is to draw attention to the empirical features of the Enlightenment and, secondarily, to their importance in the early twentieth-century philosophy of William James.

because she believes in her heart, and so believing, proselytizes: "If you feel the Power workin' in you, . . . help the others to git it" (42). This subjective manner of knowing the presence of God through the heart is an enduring American phenomenon. On the frontier, John and Charles Wesley and George Whitefield inspired a "Great Awakening" in the 1730s and 1740s. Then, in the time of the Leatherwood god, Charles Finney's inspirational Methodism took hold on the frontier, including Ohio, and created a "Second Great Awakening."[29] Such inspirational knowledge was guaranteed not by reason or experiment but by the direct experience of the divine. It was prevalent in the barnstorming revivalism of Howells's own day in such figures as Sam Jones; Reuben Torrey, who devoted himself to attacking science and the higher criticism; and Billy Sunday, on whom *Elmer Gantry* was partly modeled.[30] And it continues today among many Christian groups, including Pentecostals and the "broad tent" of those called evangelicals.[31]

Among Leatherwood's believers, there is the brand of faith exhibited by the thoughtful Peter Hingston, a Methodist and leading landowner, who holds that since "revelation had never ceased," it is reasonable to look for a "sign," and "it was not reasonable that he [God] should afterwards always withhold Himself" (40). In contrast to the inspirational approach to knowledge, Hinston's is that of a rationalist, who considers the evidence, albeit in reference to biblical precepts. Since, moreover, Braile is a skeptic, he asks irreverent questions, which he seeks to test, as when he entertains the proposition that "maybe he [Dylks] isn't *really* a man of God" but "a rascal" (22–23). Such a hypothesis, Braile reasons, "would account for a good many things," including the materialistic consideration that Dylks stays in the homes of the leading citizens in part for their good food.

Braile's values notwithstanding, the central problem of how the reader should apprehend Dylks's ministry persists. The narrator, who does not appear to know the answer to this question, nevertheless reports that the "superstition" spreads "from mind to mind" like wildfire (48). Puzzlingly, the most fervent early believers are not the ignorant and lowlier people, as one might expect, but the pillars of the settlement, the well-to-do and the

---

29. On the two "Great Awakenings" and their preachers, see Weinstein and Rubel, *The Story of America*, 66, 212–17. On Charles Finney's career on the frontier, see Sweet, *Revivalism in America*, 134–39. See also Butler, *Awash in a Sea of Faith*, 164–65.

30. McLoughlin, *Modern Revivalism*, 298–329 (Jones), 366–74 (Torrey), Sunday (402–54).

31. On evangelicals in this context, see Worthen, *Apostles of Reason*, 3, 178–79; Watt, *Transforming Faith*, 25; and Weber, "Premillennialism and the Branches of Evangelicalism," 14.

influential. Equally odd is that as Dylks's cult grows, so does the prophet's self-promotion. Inasmuch as the narrator presents these observations without explanation, an air of intellectual suspense settles over the unfolding story.

The incredibility of subsequent events mixes with a growing anxiety about the nature of Dylks's uncanny appeal. Soon there circulates Dylks's claim that "he hain't never go'n' to die" (48). There follows a series of signs that corroborate Dylks's divinity. Brother Enraghty sees a halo around Dylks's head. Then a report circulates that Dylks met Satan in the woods and shouted salvation, whereupon the Devil's horrid wings fell off as he fled. In a repetition of the Lazarus story, a sick boy afflicted by the Devil rises from his bed and calls Dylks his savior, inspiring everyone present to fall to their knees in worship, whereupon Dylks solemnly announces that "the perfect work is done" and that Satan is bound "for a thousand years" (52). There follows Dylks's daring proclamations: "I am God and the Christ in one," and "There is no salvation except by faith in me. They who put their faith in me shall never taste death, but shall be translated into the New Jerusalem" (53).

This audacious claim, the narrator reports, was controversial. The novel makes much of the dissension. With the displacement of all other sects from the temple of worship, fathers become pitted against sons and mothers against daughters. However, for Dylks's followers, this strife does not at all undercut the credibility of their god; rather, it corroborates scripture in that Dylks brings about the same dissension among families as Jesus prophesied he would do.[32] Braile, on the other hand, sits on his porch, cob pipe in hand, collects information, and invites visitors to reveal all they know: "Go on! Go on!" and "Tell you anything else?" (51, 49). Frequently he urges greater precision: "You don't happen to know just what the doings were?" and "What did Paul the Apostle [i.e., Hingston] say? Did he own up that he was Paul?" (49, 51).

Just as Dylks's credentials are scrutinized, so are Braile's in his sphere. The squire's wisdom commands an uneasy respect. Almost everyone recognizes that his way of knowing is somehow related to his distinctive philosophic knowledge. For example, when Sally Reverdy asks Janey whether she believes Washington and Jefferson were friends with Tom Paine since "the Squire says they was, but I misdoubt it, myself; I always hear them two was good perfessin' Christians" (42), she clearly shows herself troubled by Braile's discomfirmation of her belief that these two "founding fathers"

---

32. The biblical allusion is to Matthew 10:34–37, as Pattison, editor of Howells's *Leatherwood God*, notes (see 162).

were practicing Christians.[33] A similar point is made when David Gillespie, who is beside himself because his teenage daughter, Janey, has been smitten by the charismatic Dylks, confesses to his sister, Nancy, that "sometimes I'm a mind to go to his [Braile's] house and get him to tell me what Tom Paine would do in my place" (63). For Gillespie, Braile is a beckoning resource, even if a heterodox one.

These details illustrate Braile's distinctive wisdom, but they are less significant than Howells's making Braile the person through whom the various accounts of Dylks's ministry are filtered. By this means, the events of the novel are made more indirect and psychological. In other words, Howells's mode of storytelling becomes a distancing device that prompts readers to reflect upon the bizarre events in Leatherwood—as does Braile himself. Readers who contemplate the use of this device will recognize that through it Howells develops three kinds of inquiry. The first proceeds straightforwardly from the plot: what will happen next, and how will this strange story end? A second order of question arises: psychologically, what motivates Dylks to claim to be God and what motivates Dylks's followers to believe him? A third order of question is abstract: on what empirical grounds can reasonable generalizations be made about religious impostors and their flock? Or, put more comprehensively, how can this case study of an isolated frontier community contribute to a scientific understanding of the psychology of charismatic leaders and followers?

Responses to these questions appear only gradually, but they do emerge. Two private scenes introduced by Howells reveal a good deal about Dylks's psychology. In the first, Dylks returns to his wife Nancy's home and invites her to join him in his quest to establish "the perfect Godhead, male and female" (69). Nancy, although acknowledging Dylks's handsomeness, wants nothing more to do with this first husband whom she thought was dead and, in any case, does not respect, knowing him to be weak, self-indulgent, and pitiless. But when in the course of this discussion, Nancy declares that he couldn't do right if he wanted to, Dylks challenges the idea that there is any difference at all between right and wrong. All there is is what God allows, Dylks argues, and he illustrates with biblical references proving that God allows all sorts of sinful actions to take place. Therefore, he swiftly implores Nancy to "be God yourself and the right and the wrong will take care of themselves" (70).

---

33. The religion of the founding fathers points to an ideological struggle over the original identity of the United States. In their preface to *Forgotten Founders on Religion and Public Life*, xiii–xxi, editors Dreisbach, Hall, and Morrison treat this issue in its intrinsic complexity.

Though Nancy calls him "wicked," Dylks is propelled onward by those who believe in him (71). Further insight into the interdependent relationship between Dylks and his converts is revealed in a confidential conversation he has with Squire Braile. The conversation comes about after Dylks fails to perform a promised miracle of turning a bolt of cloth into a seamless garment. Following the failed miracle, a riot ensues in which a gang of disbelievers, the "Hounds," tears the fabric to shreds, prompting Dylks to flee for his life. Found cowering in a kitchen chimney, Dylks is eventually delivered up to the justice of the peace. Despite repeated demands for punishment, Braile, a reader of the statutes of Ohio as well as Blackstone's *Commentaries on the Laws of England,* declares that Dylks has broken no civil law and must be released. Making a stern speech to Dylks's "Little Flock" and then to Dylks's opponents, the "Herd of the Lost," he bids the first to get some breakfast and the second to leave the Little Flock alone and to "find the true God if you can" (105). Significantly, both sides obey him, not because they recognize his wisdom, but because they feel "the mystical force of the law in his words" (105–6). In short, Braile's order is heeded because both flocks experience it evangelically. This irony raises the contemporary problem of the proper place for such spirituality in a democratic society,[34] but the novel does not explore it further.

Near the novel's end, Dylks's imposture receives a good deal of analysis. The situation arises when the would-be god flees into the forest, where he becomes lost until he finds his long-abandoned wife, Nancy, who convinces him to seek Matthew Braile's protection. There on his porch, the town skeptic finally gets some answers to the mystery. Highlighting the justice's method of interrogation, the narrator notes Braile's system "of mentally checking off the successive facts" (116). As Braile suspected, Dylks feels trapped by the expectations of his followers. It is not even a matter of convincing them, since they eagerly believe every supernatural power he claims. On the contrary, their faith traps him in his imposture and makes him "afraid" (117). This too is the reason why Dylks consents to give his followers a further "sign" by promising another miracle (119). As the squire reflectively generalizes, "The ignorant are sure to want a sign," and Dylks feels compelled to provide it (119).

When a sobbing Dylks confesses that after a while, "you begin to believe it [that you may really be God] yourself" (118), the novel reaches a climactic moment, for Braile suddenly interjects, "Hold on!" and for the first time

---

34. Asad, *Formations of the Secular,* 183–84, employs the term *religion* rather than *spirituality*. See also Craig Calhoun, "Secularism, Citizenship," 77–83.

offers an embracing social-psychological conclusion: "It must have been so with all the impostors in the world, from Mahomet up and down" to the false prophets in the Old Testament (118), he says in a passage echoing Paine's opinions in *The Age of Reason*.³⁵ Then reformulating the psychological principle, he hypothesizes, "Their faith begins to work on the liar's own unbelief, till he takes his lie for the truth. Was that the way, you miserable skunk?" (118). The somber answer is, "It was exactly the way" (118). In this manner, the novel moves from the mystery of the Leatherwood god to a psychological explanation of the steps by which the prophet or would-be god comes to believe his own lie.

III

Having attained a measure of clarification regarding Dylks's motivations, the novel shifts focus to address sociological and psychological issues pertaining to Dylks's followers. Even after the narrator's factual assessment that Dylks's prophecies had been "falsified" (97), Dylks's followers remain undeterred in their faith in their new god. For Howells's readers, the increasingly intriguing question becomes how to explain this seemingly irrational response. One locus of interest is Jane Gillespie's continued refusal to believe that her hero god has been "proved an impostor" (97). She insists that more evidence be delivered from the body of the god himself. Since Dylks had declared it would be death for anyone to touch a strand of his flowing hair, Jane demands of her overwrought father that until someone brings her a lock of his hair, she will never stop believing. When Dylks is discovered cowering in Enraghty's home, Jim Redfield, a redheaded young man enamored of Jane and angry that Dylks has usurped his place, tears a swatch of hair from Dylks's scalp and hands it to Jane's father. Only then is a chastened Jane disabused of her misplaced faith. However, a question lingers as to why the girl remained obsessed with Dylks for so long.

Braile finds a credible explanation in human sexuality. On several occasions, the squire laments that Dylks has sex appeal such that girls and even married women are likely to fall for this "handsome devil," and there is no help for it because "the Real God put it into human nature" (57–58).³⁶ The point that Jane is not alone in her intense emotional attachment to the fallen

---

35. Paine, *Age of Reason*, 209–10, 218–21.
36. On the subject of Dylks's sexuality, see Feigenoff, "Sexuality in the Leatherwood God."

god is neatly made when Gillespie presents his daughter with the scalped swatch of hair and finds her among like-minded "sobbing women—worshipers of the outraged idol" (98). Given Braile's dedication to civil society, it appears that this form of irrationality is a limitation on the substantive rationality necessary to an optimally functioning democratic community.

A related issue is the phenomenon of crowd psychology, inasmuch as individual judgment becomes submerged in a corporate identity. At the time that *The Leatherwood God* appeared in 1916, Americans were experiencing their own brand of revivalism through the spellbinding, miracle-working evangelism of such preachers as Billy Sunday and the newly rising Aimee Semple McPherson. From this period, the subject of mass hysteria became a subject of scientific interest. Especial attention fell on the irrational frenzy repeatedly observed at camp meetings. Frederick Davenport's 1906 *Primitive Traits in Religious Revivals*, perhaps the most notable contemporary book on this theme, drew attention to the suggestibility, imitativeness, emotionalism, and general "sympathetic likemindedness" of participants in revivalist movements.[37] From Davenport's perspective, which is inescapably secular and academic, such irrationalism is a throwback to more primitive times and a setback for the progress of civilized society. In Talal Asad's formulation, this depiction of the primitive is associated with savagery, childlike states, and imagination (the unreal) against its complementary binary, reason, which is associated with maturity and progress.[38] Once again, the theorization of the historical context reveals the secular ideology beneath.

However, this ideology of the secular ought not to be read as signifying that things ideological are false, only that the ideology functions invisibly and (here) in the interests of secularism. Howells's novel may thus be seen as drawing on its authentic historical source materials (Taneyhill) to shape the narrative history and its meaning. Howells himself is concerned to interpret the behavior of Dylks's faithful flock subsequent to the Leatherwood god's offer to take them to the New Jerusalem—in Philadelphia. Many of the Little Flock respond by putting their houses in order; some even mortgage their land and, expecting to be swept up to live forever in the rapture, travel on foot with their god over the hills from Ohio to Philadelphia. Furthermore, when Dylks assures them that they need not worry about money, since he (echoing Jesus' miracle of the fish) will turn three copper coins into millions in gold and silver, the flock, behaving like a "swarm" of humanity,

---

37. Davenport, *Primitive Traits in Religious Revivals*, 1–2.
38. The concept derives from Asad, *Formations of the Secular*, 29–30.

is swept up into a mounting "frenzy," full of "sighs and groans of ecstasy" (129–30).[39]

But prophetic expectation is one thing, fulfillment another. Dylks never does perform the miracle of the copper coins, nor is his flock swept into the New Jerusalem. This part of the historical novel is told through the young Joey, who, not knowing that Dylks is actually his father, tells his mother that he expects the New Jerusalem will be "like the circus"—which, in an odd way, it turns out to be (133). Later, upon his return from Philadelphia, Joey explains how the adventure went awry as Dylks became lost, forcing his believers to sleep outdoors and even beg for food. By relating how Dylks at times cried and prayed, Joey reveals "the Good Old Man" (148) in a human but pathetic light. Soon after the pilgrims saw the lights over Philadelphia, Dylks slipped into the river and, despite the efforts of Joey and his friend Benny to rescue him, he "drownded" (146). Another mystery. To these lads, the death was accidental; to those disappointed in not finding the New Jerusalem, Dylks's death was a deliberate suicide, but to the numerous remaining faithful, Dylks did not die at all. As Joey reports, "Some said he did fetch it [the New Jerusalem] down; and they seen it, with the black horses and silver gates and velvet streets, and everything just the way he promised" (148). This account is an unsettling testament to the power of belief to shape the perceptions of an evangelical community. To them, Dylks remains their god, through whom they will be redeemed, and no one can shake their faith in him.

As for Joey's mother, the news of Dylks's death elicits a heartfelt thanksgiving. Never having knowingly violated her marriage vows, she had sent her husband Laban, the man she truly loves, away as soon as she learned that her first husband, from whose callousness and cunning she recoils, was still alive. Her behavior shows her respect for the laws of society, despite her desire to continue living with Laban. But with Dylks's death, she again feels free to love Laban and to tell Joey that though Dylks was his *"real* father," Laban is his *"true* father" (150). This restoration of Nancy's family, including her newborn babe by Laban, is emblematic of the peace that returns to Leatherwood once Dylks is gone. To similar effect, we learn that with the distraction of Dylks removed, Jane Gillespie soon marries Jim Redfield and enjoys a happy life filled with children. These stories of domestic recovery establish the novel's closing perspective on Dylks—that Leatherwood would have been better off had he never appeared.

---

39. In most of the details of the journey, Howells follows Taneyhill, *Leatherwood God,* 45–47.

IV

This judgment notwithstanding, the novel's concluding analysis of the devotional mania spawned by Dylks is reserved for the final chapter, which is remarkable for introducing yet another distancing device. The locale is again Braile's home, some twenty-five years later, in the 1850s, after the Leatherwood craze has become all but a memory. Fittingly, Howells makes the now-aged Braile central to the reflective discussion with an educated stranger from Cambridge, Massachusetts, T. J. Mandeville, who has come to learn more about Leatherwood's impostor god of the late 1820s.

Answering Mandeville's question about what has become of the Little Flock, Braile confirms the dogged persistence of the Dylks religion, observing that those who lived in the faith died in it, and those young at the time have become old and still worship Dylks. The "failure in all his miracles" was only what the disbelievers alleged (155). Indeed, some eight years after Dylks left them, a preacher appeared in Leatherwood teaching that "there was no true religion that didn't recognize him [Dylks] as God" (155). The preacher personally avowed seeing the Good Old Man go up to heaven, promising to return to establish his kingdom. So strong was the preacher's faith, so radical his doctrine, that he decried Christianity "as just a hotchpotch of Judaism and heathenism" (155).

To explain such unwearied devotion, Mandeville suggests that there ought to have been a logic, "steps of belief," besides the performing of miracles (156). Braile confirms that these steps reveal Dylks's progression from humbly teaching Christianity to claiming that he was Jesus Christ, then the *perfect* Messiah," and, finally, God himself (156). This "plan of belief," Braile hypothesizes, "has served the purpose of the imposter in all ages" (156). As for explaining the persistence of belief among Dylks's followers, Braile at last theorizes that life is hard on the frontier, and the easy promise of salvation is a powerful step to belief, as is the soothing desire to live forever. Desire to be reassured thus precedes belief. As for the actual process of conversion, Braile holds that Dylks's ministry offered a faith that was "clear to the meanest understanding. The meaner the understanding, the clearer" (156). With these words, Braile affirms his view that ignorance and ill-placed hope lay at the bottom of the Leatherwood phenomenon.

Howells, it is true, did not place his novel in the wider (expected) context of the emotion-laden revivalism of 1820s and 1830s, which spread out from the so-called burnt-over district in western New York. That would have allowed Howells to interpret Dylks's career as a natural extension of preachers propounding the importance of truth as a powerful, individual experience. That historical context might have explained Dylks's own behavior as an extreme example of an internalized individualism providing a view of the self as not only godlike but divine. The absence, moreover, of a state religion or a strong central authority in the United States to support orthodoxy could have been used to explain the proliferation of Protestant sectarianism such as we see in *The Leatherwood God*.[40]

Nevertheless, Howells discovered a fresh approach to the problem of explaining the Leatherwood phenomenon. In a letter written to Thomas S. Perry in October 1914, Howells requested that Perry tell him "something about religious impostors and false prophets; so that I can give a learned look to the last chapter of my Leatherwood God."[41] What Perry suggested, if anything, we do not know, but the result, as we have it, strikingly illustrates that Howells sought to reduce to principles the psychology of religious impostors and, in so doing, to account for their differing degrees of success. Thus, when Mandeville wonders why Dylks, unlike Mahomet, "didn't establish his superstition in universal acceptance" (157), the squire responds by observing that Dylks was no fool and was unwilling to shed his blood for his cause. Moreover, the setting in which Dylks professed his divinity was too small, too remote, for it to take hold in a big way. Weighing this judgment, Mandeville introduces the name of Joseph Smith, founder of Mormonism (the Church of Jesus Christ of Latter Day Saints), who during this period established "his superstition, which bids fair to live right along with the other false religions" (159). Braile responds thoughtfully, suggesting that it may have been easier for Smith, since he "only claimed to be a prophet," not a god. "That made it harder, maybe for his [Dylks's] superstition" (159).

On this suggestive note, the conversation and the novel end. Perusing these final pages, we observe that Howells avoids puffed-up moral pronouncements, and Braile and Mandeville offer provisional generalization subject to revision. Howells himself, we know, approached the subject of the Leatherwood God as "an insoluble problem."[42] Yet for all its tentativeness, the novel strives to present a systematic, wholly empirical interpretation of the mania that overtook Leatherwood. In this case, it seeks to develop a typological profile that might explain the behavior of past religious impostors and, presumably, of future ones as well.[43]

---

40. Throughout the paragraph I rely on Thomas, *Revivalism and Cultural Change*, 66–70.

41. Howells, *Selected Letters*, 63n5.

42. Howells, *Selected Letters*, 105.

43. Observations on the conceptual nature of science are from Rovelli, *The First Scientist: Anaximander*, 107–11. Braile's conversation with Mandeville may be read as an

Several contemporary reviewers recognized the epistemological features of *The Leatherwood God* and admired Howells's typological approach, so much so that they responded to the novel with the same eagerness to categorize, or to adduce contemporary evidence to corroborate Howells's manner of analyzing the phenomenon of religious imposture.[44] Absorbing Howells's systemizing approach to his material, the *Times Literary Supplement* began its review by claiming that "imposters may be grouped in three classes—the deliberate, cynical deceivers, the complete self-deceivers, and those in whom these two kinds of deceit are mixed."[45] It then proceeded to apply these categories systematically to the novel. Others observed that the novel's insights were as pertinent to the present time as to the nineteenth century. One reviewer referenced the novel's "essential contemporaneousness," and another noted that Howells's depiction of "credulity and hysteria" would seem "almost incredible did we not know that ... exactly similar instances have occurred in our own time."[46] The *Catholic World* objected to the subject of a *"sordid imposter"* as *"unworthy"* of the novelist but ended by affirming that the novel "illustrates well the power men like Alexander Dowie [the Scotch evangelist and faith healer who practiced in Australia and America], or women like Mrs. Baker Eddy [founder of Christian Science, which holds that bodily disease can be conquered by mind and faith], possessed to *delude the ignorant multitudes.*"[47] Similarly, the editor R. F. Wormwood was eager to draw Howells's attention to one Jacob Cochrane, a leader of a religious movement later referred to as "the Cochrane craze" because his imposture exhibited many similarities to Dylks's, including a religious fanaticism that divided churches and broke up families.[48] Like Dylks, Cochrane had "considerable natural ability," Wormwood reported, although he admitted that it is "impossible to determine whether there was more of the religious fanatic or just plain charlatan in his makeup."[49] Considered in concert with the reviews it generated,

---

exercise in scientific speculation in a manner that recalls proto-scientific speculations of the pre-Socratic Greek philosophers.

44. Not all reviewers, however. See, for example, Boynton, "Some Outstanding Novels of the Year," 508, and, on style, review of *The Leatherwood God* in *Athenaeum*, 596. At one point, Howells also complained that the American critics were receiving his work "most ignorantly" (*Selected Letters*, 109).

45. Review of *The Leatherwood God*, *Times Literary Supplement*, 548.

46. Review of *The Leatherwood God*, *New York Times Book Review*, April 30, 1916, 184, and October 29, 1916, 453, respectively.

47. Review of *The Leatherwood God*, *Catholic World*, 397.

48. Howells, *Selected Letters*, 105–6n1.

49. Ibid., 105n1.

The Leatherwood God demonstrates the ongoing construction of the new discipline of psychology, which is depicted in the very act of substituting a systematically secular set of explanations for miraculous ones.

A decade after the publication of *The Leatherwood God*, Sinclair Lewis composed a more stridently secular novel, for which he was offered a Pulitzer prize, but the novel's very secularity in depicting a research scientist's dedication to his field of bacterial epidemiology was presented as possessing spiritual meaning.

PART 2

SECULARISM RESURGENT

CHAPTER 5

A RESEARCH SCIENTIST'S RELIGION

Sinclair Lewis's *Arrowsmith*

SINCLAIR LEWIS BIOGRAPHER Mark Schorer made the important observation that *Arrowsmith* introduces an "almost entirely new subject matter into American fiction," the research scientist.[1] Two earlier twentieth-century novels, Robert Herrick's *The Web of Life* (1900) and *The Healer* (1911), had treated the medical doctor as torn between professional integrity and the temptation of generating a more lucrative practice.[2] Also, Jewett's *A Country Doctor* (1884) and Eggleston's *The Faith Doctor* (1891), previously treated in chapter 1, had dramatized the inroads that modern science and its technologies were making in the treatment of illness, which had been, ambiguously, both a scientific and spiritual endeavor. However, Lewis's *Arrowsmith* is of a different order because it extols not doctor-patient relationships but the research scientist who creates the medical knowledge that transforms society.

The novel has a second, supporting objective as well in that it challenges the entire social order in America, which not only fails to honor its

---

1. Schorer, *Sinclair Lewis*, 414.
2. Ibid., who references Herrick's *The Healer* and *The Web of Life*.

intellectuals and its scientists, but vitiates the research process by its commercialism and conventionality. Expressing a strong iconoclastic orientation to American culture, *Arrowsmith* directs much of its social satire at a generic form of lived Christian culture, which Lewis sees as inimical to the reception of new medical practices. A brief synopsis shows Lewis's wide-view critique of the medical profession and, by extension, American society.[3]

The novelist, in fact, has his protagonist, Martin Arrowsmith, experience every kind of medical practice, beginning with his visits as a teenager to the office of a small-town doctor through his student years in medical school at the University of Winnemac, and, with his loyal wife Leora by his side, his first job as a country doctor in Wheatsylvania, North Dakota. From there Martin becomes the assistant to Dr. Almus Pickerbaugh, director of public health in the middling city of Nautilus, Iowa, where after running up against strong political and cultural opposition, he accepts an appointment as a bacteriologist and immunologist at the Rouncefield Clinic in Chicago. After an article he publishes catches the attention of his former medical-school teacher Max Gottlieb, now the leading scientist at the McGurk Institute in New York, the two men are reunited, and Martin is able to pursue pure research activities full time. At his lab, Martin discovers an X Principle that proves effective in containing the spread of bubonic plague on a Caribbean island, but his success, which is accompanied by Leora's death by plague, does not bring him happiness. Instead, he continues to chafe at the institute's expectations that he follow protocol, socialize, and participate in public relations activities. Martin is also exposed to the temptations of celebrity, position, and wealth, all of which he ultimately rejects. Only when he leaves his socialite second wife, Joyce Lanyon, and removes himself, along with one fellow scientist, to a backwoods laboratory in rural Vermont does Arrowsmith find himself. In this way, Arrowsmith, like John Bunyan, makes his pilgrim's progress through medical society,[4] through its material temptations, until he finds the haven in which he can dedicate his life to scientific research. The structure is homiletic and insofar as Arrowsmith pursues a monastic vocation, his is a spiritual quest.

Despite Lewis's straightforward presentation, *Arrowsmith* poses three issues of interpretation. The first proceeds from the satiric depiction of Christian culture, which functions as a foil for Lewis's high-minded representation of Martin's and Gottlieb's dedication to research science. That is,

---

3. See, most notably, Emerson, "A Doctor Looks at Arrowsmith," 107–8, and Lovett, "An Interpreter of American Life."

4. Grebstein, *Sinclair Lewis*, 87, elaborates the comparison.

science and religion are clearly placed in polar opposition. Moreover, Martin's and Gottlieb's exacting scientific practice is capable of producing exaltation, as when the application of scientific methods to the study of infectious disease leads to the rapturous discovery of an immunizing vaccine. Lewis records this rapture through a class of images associated with Christian devotion. This transposition, in which the subjective experience of the scientist is rendered in imagery of faithful devotion, begs for exegesis, since it is built on the contradiction that the very forms of religious belief that the novel rejects are brought forward to demonstrate the spiritual exaltation that the true research scientist can experience.

A second related issue is whether the novel's spiritual affirmation of scientific research works to enhance the prestige accorded to the religious pole of the science versus religion binary, or whether it functions imperially to extend the domain of the secular. The third issue is whether Lewis's management of this devotional imagery works polemically or whether it is convincingly rendered as the genuine expression of an internal spiritual state. Since these are complex questions, I have made them part of the process of analysis over the course of the chapter.

Not in dispute but in need of exposition is the novel's informed depiction of the scientific research that Gottlieb and Arrowsmith perform in the fields of epidemiology and immunology. This achievement would not have been possible without the assistance of Lewis's collaborator, bacteriologist Paul de Kruif. Much of the dramatic tension in the novel arises from the discovery of a viable vaccine, and, as we shall see, de Kruif's firsthand understanding of scientific methods and the practice of laboratory science was crucial to the novel's success.

I

As the novel opens, country doctor Vickerson is teaching the young Martin Arrowsmith that three books are essential for any physician: Gray's *Anatomy*, the Bible, and Shakespeare. Vickerson's scientific values exalt "the universality of biology, [and] the triumphant exactness of chemistry" (5), values that become the foundation of Arrowsmith's scientific work.[5] The next we hear of him, Martin has entered medical school, where he and his lab partner, Ira Hinkley, a medical missionary and minister, are dissecting

---

5. Unless otherwise noted, page numbers to quotations from *Arrowsmith* are from the New American Library edition and appear in the text.

a cadaver, an activity that causes Arrowsmith to fall into doubt because he can find no evidence of a soul in his dissections. Hinkley, however, is completely unfazed by "Modern Doubts" (13).[6] During this process of deepening religious skepticism, Martin finds new hope as he comes to view experiments as a mode of inquiry that might otherwise be identified with theology. Medicine presents itself to him as "illumination," and he acquires the view that experiments should deal with "the foundations of life and death" (19). Soon the practice of science becomes a religious experience, as when Martin, inspired by the difficulty and precision of lab experiments, responds to his lab mate's complaint that Max Gottlieb is not religious, exclaiming, "Why, his just being in a lab is a prayer!" (29). This transference of devotional language into the laboratory may appear to be more witty than profound, but it functions appropriately as a prelude to Gottlieb's subsequent depiction as a practitioner of a new kind of spiritual truth. A lonely lab worker, he first appears as a monkish saint, demanding a perfection of technique, a seemingly inexhaustible collection of data, and the cultivation of endless patience.

This statement about Gottlieb's lab being a prayer foreshadows the rising theme that in matters of scientific experimentation the secular *is* the religious. Yet there is nothing convincing about Martin's utterance: what makes Gottlieb's lab a prayer? There is not enough information to decide the matter. However, when Martin's German-educated mentor speaks, a heterodox pantheon of heroes is invoked. Undeterred by the usual ethical norms, he entertains possibilities others would dismiss, such as why human beings should be protected from deadly pathogens while the innocent germs themselves are eradicated. This unrestrained freedom of thought prompts Gottlieb to invoke as heroes the names of "Father Nietzsche and Father Schopenhauer," along with the great European immunologists with whom he has studied, Robert Koch and Louis Pasteur, and the younger generation as well, who, through de Kruif, served as models for Lewis's book, "Brother Jacques Loeb and Brother Arrhenius" (39).[7]

By addressing these leading figures as *Father* or *Brother*, Gottlieb reveals himself to be a worshiper of a pantheon of heterodox philosophers and

---

6. In *Art of Sinclair Lewis*, 106, Dooley calls Lewis's treatment of Arrowsmith's waning faith "cavalier," which in tone it may be, but in respect to content, the satire explores the strains between scientific discovery and biblical belief.

7. These latter two scientists became known to Lewis through bacteriologist Paul de Kruif, who collaborated with Lewis on the scientific features of *Arrowsmith*. Loeb was de Kruif's idol and Svante Arrhenius was a highly regarded Swedish scientist, mentioned in de Kruif, *Microbe Hunters*, 53. On Loeb, see Fangerau, "*Arrowsmith*."

scientific saints. This hagiography shows that Lewis's objective, to render secular science as a spiritual experience, is not carried out mechanically but troublingly, complexly, from a well-thought-through conception of Gottlieb's personality. To be sure, there is something of the overzealous scientist about him, but Lewis never allows the character to collapse into the literary stereotype of the evil or demonic scientist, as in Hawthorne's melodramatic rendering of the doctor in *The Scarlet Letter*, Roger Chillingworth, whose name connotes a cold heart, congealed by envy and the desire to destroy others. In contrast, Max Gottlieb's two names translate as "great love of God," though his German identity defines him as an outsider who lives beyond the orbit of conventional America. This presentation of character demands reflection on the part of readers, who must weigh the praise of Gottlieb against his heterodoxy.

We see that Lewis endows Gottlieb with professional and personal virtues but then shows how these virtues entail limitations that dog him. For instance, Gottlieb's identity as loner and outsider contributes to his creativity. Nor is he completely alone or unloved. Unlike the celibate research scientist Dr. Ledsmar in *The Damnation of Theron Ware*, Gottlieb has a wife and daughter and establishes a lasting bond with Martin based on high scientific standards, avuncular warmth, concern, and increasingly shared values. But Gottlieb's very independence creates serious trouble for him among his conformist colleagues, who want him to produce immediate, practical scientific results. Feeling this devaluation of theoretical research, Gottlieb in turn does not collaborate.

Convincing as well is that Gottlieb's colleagues at Winnemac University, filled with envy, first demonize him as "Mephisto, Diabolist" and as a snob, atheist, and Jew (122–23) and subsequently bring a charge of disloyalty against him, causing him to be dismissed. The epithets hurled against Gottlieb reveal a lot more about the atmosphere in which he works than they do about the professor. They reveal a process of demonization that is the product of an extremely parochial culture, envy of Gottlieb's genius, and intolerance of his idiosyncratic personality. This presentation follows an inner logic; however, Lewis's narrator must present an overblown eulogy on Gottlieb as a benefactor to humanity because instead of being a mere classifier of bacteria, he seeks "the laws of their existence and destruction" (123). Through this kind of intrusion, authentic characterization is diminished by authorial hyperbole.

This said, Lewis's depiction of the overpowering constraints that American institutions impose on independent-thinking science professors is carried forward by the parallel story of Martin Arrowsmith's encounter with

Midwestern America. There the young doctor finds himself hemmed in by suspicion of the physician-scientist, whose education and worldview make him an outsider in the Christian communities he serves. In the farming town of Wheatsylvania, for instance, Arrowsmith encounters mounting resistance because the citizens are suspicious of his lack of religion and local patriotism. As one reviewer characterized this phenomenon, Lewis "lays bare the petty jealousies of the small town practice and ... shows the inability of the small town mind to dissociate between a man's skill with the scalpel and his belief in the Book of Genesis."[8] Numerous variations illustrate these insular responses, including the predictable opposition of the Christian community to normative, prophylactic scientific practices in respect to infectious diseases. Thus, after Arrowsmith misdiagnoses an outbreak of chicken pox as smallpox and urges everyone to be vaccinated, he finds that a United Brethren preacher inveighs against vaccination, hence undermining his entire scientific position. Arrowsmith subsequently becomes such a laughingstock that when a real outbreak of diphtheria emerges and he calls for antitoxin, few comply. Even after children die, the community persists in its ridicule, with the result that Arrowsmith concludes that he must find employment elsewhere.

In Wheatsylvania, Arrowsmith experiences the difficulties of working among uneducated people fixed in their ways; in his next position in Nautilus, Iowa, he faces various kinds of institutional authority. Chief among these is "the preposterous Pickerbaugh," a literary descendent of Babbitt.[9] The director of public health in Nautilus under whom Martin works, Dr. Pickerbaugh, embodies the religious conformism, hypocrisy, and opportunism that Lewis most detested in Midwestern culture. Despite his mission as a leading public health official, Pickerbaugh becomes completely entangled in religious affairs, civic campaigns, and commercialized promotions. His self-congratulatory pamphlet, *Pickerbaugh Pickings,* recommends "good health, good roads, good business, and the single standard of morality" (196). A writer of doggerel and limericks who casts himself as a poet, Pickerbaugh circulates the idea of "the Morality of A1 Health" and crows that his boosterism has brought church attendance up 17 percent (195). A shameless self-promoter, he strives to imitate the flamboyant, evangelistic methods of Billy Sunday so that the public will adopt public health habits.

---

8. Le Blanc, "Scientific Books," 633.

9. The quotation is from Lovett, "An Interpreter of American Life," 517. The similarity between Babbitt and Pickerbaugh was developed in Mencken's essay, "*Arrowsmith,*" 102.

Since Americans lack a national church, Pickerbaugh must compete for the allegiance of churchgoers by using his office to fill their every social and spiritual need.[10] Predictably, his obsession with the marketing of health and morality makes Pickerbaugh's scientific knowledge pathetically thin. His trivialization of an otherwise honorable medical profession is epitomized by Arrowsmith's exasperated declaration that Pickerbaugh's use of the word *science* in his limericks is a "sacrilege!" (206). But Arrowsmith's describing this act as "sacrilegious" is more than mockery; it is a hyperbolic way of declaring that the profession of medicine is in some real sense sacrosanct. This is the core value that is missing in Pickerbaugh's worldview and in that of the people of Nautilus.

The trivialization of science takes place, ironically, under religious auspices. Arrowsmith introduces a program on church grounds to teach the importance of laboratory testing for communicable diseases, but, ridiculously, Martin finds himself prayed and sung over. Through these rituals, the independent, evidence-driven practice of preventive medicine finds itself being absorbed in promotions of church faith. Subtle forms of religious pressure turn into coercion. The process encompasses Pickerbaugh's resolve to bring Arrowsmith to "salvation," since he has detected "traces of heterodoxy" in his assistant. After Arrowsmith expresses his support for the practice of birth control, Pickerbaugh, a man with eight daughters, answers him with "theology, [and] violence" (213, 224).[11]

Significantly, the satiric point of view that Lewis adopts in this part of the novel takes for granted the unexpressed value that church and state—which is to say in this case, science and religion—ought naturally to be separate. The results of mixing the two lead, self-evidently, to ludicrous consequences. But the normative perspective from which these satiric events are launched intimates the presence of what José Casanova describes in his theory of secularization "as an epistemic knowledge regime that may be held unreflexively or be assumed phenomenologically as the taken-for-granted normal structure of modern reality, as a modern *doxa* or an 'unthought.'"[12] Not that Lewis could or would have articulated this notion in 1925, when *Arrowsmith* appeared. Operating within this secular episteme, he sounds the alarm from just the opposite direction—that the needed separation of scientific matters of health from religious matters (and from extraneous marketplace considerations) was not being observed. Lewis is not mindless about

---

10. Jacoby, *American Unreason*, 43–44, makes the point.
11. See Mencken's chapter "On Birth Control" in *Prejudices, Fifth Series*, 9–14.
12. Casanova, "The Secular," 55.

the position he adopts; he has his rationale. Pickerbaugh is a menace not because he mixes religious with scientific matters, but because he has no appreciation for or understanding of the importance of a modern, scientific health services program.

This is the reason why Pickerbaugh's publicity-seeking practices, farcical as they are, begin in humor and end in judgment. As Lewis depicts him, Pickerbaugh shamelessly promotes the cause of public health with such religious zeal that he fabricates statistics to support the cause. To him, health is a moral crusade to be won through marketing rather than sound science. To Arrowsmith, this contaminates the scientific enterprise. Arrowsmith, in fact, poses what Lewis must have regarded as the most central value question, for it has the ring of a morality play:[13] "Yes, does it really matter? Does truth matter—... Max Gottlieb's truth?" (225). This claim to truth is framed in such a way as to pit science against the intrusions of religion, where Arrowsmith, operating within a secularizing episteme, observes a clear distinction between "true and false knowledge."[14] Put in other words, Arrowsmith asks rhetorically whether the results of science matter, where science is an activity undertaken without the contamination introduced by extraneous commercial and religious interests. In effect, Arrowsmith is operating under the ideological belief that the "privatization of religion" is a necessary precondition for the proper implementation of scientific knowledge.[15]

Pickerbaugh does not want scientific truth; he wants a marketing strategy. Given Arrowsmith's uncompromising scientific standards, there is no longer room for him at Nautilus. Thus, Arrowsmith, finding himself unable to rally supporters for his rigorous scientific prevention measures, fed up with the hostility of the churches, and worn down by community resistance, leaves Nautilus, his vision of a modern health program unrealized. Pickerbaugh, by contrast, Nautilus's most cheerful opportunist, is last seen rising beyond expectation. Hailed in the local paper as the first scientist to be elected to Congress, he enjoys a victory as shallow as it is wide, for the local byline reads, "*Side-kick of Darwin and Pasteur / Gives new Punch to Steering / Ship of State*" (254).

---

13. *Arrowsmith* has repeatedly been called, at least in part, a morality play. See, for instance, Doctorow, afterword to *Arrowsmith*, 454.

14. For a discussion of religion in the public sphere, see Calhoun, "Secularism," 77.

15. I adapt an aspect of the theory of secularization expounded by Casanova, "The Secular," 60.

II

Arrowsmith's path proves difficult and lonely. After securing a research appointment at the Rouncefield Clinic in Chicago, he again feels misplaced because of the director's requirement that his research (like Gottlieb's) should end with practical, immediately useful—and remunerative—results. Fortunately, Max Gottlieb, now a celebrated researcher at the McGurk Institute, notices one of Martin's publications and brings about his former student's transfer to McGurk. The reunion of the two scientists injects the novel with new life and the prospect of a fully articulated scientific ideology.

Spurred on by Gottlieb's personal example, Arrowsmith begins to work out his own core values. Exhilarated by the prospect of a life of research, he utters the most quoted passage in the novel, the scientist's prayer: "God give me unclouded eyes and freedom from haste. God give me a quiet and relentless anger against all pretense and all pretentious work and all work left slack and unfinished. God give me a restlessness . . . till my observed results equal my calculated results . . . God give me strength not to trust to God!" (280). Except for the last line, which is often read as another of Lewis's oxymoronic zingers, critics tend to cite the passage as if it spoke for itself.[16] Such a response would be reductive, however, for the ideological point is that the prayer underscores Martin's own agency, not God's. By virtue of his disciplinary creed, Martin is to trust his calculations and results to no external power. He must also possess, strangely enough, the religious virtue of piety in that the experimental process and the results are hallowed because they are attained neither with pretense nor fakery.

Lewis found a way to dilate upon this crucial idea by creating a complement to Arrowsmith's statement of values in Max Gottlieb's own speech, called "the religion of a scientist" (278). In it Gottlieb maintains that the vocation of a scientist is unlike any other; it changes the nature of its "victim" because it makes the scientist "intensely religious," refusing to accept quarter-truths (278). It spurns American boosterism and European privilege, and it "hates" two kinds of religious pretenders to knowledge, "the preachers who talk their fables" and the "ridiculous faith-healers," who, along with the pseudo–social scientists, make only "guesses" (279).

Not all of Gottlieb's claims for science speak to its epistemological status; several are unexpectedly civic. The idea that science spurns privilege

---

16. Schorer, afterword to *Arrowsmith*, 435; Van Doren, "Sinclair Lewis and the Revolt from the Village," 88. But see the comments of Dooley, *Art of Lewis*, 109.

is a democratic value that ties science to freedom of information as well as to individual achievement, not birth. These values are open to the kind of criticism Walter Lippmann presented when he wrote that Lewis was really describing a meritocracy because, in reality, the scientific profession he presents is open only to the talented few; ironically, the profession reveals itself to be much like the Protestant concept of special election because only the few can be saved.[17] Similarly, the fact that dedicated scientists observe high standards underscores the notion that they belong to an elite meritocracy.

On the epistemological side, Gottlieb considers two kinds of knowing, both religious. The preacher, who represents the written word, biblical and doctrinal, is dismissed *tout court* as a dealer in fables. For Gottlieb and, one suspects, Lewis as well, there is only one kind of genuine knowledge, only one discipline capable of approaching the truth, and that is the scientific-secular. Faith healers, who deal not in knowledge acquisition but in the discipline of mind and spirit to bring about healing, are simply frauds. Again, for Gottlieb only one kind of knowledge exhibits a real value. He will not even concede the mind-body communication system that novelists Eggleston and Scott acknowledge as genuine in the placebo effect. Gottlieb's secularism operates as an ideology, a regime of truth that admits no rival.

Yet, for all of the novel's secular ideology, the generic idea of the spiritual is not called into question. To the contrary, Gottlieb aptly describes a scientist's religion as a subjective state that can transform the "victim" through an intense inner experience.[18] This account returns the reader to the seeming contradiction that Lewis constructs a field of devotional imagery to convey the inner experience of a scientist at the exultant moment of discovery, when an experiment comes to a successful conclusion. A promising approach to this problem is Charles Taylor's account of the spiritual experience, which for the religious person is felt as a sense of "fullness" or completeness. Taylor acknowledges that the feeling is of the same order as that which is available to the nonbeliever. Taylor argues that for believers, that sense of transcendence is experienced as coming from another place, from something larger than the self, "beyond human life," whereas unbelievers "understand fullness in terms of a potentiality of human beings understood naturalistically." He goes on to argue that unbelievers locate this experience in "the self-sufficient power of reason." But this latter distinction, which locates the religious experience for nonbelievers in reason,

---

17. Lippmann, "Sinclair Lewis," 89, makes the point.
18. Hungerford, *Postmodern Belief*, xiv–xvi, theorizes the experience of inward transformation, even without belief.

seems to me unnecessarily restrictive. Certainly Gottlieb's own account of this inward process is one that speaks of the experience not as a rational one at all, but as an undermining and transforming of the ordinary self. From these considerations, it appears that the experience of spiritual fullness can belong to believers and unbelievers alike. Furthermore, Taylor's account of how in giving "this power full reign" one comes "to live by it" is exactly what Gottlieb and Arrowsmith come to feel and do.[19]

Laurence Veysey's *The Emergence of the American University* lends credence to the authenticity of the reverent portrayal of scientific research at the turn of the twentieth century. Quoting from well-known contemporaries at the time such as Thorstein Veblen and Hermann von Holst, Veysey generalizes, "For the intense seeker after new knowledge, research soon came to possess many of the emotional characteristics of a religion."[20] If the inner experience that Arrowsmith and Gottlieb describe is not only plausible but historically grounded, then what remains to determine is Lewis's purpose in depicting the allegiances of the research scientist in religious terms. In the interplay of the religion-secular binary, the question is whether that interaction contributes to or detracts from the power of religion itself. Here it should be recognized that Lewis's strategy is, indeed, to demonstrate, as Dooley charged, that science can replace religion. Since Lewis's disdain for formal religion is unrelenting, his purpose is to enhance the prestige of the scientific enterprise and thus to extend its reach over religion in the world. Furthermore, his prescription of science as salvation sets forth a new kind of allegiance that, if nourished, would draw the credulous away from myth and align their spiritual aspirations with a profession that Lewis championed as producing genuine knowledge.

Since the formation of scientific knowledge was so important to Lewis's purpose, it was crucial that his novel accurately present the actual practice of scientific research. Lewis's success in achieving this goal was much praised. Even in the early months following publication, reviewers such as Stuart Sherman of the *Herald Tribune* exclaimed, "I suppose there is more science and scientific talk in 'Arrowsmith' than in any other novel that has hitherto appeared in the world." Not content with that, he continued, "With all explanations made, the amount of his special information is astonishing. Still more astonishing, the special information nowhere clutters the story: It is all at work."[21]

---

19. Throughout the paragraph, I cite from Taylor, *Secular Age*, 7–9.
20. Veysey, *Emergence of the American University*, 150.
21. Sherman, "A Way Out: Sinclair Lewis Discovers a Hero," 2.

These features owe much more than most readers recognize to Lewis's collaboration with the young bacteriologist and pathologist Paul de Kruif. Like Lewis, de Kruif was a proponent of reform in the medical profession and had written a series of articles on the subject for the *Century Illustrated Monthly*, which led to his dismissal from the Rockefeller Institute.[22] The two took easily to one another, and de Kruif convinced Lewis to write a novel about medicine. He also agreed to accompany Lewis on a two-month Caribbean cruise to assist the novelist in writing about scientific matters, particularly in mapping out a plague in the West Indies where they were traveling.[23]

Even by conservative estimates, de Kruif's contributions to *Arrowsmith* were considerable, which is presumably why Lewis agreed to a contract giving the young scientist 25 percent of the royalties *Arrowsmith* reaped.[24] De Kruif was also to share top billing with Lewis as coauthor, but later Lewis's publisher decided against this part of the agreement.[25] Instead, Lewis composed a graceful prefatory acknowledgment of de Kruif's aid, an interpolation that appears only in some modern editions—which may help to explain why many modern readers are not aware of the collaboration.[26] The disagreement over how to acknowledge de Kruif's contribution created a breach that never healed. Nonetheless, de Kruif went on to publish *Microbe Hunters* (1926), a nonfiction book that earned $1,202,913; made heroes out of scientific discoverers; and catapulted the author into a long, successful career as a popular science writer.[27]

So individuated were the scientific personalities de Kruif described to Lewis, several of them famous, that knowledgeable contemporaries worked out the probable identities of those who served as models for the scientists and administrators in the novel, including Max Gottlieb and Arrowsmith himself.[28] As a *roman à clef*, *Arrowsmith* was important to some, but to the

---

22. Hutchisson, "Sinclair Lewis, Paul De Kruif, and the Composition of *Arrowsmith*," 50, and Charles E. Rosenberg, "Martin Arrowsmith," 448–49.

23. Information in the paragraph on Lewis's and de Kruif's collaboration and relationship is drawn from Lewis, *From Main Street to Stockholm: Letters*, 121–26, and Schorer, *Sinclair Lewis*, 339–40, 364–68.

24. Schorer, *Sinclair Lewis*, 361.

25. Hutchisson, "Sinclair Lewis," 50.

26. Lewis, *Arrowsmith* (1st ed.). The acknowledgment begins, "To Dr. Paul H. De Kruif I am indebted. . . ." See Schorer, *Sinclair Lewis*, 406–7.

27. For sales figures, see Hackett, *60 Years of Best Sellers*, 21. For discussion of de Kruif's fame and importance, see Gonzalez-Crussi, introduction to *Microbe Hunters*, vii–xiv.

28. Verhave, "*Arrowsmith*," and Schorer, *Sinclair Lewis*, 418–19.

great bulk of readers it was the revelation of the research scientist's habits and training, the actual experiments, and the authenticity of the novel's scientific information that was so admired. Much of this Lewis learned from de Kruif, as we have seen, but some part at least came from Lewis's father, who was a country doctor.[29]

As a presentation of scientific concepts, *Arrowsmith* is impressive. Its account of the concept behind the control group, for instance, is handled with pedagogical clarity and ethical sensitivity, as when Arrowsmith faces his great ethical dilemma in St. Hubert near the end of the novel. The novel also explores the idea of antitoxin as the basis for a vaccine. In taut scenes it explains how a healthy elderly woman who had been cured of typhoid years earlier was nonetheless a carrier. Later it explicitly introduces, and enacts, a "quarantine" (238). The central concepts of inoculation and immunization are explored throughout the novel. Along the way, the tools of the research scientist—the omnipresent microscope, the "Bunsen" burner, the "reagent," the incubation of bacteria "*in vitro*" (271, 122)—are all accurately introduced. A host of diseases, including typhoid, tuberculosis, cholera, influenza, diphtheria, and even syphilis—and sometimes their pathology, prevention, or cure—all ease into view. Moreover, the names of famous bacteriologists earlier hailed as "Father," including Koch and Pasteur, later reappear in reference to their discoveries. In these several ways, Lewis's novel becomes pedagogical as it celebrates its scientific heroes. Without doubt, the novel's compelling power proceeds from its painstakingly accurate detail. Such detail, we know, appears in Lewis's notebook for *Arrowsmith*, which displays five pages garnered from conversations with de Kruif, entitled "BACTERIOLOGICAL NOTES."[30]

In addition to the technical scientific knowledge displayed in Lewis's novel, members of the medical community identified a historical layer as well. Writing in *Medical Humanities*, Heiner Fangerau argues that Arrowsmith's career follows in parallel the history of modern medicine.[31] It begins by singling out Lewis's portrayal early in *Arrowsmith* of the older experimental healing practices of Doc Vickerson, then moves on to show Max Gottlieb's "quantifying, mechanistic philosophy of science," which was so important to the achievements of scientific bacteriology, and finally depicts the ascent of the great research laboratories, with their emphasis on teamwork and public relations.[32] To Fangerau's account may be added an

---

29. On Lewis's father, Dr. Edwin Lewis, see Schorer, *Sinclair Lewis*, 12–13.
30. Hutchisson, "Sinclair Lewis," 52.
31. Fangerau, "*Arrowsmith*," 83–84.
32. Ibid., 84. See also Charles E. Rosenberg, "Martin Arrowsmith," 454–56.

intermediate layer of medical history (which Lewis treats satirically), the Pickerbaugh-Arrowsmith episodes, in which strict public hygiene protocols based on improved understanding of germ theory successfully prevents the spread of disease.[33]

III

Despite Lewis's accomplishments in *Arrowsmith*, his novel has faced sharp criticism for failing to provide a satisfactory philosophic rationale for the exceedingly high value accorded to research science. The reciprocal charge, that it denigrates religion, is also prevalent. D. J. Dooley's *The Art of Sinclair Lewis* locates the source of the problem in Lewis's treatment of science "as a worthy successor to religion." Dooley's charge is that the philosophic ground for this exaltation is far more "brisk" than reflective or cogent. Do we really believe, he writes, "that the cure of the sick is of small consequence in comparison with the search for the fundamental laws of nature? Lewis gives the impression of having gone deeply into the problem of the rational foundation for devotion to science," but he fails to present a satisfactory explanation.[34]

Although it might be easier to yield the point since Lewis is a novelist rather than a philosopher, that would concede too much. If Lewis exalts the process of scientific discovery, he does so by complicating the reader's response to what science is, in one set of places likening it to a spiritual experience while in others satirizing religion as a practice and as a way of knowing the world. Thus, Arrowsmith affirms that embedded in the mundane activities of the laboratory is the search for the "fundamental laws" that the scientist "exalts above temporary healing " (118). In the search for nature's fundamental laws, the researcher feels a kind of religious exaltation in pursuing a transcendent goal that surpasses the experiment of the moment. It is another expression of that inner sense of "fullness," which, as we saw earlier, Taylor describes in his theorization of a believer's transcendent experience—except that it is an unbeliever who experiences this transcendence. In this matter of spiritual transcendence, there is no intention of the part of either Arrowsmith or Gottlieb to substitute a secular experience of spirituality for a religious one; for them they are the same inward experience.

---

33. Starr, *Social Transformation of American Medicine*, 135.

34. Quotations throughout the paragraph to this point are from Dooley, *Art of Lewis*, 107–9.

As for embracing miracles, *Arrowsmith* resists. When Gottlieb teaches that you can't be a "miracle man" and a scientist too (316), he puts on full display the secular-religious binary, with its devaluation of religion as something intrinsically opposed to knowledge. In *Arrowsmith,* the two value systems are incompatible because a miracle means suspension of the physical laws of nature, the opposite of Gottlieb's belief that these laws are never suspended. This prevalent secular view is epitomized by astronomer Carl Sagan, who depicted the scientific endeavor as "a candle in the darkness"— the only kind of knowledge, he argued, to which we have access.[35]

Lewis's spirited apology for research science may be viewed as correcting the overemphasis in America for applied knowledge, for the practice of science would be virtually impossible without the prior discoveries issuing from basic research. Many contemporary reviewers endorsed the wisdom of *Arrowsmith* on the ground that the novel communicates the intrinsic values of scientific research in a world otherwise filled, as Lewis presents it, with hokum and shallowness. For instance, Robert Morss Lovett concluded his review with the stirring observation, "If he [Lewis] has sacrificed the reality of fiction, it is in the interest of the reality of a public cause which gives largeness of view and significance to Arrowsmith."[36] Henry Canby, assessing the grand passion of the novel's two main researchers, declared there to be little difference between the heroes and the villains except that "Lewis's heroes work at something greater than themselves."[37] More blandly, Clarence Gaines asserted that Lewis "discovers in *science* a reality that is worthy of respect."[38]

There is, finally, a fourth kind of evidence that issues from the novel itself. Far from being shallow, *Arrowsmith* draws attention to the damaging as well as salutary consequences of pursuing a life uncompromisingly dedicated to research science. Thus, the incorruptible Gottlieb is also a flawed, tragic figure whose single-mindedness and incorruptibility conspire to produce his fanaticism. Taking notice of the complexity of his character, one contemporary reviewer wrote that Gottlieb is a Puritan with something of "religious fanaticism" in his soul.[39] How better to describe a man who contemplates letting loose "amiable" pathogens on the world so as to solve its economic problems (38)?

---

35. Sagan's title phrase in *The Demon-Haunted World: Science as a Candle in the Dark,* 26–27.
36. Lovett, "An Interpreter of American Life," 518.
37. Canby, "Fighting Success," 112.
38. Gaines, "Some Modern Novels," 165.
39. Hazard makes the observation in "The Frontier in *Arrowsmith,*" 113.

Similarly, Lewis affirms that although Martin is perceived to be a truth-seeker, he is "in no degree a hero" (43).⁴⁰ The novelist then proceeds to dramatize the problematic nature of Arrowsmith's choices and his values. Subjecting his protagonist to an ethical crux, the novelist has the young scientist decide whether or not to establish the efficacy of a serum (vaccine) he has developed by administering it to one portion of the plague-stricken population while withholding it from another. His decision to use human beings as a control group for his new vaccine places the acquisition of scientific knowledge above the immediate needs of suffering humanity. Thus it is with considerable irony that once Arrowsmith, under strong pressure, relents, he is hailed as a hero and dubbed "savior of all our lives" (396). With equal self-centeredness, he also abandons his second wife and their child for the secluded life of scientific experimentation. In this manner, Lewis reveals that Gottlieb and Arrowsmith subscribe to a problematic ethics that is, ironically, the direct consequence of their scientific idealism. This critique, it may further be observed, is rooted in a normative ethics consistent with Judeo-Christian teaching. Taken together, this multifaceted set of critical observations reveals *Arrowsmith* in a more complex light, which breaks out of the binary oppositions that originally envelop the novel.⁴¹ In so doing, the novel presents its own critique of the values by which it stands.

IV

Given the cultural significance of *Arrowsmith*, it is not surprising that Lewis's novel attained seventh place on the best-seller list for fiction in 1925.⁴² However, Lewis's refusal to accept the Pulitzer prize after being offered it for *Arrowsmith* reveals a great deal about the author's disdain for those institutional forces in America that promote conformism, including the Pulitzer Prize Committee. To some degree, Lewis appears to have rejected the award because he was smarting over not having previously received the award for *Main Street* or *Babbitt*. But ideological principles and a public identity were also at stake. In a letter to his publisher, Lewis was clearly

---

40. Many critics recognize the problematic nature of Arrowsmith as hero. See Canby, "Fighting Success," 112; Van Doren, "Sinclair Lewis and the Revolt from the Village," 89; Sherman, "A Way Out: Sinclair Lewis Discovers a Hero," 1–2; and Charles E. Rosenberg, "Martin Arrowsmith," 447.

41. Hamner, "Damning Fundamentalism," 266.

42. Hackett, *60 Years of Best Sellers*, 139.

concerned about "selling out," recalling that the Pulitzer was awarded to the novel "best portraying the highest standards of American morals and manners." But the actual wording, as Lewis's formal letter to the Pulitzer Prize Committee shows, was "the highest standards of American manners and *manhood*" (italics mine). Lewis's mistaken recollection of the word *morals* dramatically illustrates his sensitivity to the committee's role in validating social norms, especially through manners—the very thing his fiction, including substantial portions of *Arrowsmith*, flamboyantly challenges. As a novelist who was then planning *Elmer Gantry*, an exposé of religious hypocrisy; a public figure whose companions included atheists H. L. Mencken and Clarence Darrow; and, furthermore, a public speaker who had dared God, if he exists, to strike him dead in fifteen minutes, Lewis was heavily invested in resisting status quo institutional authority in America, especially religion.[43]

Furthermore, he associated the Pulitzer Committee with the authoritarianism of the Catholic Church. In his letter to the committee he brandished a religious imagery of insult, accusing it of acting like a "pontifical body" and as "a college of cardinals."[44] Beneath this obvious attack lay Lewis's disdain for the culture of the United States, with its conventional manners, morals, and devaluation of free-thinking intellectuals.

Lewis was himself such a person, and his novels show it. *Arrowsmith* charts the ascendency of scientific medicine in America, but it does so as an exposé of the corrupting entanglements to which its practice is subjected. A chief object of his satire was the practical culture of Christianity in the Midwest, where science is hemmed in by religious opposition of varying sorts. Although Christian churches suffered a relative loss of cultural prestige in the 1920s, they were able to maintain a firm grip on their communities through their enduring cultural authority. When Lewis found his own novel subject to that cultural authority, he learned how long that reach was. The occasion of this object lesson was the publication of *Arrowsmith* in serialized form (June 1924 to April 1925) by the *Designer and the Woman's Magazine*. Its editors, though eager to publish the novel, became apprehensive about the reactions of their middle-of-the-road, mostly female readers to the novel's satire. Consequently, they excised a large number of passages in the manuscript. Lyon Richardson, who made a thorough study of the excisions, wrote, "Throughout *Arrowsmith* there is no favorable response to religious

---

43. Throughout the paragraph facts and quotations are drawn from Schorer, *Sinclair Lewis*, 374, 445–46, 451–53. Besides appearing in Schorer's book, the text of Lewis's letter to the Pulitzer Committee is reproduced in Lingeman, *Sinclair Lewis*, 279–80.

44. Schorer, *Sinclair Lewis*, 452–53.

institutions or to persons affiliated with them." This the editors clearly saw, and they moved to soften Lewis's portrait of middle-American homes. Thus readers of the *Designer* did not find Pickerbaugh's "Health Hymn," satirically rendered for the Congregational Festival, nor the depiction of Pickerbaugh's home as suggesting an aura of "overpowering Christian Domesticity" (202–3, 206), because they had been removed. Similarly excised was Leora's snide opinion that Martin might consider becoming "a Respectable Citizen" and church member (217). Among the many other censored passages was the death-bed exclamation of Arrowsmith's good friend and devoted scientist, Dr. Sondelius, who wants to show "how an agnostic can die!" (381). Seldom has there been such palpable evidence as this of prepublication editorial censorship undertaken to avoid arousing the ire of upstanding Christian households.[45]

This fate, it must be remembered, did not befall the publication of the novel as a book, whose audience was more diverse. Nor has *Arrowsmith* lost its generative cultural energy. Although the novel has undergone numerous transformations, it continues to exert influence down to the present day. Thus, a highly successful film version of *Arrowsmith* appeared in 1931 with an all-star cast featuring Ronald Coleman playing Martin, Helen Hayes as his wife Leora, and A. E. Anson as Gottlieb. The film was nominated for four Academy Awards, including best picture and best screenplay adaptation.[46] Predictably, the film preserves Arrowsmith's idealism but sets aside the novel's satire of religious mores. Nevertheless, it raises the crucial ethical issue brought about by Arrowsmith's extreme reluctance to compromise the results of his plague experiment. Before giving into relentless pressure, Arrowsmith was intent on giving the life-saving vaccine to some, while withholding it from others in the control group.

Over the next twenty years, *Arrowsmith*, in concert with de Kruif's biographies of scientists in *Microbe Hunters*, appears to have inspired a spate of biographical films dramatizing—and teaching the public about—the trials and triumphs of research scientists battling disease.[47] These films include, among others, *The Story of Louis Pasteur* (1936), with Paul Muni, and Paul

---

45. Throughout the paragraph, information about *Designers* is drawn from Richardson, "*Arrowsmith*: Genesis," 234–35. Richardson's page references from *Arrowsmith* have been adjusted to conform to the edition used in this chapter.

46. *Academy Awards Index*, 17, 83. The other two fields in which the film *Arrowsmith* was nominated were in cinematography and art direction/set decoration (111, 127).

47. Indirect support for this interpretation comes from Schorer, *Sinclair Lewis*, 407n., who states that when *Arrowsmith* was in the planning stages, the film agent turned to de Kruif rather than Lewis for advice.

Ehrlich's *The Magic Bullet* (1940), with Edward G. Robinson. The films in the group, along with the popular magazines on the subject, feed the narrative of basic research as an "exact science."[48] They also showcase the immense prestige that research science attained in the mid-twentieth century, along with the consolidation of its medical authority.

More than any other Lewis novel, *Arrowsmith* continues to be read in our own time and to generate cultural energy by producing controversy as well as approval. It has even entered the medical journals. There it is especially valued for its prescient presentation of the tensions between research science and practice. Since 1945, some 145 citations or titles featuring "Arrowsmith" have been entered in the Science Citation Index and the Arts and Humanities Index.[49] Surprising to contemplate, most of these are in medical journals, with the highest number of citations appearing in the years 1985, 1996, and 2000.[50]

The influence of *Arrowsmith* in the scientific community also extends to its power to model scientific ideals and to inspire. In a 1999 biography of the fabled fruit-fly geneticist Seymour Benzer, Pulitzer prize–winning author Jonathan Weiner recorded the lifelong inspiration Benzer drew from reading *Arrowsmith* as a student. Weiner's book *Time, Love, and Memory* dramatizes the novel's influence on Benzer in no fewer than twelve discrete passages. In what amounts to a leitmotif, the biography retells Arrowsmith's story even as it relates Benzer's own. More profoundly, it makes the novel live again as a model for the faith of a modern scientist, for Weiner attests that for Benzer, *Arrowsmith* "was almost a prayer book, because it showed science as an adventure, a romance, and a pure faith, a way to live a life." Poetically, Weiner also describes old Gottlieb emerging from his laboratory late at night with a threadbare coat, uttering his mantra: "I make many mistakes. But one thing I keep always pure: the religion of the scientist."[51]

In citing these words, Weiner identifies the impact of Arrowsmith and Gottlieb on Benzer's spiritual development. Weiner thus provides cogent evidence that the values Lewis depicts in his novel became for Benzer transformational. Throughout his long career, which took flight in the 1950s and lasted into the early twenty-first century, Benzer held convictions about the disinterested pursuit of knowledge and the refusal to succumb to the blandishments of careerism or material success that have affected the outlook of

---

48. On the ascendency of medicine as an "exact science," see Hutchisson, "*Arrowsmith* and the Political Economy of Medicine," 114.
49. Fangerau, "*Arrowsmith*," 86.
50. Ibid.
51. Throughout the paragraph I cite from Weiner, *Time, Love, and Memory*, 36–37.

several generations of science students. Through Benzer and former graduate students who later entered the science profession, a new generation of students became readers of Lewis's novel.[52] This is cultural power of an exceptional sort. The lasting message it conveys is that Benzer's career did not bring about a loss of faith; it inspired a life-guiding belief system based on faithful devotion to research science.[53]

Surprising as it may appear, this analysis is consistent with Charles Taylor's observation that a hallmark of "the Western march toward secularity is that it has been interwoven from the start with this drive toward a personal religion."[54] For Benzer and unnamed others, *Arrowsmith* expresses the spirituality and reverence associated with the full heart and transfers it to the domain of scientific research.

Among Lewis's major novels of the 1920s and 1930s, *Arrowsmith* is unusual because it praises more fully than it satirizes or critiques. In his next novel, *Elmer Gantry*, Lewis reversed the emphasis. In that unrelenting satire, to which I now turn, Lewis poured into his revivalist preacher the personal qualities he most detested, and in so doing sought to discredit all those conservative cultural forces, including the Bible colleges, that impeded scientific progress and modern secularization.

---

52. I learned from Dr. Michael Shiflett, neuroscientist at Rutgers-Newark, that in 2007 his postdoctoral professor at UCLA, Dr. Alcino Silva, recommended *Arrowsmith* to his postdoctoral students, as did Dr. Robert Brown. Through Brown, Shiflett and numerous classmates also learned about and read Weiner's biography on Seymour Benzer.

53. Throughout the paragraph data on Benzer's relationship to *Arrowsmith* and its circulation among his graduate students and others is drawn from Weiner, *Time, Love, and Memory*, 36–37, 63, 204–5, 212–13.

54. Taylor, "Western Secularity," 38, and for Taylor's definition of "secularization," see 32.

CHAPTER 6

SATIRIZING FUNDAMENTALIST EDUCATION AND REVIVALIST PREACHERS

Sinclair Lewis's *Elmer Gantry*

SINCE *ELMER GANTRY* (1927) was composed soon after *Arrowsmith* (1925), it is illuminating to compare briefly their strategic presentation of science and religion. If these novels are thought of as photographic images, *Elmer Gantry* would look very much like a negative of the earlier novel. Whereas *Arrowsmith* foregrounds the mainly admirable research scientist, Arrowsmith, setting his earnestness against a background of Christian conventionality and commercialism, *Elmer Gantry* reverses this emphasis. It foregrounds the opportunism and hypocrisy of its revivalist preacher while relegating to the background the novel's liberal, scientific, and humanistic values. Considered together, the two novels offer an extensive examination of the clash in American culture in the 1920s between secular materialists and Christian fundamentalists, whose numbers included not only dogmatists, but also evangelicals who emphasized the transformative powers in heart and spirit of the direct experience of God.[1] Viewed more

---

1. Worthen, *Apostles of Reason*, 3–7, points to the variety of evangelical faiths—characterized as "heart religion"—that emerged from the Reformation through the Scopes trial.

abstractly, *Elmer Gantry* became the occasion of a struggle over the meaning of Lewis's novel, a struggle played out on a national stage as a contest between competing ideologies, each with its own epistemic discourse and its own educational system.

Published in 1927, the novel was composed in the still-heated aftermath of the 1925 Scopes "monkey" trial. As soon as it appeared, it was interpreted as a second *casus belli*, further polarizing an already polarized society. Reviewers divided along sharply partisan lines. Newspapers inflamed the divisions. For instance, the *New York Evening Post* in the first page of its *Literary Review* juxtaposed two diametrically opposed assessments of Lewis's new novel. In admiring tribute, W. E. Woodward presented his review under the headline, "'Elmer Gantry' Is Truth As a Study in Hypocrisy," while on the opposite side of the page was an article by nationally recognized Baptist minister John Roach Straton, emblazoned with the headline, "'Elmer Gantry' Is Bunk, Vanity and Vulgarity."[2] Sprinkled with pungent mockery, Straton's essay described the "malodorous literature" produced by the "malodorous flock" of Lewis's friends and supporters, whom he singled out as the intellectual infidels Clarence Darrow and H. L. Mencken, along with left-leaning historian Rupert Hughes. Going on to accuse Lewis of defaming the clerical profession, Straton declared that the novel's two most important preachers, Gantry and Sharon Falconer, are "preposterously impossible" and that they bring "all fair minds" to revulsion.

Although Lewis's novel established the subject of the debate, partisans struggled to control the interpretation, which turned on the representation of Elmer Gantry himself, as it still does today. Among conservative and moderate ministers, the repeated contention was that Gantry is not a truly representative preacher type. This particular contest, it is important to remember, was enacted against the background of the cultural divide between fundamentalists and modernists, which in *Elmer Gantry* takes the form of Lewis's attack on Christian fundamentalist higher education. After considering this pervasive theme in the novel, I take up the issue of Elmer Gantry as a representative type, drawing attention to his upbringing and to the contemporary controversy about the kind of person that enters the ministry. A concluding section on the film version of *Elmer Gantry* (1960) argues that the novel's polemical edge was blunted by the film director, Richard Brooke, who worked to soften and mediate the challenging religious and scientific issues the film script placed before its mass audience.

---

2. W. E. Woodward, "'Elmer Gantry' Is Truth," 1, 10, and Straton, "'Elmer Gantry' Is Bunk," 1, 10. Quotations throughout the paragraph are from Straton, 1, 10.

I

Elmer Gantry, probably the most polemical novel Lewis ever wrote, signals its unconventionality from its first sentence. It opens in the year 1902 with the announcement that divinity student Elmer Gantry is drunk in a barroom brothel. Both he and his roommate, Jim Lefferts, attend Baptist-founded Terwillinger College in Kansas, but Jim is an atheist who relishes asking uncomfortable scriptural questions of the college president. This pairing enables Lewis to mount a satiric attack on Gantry as a crass opportunist while using Lefferts, a reader of the popular atheist Robert Ingersoll, to instigate arguments disputing the inerrancy of scripture and the miracles in the New and Old Testaments.[3]

Two illustrations of the method will suffice. Lefferts disingenuously inquires of college president Dr. Quarles why Joshua needed to have the sun stand still, since he was blessed with trumpets to blow down the walls of Jericho. Pursuing the point, the pretend believer asks why, if the Bible speaks of exorcism as the way to cure possession by devils, Baptist doctors continue to diagnose "devil-possession instead of T. B." (10).[4] All is partisan guerilla warfare as Lefferts makes quick strikes at the citadel of biblical belief and then moves on. The plan of attack is always the same: invoke the arguments of the biblical higher critics and expose as superstition or myth supposedly miraculous passages in the Bible.[5] It is easy to tell that Lewis is part of a movement because his satiric treatment of Old Testament stories draws upon an arsenal of familiar arguments. Famously, the invocation of the battle of Jericho references the example Darrow used at the Scopes Trial to make the point that whoever wrote "The Book of Joshua" believed that the sun travels around the earth, and thus the scriptures cannot always be literally true but must be subject to construction.[6] In this manner, Lewis created a narrative that flamboyantly put scriptural literalism, or infallibilism, on trial a second time.

---

3. Lewis invokes Ingersoll's essay, "Some Mistakes of Moses," whose censorious tone is much like Paine's in *The Age of Reason*. For discussion of Ingersoll's essay, see Anderson, *Robert Ingersoll*, 100–102. On the New and Old Testaments in *The Age of Reason*, see Kuklick, *Thomas Paine: Political Writings*, 216–26.

4. Lewis, *Elmer Gantry* (Harcourt Brace edition, 1927). Page references to quotations from this novel appear in the text.

5. For a history of this subject in Great Britain, see Cameron, *Biblical Higher Criticism*; for the United States, see Brown, *Rise of Biblical Criticism in America*.

6. For Darrow's close questioning regarding Joshua, see the court transcript in *World's Most Famous Court Trial*, 285–87. The Joshua story was a recurring target for the biblical higher critics, who applied their scientific knowledge to its refutation. See Jacoby, *American Unreason*, 21–22.

Near at hand as well are the author's seemingly inexhaustible ways of ridiculing fundamentalist beliefs. One such scene uses Jim Lefferts's father, conveniently characterized as a medical practitioner and atheist, to take down in argument the detestable Eddie Fislinger, the divinity student who always makes sure that his fundamentalism is more rigorous than anyone else's. With mock deference, Dr. Lefferts gets Fislinger to proclaim that he believes everything in the Bible, whereupon the doctor challenges Eddie's every assertion. Playing off biblical literalism against empirical experience, Lefferts assumes the guise of the zealot, demanding to know how Fislinger could possibly disbelieve the doctrine of infant damnation. Once Eddie protests that this doctrine is not Baptist, the doctor, in a rant, quotes the biblical verse that proclaims everyone is either "washed in the blood of the Lamb" or is not (33). The phrase is meant to reveal Christianity in its most barbarous aspect. With this mimicry of pulpit harangue, the doctor declares that salvation is made possible through baptism and that every unbaptized baby "must burn in hell" (34). The jest of outdoing the religious zealot in the extremity of his belief is a tried form of poetic justice. The satiric bite, it is true, leaves its mark in both of the illustrations I have provided, but the humor becomes personal and depends on an unfeeling practical joke. Still, Fislinger's comic comeuppance provides the occasion for Lewis's burlesque of the logic that celebrates infant damnation as a beautiful religious principle.

These attacks on specific points of Baptist doctrine give way to a more comprehensive critique of the curriculum delivered in Bible colleges as contrasted with progressive ones across the land. From the turn of the century, public and private institutions were changing fast as new sciences took their places in the curriculum and resistant Bible colleges, feeling the pressure, began to rethink their options.[7] Lewis's emblem for the problem is Terwillinger College's Bible History room, whose only wall decoration is a map of the Holy Land. That curriculum turns out to be not so much medieval as obscurantist. According to Elmer's proud summary, his studies feature "hermeneutics, chrestomathy, pericopes, exegesis, homiletics, liturgics, [and] isagogics," along with several ancient and remote languages (76). To modernists, this was a useless, moldy curriculum.

Before the turn of the twentieth century, Bible colleges found themselves caught between the desire to provide a moral education, insulated from godless materialism and the urge to demonstrate that they were up-to-date.[8] Similarly, they wanted to teach Christian doctrine while also show-

---

7. Worthen, *Apostles of Reason*, 99–101.
8. Ibid., 100.

ing their conversancy with the achievements of science. Thus, Terwillinger College president Quarles invokes the term *science* all the time, as when he admonishes Elmer that a Baptist preacher "must found his work on good hard scientific *facts*—the proven facts of the Bible" (64). He even boasts that we know the "substitutionary atonement"—the doctrine that Jesus' death redeemed humankind from the consequences of the Fall—"to be true, because it works" (64). The scene is a splendid example of the growing prestige of science, which impels the sectarian president to invoke the name absent the substance—all to bolster the Bible college's reputation as an up-to-date institution.

The reader comes to realize that this representative Bible college induces an impaired sense of reality. To drive home this point, Lewis makes unabashed use of anachronism. He has one aged faculty member become so enthused about the new vocations of medicine and advertising that he predicts men will in forty years be flying in airplanes. To this the college dean, in a clear echo of Paley's argument from design, retorts, if God had meant humanity to fly, "he'd have given us wings. . . . Never does to oppose the clear purpose of the Bible" (68). The ridicule settles on the pretentiousness of the Bible college president, even as he shows himself to be locked into scriptural exegesis to interpret future events. Of course, the main comic point is that by 1927, when *Elmer Gantry* was published, the prediction that men would never fly had already been demonstrably falsified years earlier.

Considered in the larger context of Lewis's time, the number of Bible colleges of a fundamentalist stripe had by 1930 already reached over fifty, and they were growing.[9] By 1950 another ninety-five had started up, and by that date they were adjusting to the need not just to defend fundamentalist beliefs but to prepare Bible students for useful careers.[10] To contrast this insular model of education among Bible colleges with a progressive model, Lewis juxtaposed a liberal ideal of public higher education. The two goals of the latter model were to prepare students for life in the modern world and to enlarge their personal horizons. To dramatize these goals, Lewis introduced two characters, the truth-seeking classmate of Elmer's, Frank Shallard, and Bruno Zechlin, the agnostic professor of Mizpah Seminary who is a student of German rationalism in the field of biblical exegesis. Shallard, son of a mild Baptist minister, is an Oberlin College graduate whose Christian upbringing has been enriched by reading Plautus, Homer, calculus, and the history of the French Revolution, and by playing basketball—in short,

---

9. Hadden and Shupe, *Televangelism*, 112.
10. Ibid., and Worthen, *Apostles of Reason*, 99–101.

by a liberal education. Part of that education aimed at establishing a skeptical attitude to claims regarding the Bible's infallibility. In this spirit, Shallard inquires how the New Testament could possibly state that no man has ever seen God, since the Old Testament records that Moses and others saw Him many times. Faced with this earnest, thoughtful question, Dr. Zechlin, in an echo of Dr. Max Gottlieb in *Arrowsmith*, replies that "Doubting" is a good thing because it frees the student from the illusion of the instructor's infallibility (121). Doubt and thus open-mindedness are qualities valued by progressive thinkers.

This secular agenda, it must be remembered, was brought about in reaction to the early history of American colleges, in which Christian teachings were integral to the college experience. Among college professors and administrators in the early nineteenth century, the main concern was not whether to teach the Holy Scriptures, but whether to teach them critically.[11] Lewis's choice was the latter, and his novel actually identifies the books that stimulate independent thinking. Several titles record the loss of traditional faith and the regaining of new purpose in the light of the higher criticism. Thus, Zechlin lends Frank Shallard Ernest Renan's *Life of Jesus* (1864), along with more recent approaches such as Adolph Harnack's *What is Christianity?* (1901) and George A. Coe's *The Religion of a Mature Mind* (1902). This informal reformist curriculum is rounded out by books recommended by Zechlin or by the Preachers' Liberal Club. The result is that Shallard becomes knowledgeable in a variety of fields, sociological, religious, and mythological, consuming such works as Frederick Davenport's *Primitive Traits in Religious Revivals* (1905), William James's *The Varieties of Religious Experience* (1902), Nathaniel Schmidt's *The Prophet of Nazareth* (1905), and James Frazer's *The Golden Bough: A Study in Magic and Religion* (1890). Science's battle with theology is represented by A. D. White's *History of the Warfare of Science with Theology* (1896). Shallard, for his part, shows himself to be a self-starter who also devours challenging novels and about fifty science books, believing that "there is nothing wicked in looking straight at life" (382).[12] This last observation, in which Shallard learns to know what he thinks without parental supervision of his reading, is the model that Lewis opposes to the deliberately restrictive one of the Bible colleges. That modernist goal of fostering an independent-thinking person is, of course, a constitutive feature of secularism, tied as it is to the secular-religious binary, and it is at odds with

---

11. See Brown, *Rise of Biblical Criticism*, 10–11, and on William Ellery Channing, 60–74.

12. Throughout the paragraph, the book titles cited are from Lewis, *Elmer Gantry*, 121, 123, 246.

the communitarianism of religious leaders whose preeminent goal is to save souls.[13]

On social grounds, Lewis bears down on an unreformed fundamentalist college curriculum by treating it as a form of escapism from modern problems. Suspicious of modern intellectualism and wary of the new sciences, many Bible colleges hold that "a proper school should teach nothing but bookkeeping, agriculture, geometry, [and] dead languages" (389). With humorous point, the modernists opposing them encourage the dynamic fields of learning, from biology to history to psychology, all of which threaten the convictions of the conservative clergy. In drawing this contrast, Lewis does not hesitate to employ ad hominem attacks. For instance, the reason given for psychology being on the list of liberal courses is that it impugns the supposed superiority of Baptist preachers "fresh from the farm" to become "trained laboratory researchers" (389). This smirking depiction reveals the novelist absorbing Mencken's elitist disdain for the "boobocracy" of undereducated, rural Americans, especially its clergy,[14] and it also happens to replicate the overweening sense of superiority other modernist intellectuals directed at William Jennings Bryan for taking, in a widely quoted argument, the nonelitist position that educational decisions on such matters as the teaching of evolution should rest with the majority and not with the experts, such as the scientists.[15]

This is the core of the issue, secular knowledge versus moral authority, and it culminated in a series of cultural battles initiated in multiple states by fundamentalists determined to ban the teaching of evolution.[16] But to Lewis's credit, instead of fixing on the specific issue of evolution in the schools, he undertook a broader approach to the clash of cultures enacted in Dayton by foregrounding the comprehensive subject of the need for a modern curriculum.

---

13. Taylor, "Western Secularity," 49.

14. Prominent on Mencken's list of *boobs*, from which an American "boobocracy" was recruited, were ministers from such denominations as the Methodists, Presbyterians, Baptists, and evangelists, for whom he expressed scorn. See Angoff, *H. L. Mencken*, 126–27, 138. On the aspiring Americans "in from the barnyard," see Mencken, *Prejudices, Fifth Series*, 114–15. See also Schorer, "Sinclair Lewis and the Method of Half-Truths," 52.

15. Larson, *Summer for the Gods*, 37–40. The idea that professionals (experts), not the general public, should have the academic freedom to decide the curriculum and who should be admitted to the ranks was formulated by Bertrand Russell. For discussion, see Pagliucci, *Denying Evolution*, 84–87.

16. Shipley, *War on Modern Science*, published in the same year as *Elmer Gantry*, describes the state-by-state effort of fundamentalists to curtail or remove the teaching of evolution from the public school curriculum.

For Lewis it was a Renaissance "battle of the books," revived for the twentieth century with Rabelaisian relish. Only a few critics saw this dimension of Lewis's novel. Among the discerning few was Carl Van Doren, who held that the weight of Lewis's satire falls, not on the Protestant churches *per se* and not so much on individuals as "upon an educational system that permits an ignorant boor to pass as educated, and a cunning animal, too thick-headed to be skeptical, to profess a theology that he does not understand."[17] With equal vision, Joseph Wood Krutch saw the institutional implications of Elmer's rise, writing that Elmer's career "is an indictment of the church as a whole at least in so far as it shows how the mechanism of the church permits the rise of such a man and demands of its servants no qualities which viciousness cannot convincingly imitate."[18] These commentaries demonstrate that Lewis's engagement with the topical religious issues of his time was thoughtful and comprehensive in its vision of reform. But that has never quelled the controversy.

II

For most reviewers, the crucial issue was the justness of Lewis's portrayal of Elmer Gantry as a type of preacher. Among those who faulted Lewis's capacity to represent the inner life of his characters was Mark Schorer, who wrote that Lewis's "framework of feeling, is extremely narrow, hardly wider than the material it contains."[19] Rebecca West, in rhetorically pungent mode, observed, "Mr. Lewis . . . has not entered into imaginative possession of those qualities the lack of which he derides in others."[20] Edwin Muir framed this criticism in terms of genre confusion, pointing out that Lewis makes Elmer into a "national type," but with "every attempt to particularize him," as befits the novelist, "his effectiveness is lessened."[21]

But as cultural critique, "type" is precisely what the novelist strove to establish. Elmer is the product of his Midwestern circumstances, and in his world those circumstances are persuasively general. That is to say, *Elmer*

---

17. Van Doren, "Vicious Ignorance," 637.
18. Krutch, "Mr. Babbitt's Spiritual Guide," 292. See also Gilman, "Pulpiteer of the Middle West," 4.
19. Schorer, "Sinclair Lewis and the Method of Half-Truths," 50–51.
20. West, "Sinclair Lewis Introduces Elmer Gantry," 42.
21. Muir, review of *Elmer Gantry*, 85. See also Blair, "Treasure Trove," 240. Dooley, *Art of Sinclair Lewis*, 128–30, offers an extended critique of the depiction of Elmer Gantry as neither steadily satiric nor realistic.

Gantry offers a cohesive sociological explanation of how men such as Elmer come to be. The root cause can be traced to the barrenness of Elmer's environment, and to the uniformity of available ideas. Elmer's upbringing is also portrayed as peculiarly restricted. To begin with, the only person for whom Elmer ever felt deep affection was his mother, who, we are pointedly informed, "was owned by the church" (28). Elmer himself is the product of the church. As a denizen of the pretentiously named village of Paris, Kansas, he hears no music, and no oratory, except that of his church. Beyond the church, he was reared on the William Holmes McGuffey Readers, the hugely popular, enormously influential Christian primers that sought to inculcate conservative principles of morality into young minds. McGuffy himself was a Presbyterian, and his Readers showed no recognition of progressive educational ideas; instead, they championed traditional moral virtues and taught that the drive for wealth through good business was commendable.[22] Unstated is that Elmer was never exposed to the wide world of literature or to scientific thinking.

Elmer's personal library, in his student days, tells the same story. It consisted of his Bible (with its stirring stories of heroism and domination), weekly texts on the Bible and church history, and a volume of great orations. In college, his one public speaking course filled him with grandiose ideas because, we are told, it was designed to produce speeches on "the Purpose of God in History" and the glorious American Constitution (54). Puffed up and ambitious, doted upon and undisciplined, Elmer does what he needs to do to advance. His lack of integrity is displayed early by his faked public rebirth in the spirit and his plagiarized sermon from the prose poem "Love," by the atheist Robert Ingersoll (57). Both proceed from such an upbringing as Elmer's, and both are indicative of Lewis's major goal of using Gantry to "discredit both fundamentalism and evangelism."[23]

The flawed nature of Elmer's interior life is evident from his purloined sermon on love, which merely mimics the joy of the evangelized soul. Its pretend "fullness" is the opposite of authentic spiritual experience, as Charles Taylor describes it, and also of the temporal *"work* of love," as Lori Branch describes it in her book.[24] Considering that Elmer lives in

---

22. Commager, foreword to *McGuffey's Fifth Eclectic Readers*, v. On McGuffy's Presbyterian faith, see Minnich, *William Holmes McGuffey*, 157. On morality and attitudes toward business, see Billman, "McGuffey's Readers and Alger's Fiction," 617. Billman also establishes the popularity of the Readers from 1836 to beyond the mid-twentieth century (614). An inventory of McGuffey's Primers through the Sixth Reader, covering the dates 1836–1920, appears in Minnich, *William Holmes McGuffey*, 186–93.

23. Hyland, *Evangelism's First Modern Media Star*, 183.

24. Taylor, *Secular Age*, 8–9, and Branch, *Rituals of Spontaneity*, 223.

a tight-knit religious community, it is not surprising that he should seek recognition in just this way, but, as we have seen, he lacks the foundation that would make authentic spirituality real to him. Taken together, Elmer's wildness, single-parent parochial upbringing, and the poverty of his experiences at home and in church are sufficient to explain his personality as being bound by his ministerial ambitions without being liberated.

However, not all people are so hemmed in. Lewis shows this in the education of Elmer's classmate Frank Shallard, who models an alternative upbringing. Open-minded and exploratory in his approach to knowledge, Shallard, as we have seen, is profoundly influenced by his liberal education and self-directed reading program in the sciences and humanities. If people are substantially the product of their circumstances, the most salutary upbringing, Lewis seems to say, is a liberal one, for by being broad it is most open to possibility.[25]

Lewis was widely acclaimed for the painstaking data collection that informs his novels. In *Elmer Gantry,* Lewis's subject was the topically hot one of evangelical preachers; Lewis's manner of data collection added immensely to the novel's persuasiveness. Some reviewers attempted to turn the strength of this realistic satire into a signal weakness. Walter Lippman denigrated the negative details in what he called Lewis's "clipping files," and, similarly, Emily Blair objected that Lewis constructed his title character "out of the newspaper accounts of certain sensational evangelists."[26] But Joseph Krutch, who perceived more than the making of Elmer's character, praised the novel for "a completeness of documentation not less than amazing" and for "a power of mimicry which, so far as I know, no living author can equal."[27] This power of mimicry, put on display the real-life foundation, the verisimilitude, of Lewis's novel.

Lewis's method was also a good deal more rigorous than that of making characters out of file clippings. To prepare for writing his preacher book, he took the extraordinary step of living with a Kansas City minister, the Unitarian agnostic L. M. Birkhead.[28] Many of the details of that preparation are known through Birkhead's memoir, *Is Elmer Gantry True?*, which presents an extensive account of Lewis's painstaking efforts to learn everything he could about a preacher's life. From it we learn that Lewis wrote that he met weekly for a number of weeks with his "Sunday School class" of fifteen

---

25. For a contrary view that considers the evidence for Elmer as an "autonomous" person, see Conroy, "Sinclair Lewis's Sociological Imagination," 357.
26. Lippmann, "Sinclair Lewis," 93, and Blair, "Treasure Trove," 92.
27. Krutch, "Mr. Babbitt's Spiritual Guide," 292.
28. Schorer, *Sinclair Lewis,* 441–42.

to twenty liberal Kansas City ministers, attended their functions, heard them preach, probed their beliefs, challenged their conduct, and listened to their intimate problems, for they looked up to the famous novelist and were eager to share confidences.[29]

Critics could ask, as did W. E. Woodward, whether Lewis's novel was more journalistic than literary, but in making their invidious observation they unknowingly conceded a great deal, for as Carl Van Doren declared, "That is precisely what it is, high-powered journalism making news of the religious world."[30] Let us accept, then, the observation that *Elmer Gantry* was conceived as a journalistic intervention and also that it was written in anger as a "lambasting [of] religion," completed in drunkenness, and published amid fierce protests.[31] As such, it became a journalistic event all its own. In this development, Lewis must be viewed as an agent provocateur. Even as he gathered his materials in Kansas City, he assumed the role of antagonist, mounting a church pulpit and delivering his atheistic taunt, whereby he pulled out his watch and dared God, if he exists, to strike him dead in a span of fifteen minutes.[32] It was a gesture of contempt that reviewers repeatedly recalled, and it put the spotlight on the author as an active opponent of, not just a commentator on, mainstream religious belief.

Not only had Lewis made a spectacle of himself as the atheist who denied the power of miracle; he had made a dispassionate reception of his impious novel impossible. Aware even before publication of the gathering storm his book was creating, Lewis contemplated fleeing the country.[33] He was right to be anxious. Upon publication, the novel was banned in Boston and other cities, and the author's life was repeatedly threatened.[34] Of course, the banning drove sales way up (100,000 in the first days), and Lewis's publisher cabled, "Reviews violent either way. Clergy hot. Reorders already."[35] Having been made a Book-of-the-Month Club selection, the infamous novel became the number-one best seller for fiction in 1927, even though its sales soon fell off sharply.[36]

---

29. Birkhead, *Is Elmer Gantry True?*, 7–13; Schorer, *Sinclair Lewis*, 448–50, and Lewis, *From Main Street to Stockholm: Letters*, 202, 216–17 (which shows that Lewis stayed in Kansas City from April 4 to at least May 11, 1926).

30. Woodward, "'Elmer Gantry' Is Truth," 1; Van Doren, "Vicious Ignorance," 637.

31. The quotation is from Lewis's correspondence, *From Main Street to Stockholm: Letters*, 230; the other details are from Van Doren, "Vicious Ignorance," 637, and Schorer, *Sinclair Lewis*, 465, 473–74.

32. Schorer, *Sinclair Lewis*, 447.

33. Lingeman, *Sinclair Lewis*, 300.

34. Schorer, *Sinclair Lewis*, 473–75.

35. Lewis, *From Main Street to Stockholm: Letters*, 235.

36. Schorer, *Sinclair Lewis*, 473, and Hackett, *60 Years of Best Sellers*, 143–44.

The circumstances surrounding the publication of *Elmer Gantry* made the issue of whether it was true to life crucial. When Birkhead asked whether *Elmer Gantry* was true, he put his finger on the question that most reverberated among the American public. Lewis's wife, Gracie, had called the novel "devastating," but was it really?[37] So much of the novel's force depended on its veracity. Were it untrue, this topical novel could not easily function either as cultural critique or as exposé.

Providing an insider's view of the life of Protestant ministers, Birkhead's memoir corroborates the sociological accuracy of Lewis's portrait of Elmer as an ignorant country boy become preacher. As the memoir discloses,

> Preachers are profoundly ignorant of life. They are trained not to know what life is like. It begins with the "Call," when the preacher is set apart from life and from the world. It continues in the theological seminaries which insist that the students for the ministry stay as far away as possible from life and the world. (33)

Taking seriously the image of the clergy that *Elmer Gantry* presents, Birkhead confessed that a great many preachers are more "coarse and vulgar" than Gantry himself. As a liberal, he openly decried the circumstance that "the majority of preachers in America" are full of "bigotry," and he illustrated the contention by reporting that a number of them responded to *Elmer Gantry* by calling Lewis an "ignoramus" or, in one case, by burning the novel. These details are but the symptoms, Birkhead contended, of the decadence of contemporary Protestantism, which, he wrote, is also given to contaminating commercialism, showmanship, fakery, and dishonesty. More disheartening still is the contamination from within that is prompted by the demand for complete doctrinal purity. In view of this rigid requirement, many candidates for the ministry conceal their real beliefs and are carefully instructed in how to avoid disqualifying disclosure. All these are features of Lewis's exposé and, in view of Birkhead's confirmation of their contaminating presence in American Protestant churches, lend credence to the justice of Lewis's sweeping satire.[38]

As a modernist with religious convictions, Birkhead declared, "Ministers should have some real training in the scientific spirit."[39] As for the pitiful training young ministers receive and for the shameful outcome of

---

37. Lewis, *From Main Street to Stockholm: Letters*, 231.
38. Quotations throughout the paragraph, unless otherwise noted, are from Birkhead, *Is Elmer Gantry True?*, 19–20, 22, respectively.
39. Ibid., 37.

their education as human beings, he declared flatly that the remedy was to "destroy the theological seminaries. They belong to another day."[40] They should have real-life training and proficiency in a vocation beside the ministry. In making these proposals, Birkhead was probably influenced by the pedagogical perspective Lewis expressed in the novel, but the remedies he recommended were his own. In the world of fundamentalist education, reform proposals were often viewed as subversive, as is demonstrated by the widely imitated Moody Bible Institute, whose curriculum included "the indoctrination of youth in pre-scientific biblicism and in anti-modernist culture."[41]

Further evidence of the reality underlying the satire of *Elmer Gantry* comes from another direction. It inheres in the facts that Lewis patterned his portrayal of three major characters on real-life people. Immediately following the novel's publication, readers and reviewers shared the belief that despite Lewis's denial, Sharon Falconer, the novel's leading female evangelist, was modeled upon fundamentalist revivalist Aimee Semple MacPherson, with some additional detail, many readers thought, provided by the faith-healing child evangelist Uldine Utley.[42] Among the most flamboyant of the evangelicals, MacPherson was an astute businesswoman, beautiful, with long hair, flowing robes, and a commanding preacher's voice that could nevertheless send out subtle vibrations of exoticism.[43] Her faith-healing practices included encouraging audience members to believe that hallucinations and visions induced by the revival atmosphere were divine realities.[44] These are all features that Sharon Falconer possesses in the novel, including the combination of beauty, sexuality, and business acumen. So close were the purported parallels between Falconer and McPherson that when McPherson was thought to have drowned, Lewis, who steadily denied the resemblance between Falconer and McPherson, decided to change Falconer's sudden death from drowning to burning.[45]

The more significant ideological point is that Lewis's driving motive was to expose the faith-healing practices of barnstorming preachers. This was precisely the place where belief in modern miracle and God's presence

---

40. Ibid.
41. Cole, *History of Fundamentalism*, 246–47. On the history of the Moody Bible Institute, founded in 1879, see Morris, *History of Modern Creationism*, 62–63.
42. Maurice, "History of Their Books: Sinclair Lewis," 53, and Schorer, *Sinclair Lewis*, 460. On Uldine Utley, see Birkhead, *Is Elmer Gantry True?*, 49–56.
43. McLoughlin, *Billy Sunday*, 287, and Lingemann, *Sinclair Lewis*, 272–73.
44. Birkhead, *Is Elmer Gantry True?*, 39.
45. Lingemann, *Sinclair Lewis*, 283–84, and Schorer, *Sinclair Lewis*, 460–61.

clashed with the materialist principles that provide the foundation for modern medicine. In this respect, Lewis's exposé places him in a direct line with Edward Eggleston's exposé in *The Faith Doctor* (1891) of faith cures, faith doctors, and séances—all accompanied by Bible reading and all revealed as fraudulent.[46] Lewis's novel differs from Eggleston's in that the satire in *Elmer Gantry* cuts broadly across American revivalist culture, whereas *The Faith Doctor* aims at bringing about specific reforms in public health procedures.

Although Lewis stood to gain ground with his public had he admitted that his novel shadowed real people, he could also have opened himself to lawsuits. But whatever motivated his denial, Lewis benefitted from the presumption that he had written a *roman à clef*. This was true not only of Sharon Falconer but of his title character as well. The presentation of Elmer beginning his career as a country rube with a down-to-earth style, masculine charm, and football prowess surely shadowed the career and personality of Billy Sunday, that "rube of the rubes" who had been a successful professional baseball player with the Chicago White-stockings.[47] Sunday's connections with big business, indirect connections with the Ku Klux Klan, and concerted attacks on liquor drinking all have their counterpart in Elmer Gantry's associations and activities.[48] In addition, Sunday, like Gantry, opposed the academicians and philosophers of the higher learning and rejected the theory of evolution, holding that species never change.[49] Besides, hadn't Lewis encouraged his readers to make such contemporary connections when he had Elmer steal a prose poem from Robert Ingersoll in imitation of Sunday's having paraphrased one of Ingersoll's best sermons?[50] Indeed, in *Babbitt* (1922), Lewis had gone so far as to shadow Billy Sunday, the former baseball player turned preacher, with an ex–prize fighter turned evangelist, whom he named "Mike Monday" to play on Sunday's name as a day of the week.[51] Once again, these details in parallel establish a firm

---

46. Eggleston, *The Faith Doctor*, 193–212.

47. The quotation is from the title of the first chapter of McLoughlin, *Billy Sunday*, 1–34. On Sunday's baseball career, see McLoughlin, *Modern Revivalism*, 403, and Martin, *Hero of the Heartland: Billy Sunday*, 65–79.

48. McLoughlin, *Billy Sunday*, 232–35, 274–76; Martin, *Hero of the Heartland: Billy Sunday*, 86–87.

49. Bruns, *Preacher: Billy Sunday*, 125–26.

50. McLoughlin, *Billy Sunday*, 26. For discussion, see Grebstein, *Sinclair Lewis*, 101.

51. See Grebstein, *Sinclair Lewis*, 100–101, who lists Dr. William L. Stidger and Dr. John Roach Straton as having provided additional details in the making of Elmer Gantry. See also Lewis's correspondence with Stidger in Hyland, *Evangelism's First Modern Media Star*, 182–99.

connection between fiction and reality, and they support the author's substantive purpose of dramatizing the anti-intellectualism and hostility to scientific knowledge rife among fundamentalist ministers.

Even when a character is not subject to satiric undercutting, as is the case with Lewis's representation of the liberal preacher Frank Shallard, the shadowing device adds resonance to the portrayal. Shallard, who is not generally considered to be drawn from a living person, actually recalls the travail of Harry Emerson Fosdick, the liberal Baptist minister who resisted the increasingly militaristic fundamentalists in the early 1920s by composing a sermon that he published as a pamphlet entitled "Shall the Fundamentalists Win?"[52] In *Elmer Gantry*, the title of Shallard's sermon, "Are the Fundamentalists Witch Hunters?" (389–90), enticingly echoes Fosdick's own. Then, too, several broad themes in Fosdick's life are picked up in the rendering of Shallard's. The initial circumstance that generated Fosdick's protest was the Baptists' decision in 1922 to compel unity of belief in the Christian "fundamentals" and, in effect, to forego the hallmark of Protestantism—individual freedom of scriptural interpretation. Fosdick particularly objected to the intolerance of compelling belief in five doctrines, including the miracle of the Virgin Birth, "substitutionary atonement," and inerrancy of scripture, all of which made it difficult for reformers like him, who supported modern scientific inquiry and endorsed the teaching of modern biology, to conform.[53]

Shallard's sermon, delivered under the auspices of "the League for Free Science," explicitly references fundamentalist hostility to evolution through Shallard's public recollection of how one fundamentalist declared that "evolutionists were literally murderers, because they killed orthodox faith" (391). Like Fosdick, Shallard clearly reflects the influence of the higher biblical criticism when he reveals his modernist belief in Jesus, not as the son of God, but as a great teacher. Shallard's confession about his doctrinal doubts—his inability "to believe literally in Purgatory and the Immaculate Conception, [and] the Real Presence"—reveals the same thing (387). Furthermore, his refusal to affirm these theological doctrines is the act that causes him, like Fosdick, to be investigated for deviant beliefs (in effect, heresy) and to be repeatedly called out by the Reverend Elmer Gantry as a leader of "atheists" (385), a charge similar to Sunday's denunciations of Fosdick for agnosticism and modernism.[54] Like Fosdick, Shallard fights back,

---

52. Marsden, *Fundamentalism*, 171.
53. Ibid.; Cole, *History of Fundamentalism*, 112.
54. McLoughlin, *Modern Revivalism*, 446; Marsden, *Fundamentalism*, 173.

and his courageous sermon functions, not as self-defense, but as an urgent warning to his audience and, implicitly, to the readership of the novel. Everyone, he pleads, must recognize the "menace of the Fundamentalists' crusade" and the tyranny they would bring to the country (390). Like Fosdick as well, Shallard loses his battle to hold off the witch-hunters, but the fate meted out to him is entirely of Lewis's own making. Viciously beaten up by the vigilantes of orthodoxy—a gang of toughs, really—he loses his right eye and much of the vision in his left, and becomes a broken man.

This deliberate darkening of events may strike readers as excessive, but apprehensions that the Ku Klux Klan would continue to rise or, with H. L. Mencken, that mob rule would overcome more reasoned voices, were real enough.[55] After all, Lewis was later to write *It Can't Happen Here* (1935), a novelistic homily of sorts about American democracy being overrun by forces of the radical right and turned into a fascist dictatorship. Other assessments nearer at hand come from scholars who remark on the disposition to violence inherent in absolutist belief systems. In Lori Branch's succinct framing, "the disavowal of belief and the claim to rational certainty in modernity has been the basis of all manner of fundamentalisms and violences."[56] Appleby, writing about fundamentalist leaders around the world as being given to an absolutist, dualistic worldview, states that they typically are "drawn toward extremism, that is, toward extralegal, often violent measures to realize a meaningful victory over their enemies."[57] However readers may respond to Frank Shallard's fate, the cultural context revealed by religious scholars supports, albeit indirectly, the plausibility of Lewis's plot-making.

III

The 1960 blockbuster screenplay *Elmer Gantry* tells us more about the long-term cultural power of the novel in a new incarnation. It also reveals more about the fortunes, as it were, of the secular-religious binary in the latter part of the twentieth century. Writing in 1927, W. E. Woodward predicted that the character of Elmer Gantry would take a prominent place among Lewis's gallery of type characters: "He is destined to become a descriptive adjective, a synonym for loud-mouth, vulgar, soul-saving, cash-register

---

55. Mencken believed aristocratic government superior to democracy. Underlying his view, which Lewis partly absorbed, was apprehension about mob rule. See Mencken, "At the Mercy of the Mob," 127.

56. Branch, *Rituals of Spontaneity*, 222.

57. Appleby, "Rethinking Fundamentalism," 232.

religious hypocrisy," and Woodward was right—after a fashion.[58] The 1960 film adaptation of *Elmer Gantry*, in which Burt Lancaster played the title role as the fast-talking, hard-drinking, womanizing, revivalist hypocrite, secured this identity. For his commanding performance, Lancaster received the Academy and the Golden Globe Awards for best actor, while screenwriter and director Richard Brooks received the Academy Award for best writing of a screenplay based on material from another medium.[59]

These accolades showed the enduring cultural power of *Elmer Gantry* in another medium. The meaning of its persisting cultural significance is another matter. Film reviews comparing Gantry's character in the original to the adaptation praised the latter for toning down those features that made Gantry "an incredible monster, a walking catalogue of vices" and for showing him capable of love while still portraying him as "a liar, a cheat, an adulterer, ignorant, loud, course [sic], cruel, unscrupulous, sacrilegious."[60] For viewers, this more romantic rendering of Lewis's hard-driving satire appears to have been more acceptable. The change worked to make the movie more acceptable to viewers with religious qualms.

New York Times reviewer A. H. Weiler also identified a second important change, namely that screenwriter Brooks steered clear of Lewis's tendentious "pamphleteering" while giving "point and action to the sprawling, contentious work."[61] On this theme, *Variety* declared that the film "aspires to be as provocative as was the book in 1927."[62] The fact that Brooks held the property rights for five years, reworking the manuscript for two years before going ahead with this Hollywood production, attests to the dangers posed in the mass market by the film's religious subject matter.[63] This circumstance shows that even in 1960, the battle for the meaning of *Elmer Gantry* had not been decided. It was not even clear that the novel's pronounced secular perspective had survived its transformation into the mass-culture film market.

Even after the screenplay's acceptance, Brooks, as screenwriter, found himself fending off the Production Code censors because his manuscript didn't show any "decent religious people," and he had to avoid offending the Roman Catholic Church's Legion of Decency, so he decided to open the

---

58. Woodward, "'Elmer Gantry' Is Truth," 1.
59. *Academy Awards Index*, 35, 95.
60. Arthur Knight, review of the film *Elmer Gantry*, 159–60. See also Beckley's review of *Elmer Gantry*, 161, and Weiler's, 257–58.
61. Weiler, review of *Elmer Gantry*, 257.
62. "Pry," "Elmer Gantry," 161.
63. Daniel, *Films of Richard Brooks*, 132–33.

film with a disclaimer about dishonest revivalists.[64] That opening announcement, starkly presented in white letters against a black background accompanied by a drumroll, carefully takes the position that "the conduct of some revivalists makes a mockery of traditional beliefs and practices of organized Christianity!"[65] Pointing to the "highly controversial nature of this film," the producers urged that children be prevented from seeing it. In this way, Brooks worked hard to avoid having his film labeled *antireligious*. Nonetheless, the movie exhibited a critical rather than a reverential attitude toward American revivalism. Consequently, the letters from religious leaders described the production as "communist propaganda" and "a tragedy for Protestantism and religion in general."[66] But the very fact that Brooks made the major adjustments he did amply demonstrates the strong religious interests that the movie had generated. Religious interests had not been marginalized; their oversight conditioned the film's production.[67]

True to the novel, the film joins the controversial issues of science and evolution to religious fraud and the credulity of the faithful. A pivotal but underappreciated alteration made in the screenplay was the enlargement of the role of Lewis's atheist, Jim Lefferts (played by Arthur Kennedy), into an acerbic, Mencken-like journalist (not a schoolmate of Elmer's). Lefferts's skepticism, sustained throughout the film, helps shape audience response to Elmer's energetic but uninformed and anti-intellectual characterization of evolutionary science. Brooks, who strategically maps out Lefferts's position as Elmer's antagonist, makes the newsman a Pulitzer prize winner for his articles on evolution, an achievement that Elmer trivializes by declaring that Lefferts couldn't really believe the stuff he writes. How could he, for if men are made in God's image, Elmer argues, God himself would be a gorilla! This glib anti-intellectualism is fully defined in Elmer's presentation of himself as "not smart like some of the smart-alecky professors."

This deprecation of the academic profession, and especially science learning, rises to a theatrical point when Gantry, with mocking demagoguery, introduces a live chimpanzee to a public gathering as "your great-great-grandfather." Throughout the scene, Elmer's talent for showmanship and circus rather than intellectual depth are on display. By contrast, Brooks's

---

64. Ibid., 137, 143.

65. *Elmer Gantry*, written and directed by Richard Brooks. Quotations are from the film and have no page numbers.

66. Daniel, *Films of Richard Brooks*, 142.

67. I am responding in the negative to the first of two kinds of secularist ideologies described by Casanova, "The Secular," 66–67, in which several "philosophies of history . . . relegate religion to a superseded stage" of historical development.

Lefferts is intellectual and possesses a genuine ethical sensibility. Not only does he acknowledge his doubts about God, but he declares that under Gantry's leadership, conformity of opinion is enforced so that people are not allowed to doubt or to think—and yet even Darwin had doubts.

Through this counterpoint between Elmer and his journalistic commentator, the screenplay takes its ideological stand. But unlike Lewis's novel, which launches a frontal assault on evangelical beliefs, Brooks's film generally avoids polemics. Instead of inveighing against faith healing, it depicts the practice equivocally, and readers are left to judge for themselves. Similarly, it dramatizes the financial motivations that loom large in the spiritual decisions of the Protestant churches in Zenith but lets the images speak for themselves. In these respects, the mass-market film recreates the intellectual edge of Lewis's satire without moralizing or reducing the message of the film to binary alternatives.

Elmer Gantry has also participated in the media transformations that revolutionized the way evangelizing movements delivered their message. By the 1950s, the big-tent revivalism in the 1920s had turned into mass-market television evangelism (televangelism). Yet the cultural potency of the name "Elmer Gantry" remains as strong as ever. As audiences for Billy Graham began to spread beyond his original fundamentalist base, a secular press reviewed his revivalist activities, ever mindful of the Elmer Gantry stereotype, which hovered "between hucksterism and soul saving."[68] Hadden and Shupe's 1988 study, *Televangelism*, actually devotes its opening three pages to the negative image summoned up by the name "Elmer Gantry" and then proceeds to assert that the revivalist scandals of the 1980s "so [fit] 'mainstream' America's preconceptions that a large proportion of those who have never switched the dial are convinced that the caricature is literally true to life."[69] This, too, is convincing testimony of the cultural staying power of Lewis's Elmer Gantry.

Nor is this staying power the sum of it all. During the 1980s, numerous Pentecostal preachers—that is, those whose ministries emphasize Christian conversion and spiritual renewal through the Holy Ghost rather than dogma—introduced what is called the "health and wealth gospel," which was accompanied by highly publicized preacher scandals, both sexual and fiscal, that continue to corroborate Lewis's original representation of preacher Gantry.[70] Professional mass broadcasters and preachers who

---

68. Steven P. Miller, *Billy Graham*, 21.
69. Hadden and Shupe, *Televangelism*, 3.
70. On Pentecostal Christianity, see Hollenweger, *Pentecostals*, 4, 9–12. On the health-wealth gospel, see Giuliano, *Thrice-Born*, 19.

have subscribed to this health-wealth worldview include celebrity televangelists Jim and Tammy Bakker, Kenneth Copeland, Ernest Angley, Benny Hinn, Oral Roberts, and Pat Robertson.[71] Jim Bakker's ownership of four Mercedes-Benz automobiles, two antique Rolls-Royces, and several mansions drew attention (some of it from the Christian community itself) to the excesses to which this wealth teaching has lent itself.[72] A highly visible federal grand jury was convened in June 1987 to investigate, and by September of that year the House Ways and Means Committee launched an investigation into the financial accountability of religious organizations.[73] Just as damaging were the extramarital sexual affairs and mutual recriminations into which surprising numbers of preachers fell. Whether representative or not, both kinds of scandal have provided the public and the press with sensational examples of misbehavior that continue to remind people of the Elmer Gantry prototype. But even as these scandals have become nationalized, they demonstrate that religion in many of its expressions has succeeded in penetrating America's lucrative mass markets. In other words, through the late twentieth century at the least, the secular-religious binary that numerous scholars of religious studies have theorized is not nearly as settled on the side of secularism as many theorists believe.

Separated by some twenty-three years, *Elmer Gantry* the film and *Elmer Gantry* the novel embody persisting religious conflicts in mainstream American culture. Predicated on events of the 1920s, the 1960 film was produced during the Christian revivalist movement led by Billy Graham and Oral Roberts in the 1950s—and it anticipates the mass-market revivalism of the 1980s. The interconnections of these periods are strong because the teachings of Graham and Roberts drew from and emerged out of the fundamentalist movement of the 1920s. The result was that 1950s televangelism rejected evolution, endorsed the authority of the scriptures, and urged the implementation of Christian principles in politics and society.[74]

During this same decade, the 1950s, there also appeared two converging forms of authoritarianism, one religious and the other inextricably associated with Senator Joseph McCarthy. These developments formed the contemporary context against which not only the *Elmer Gantry* film, but also the 1955 play and 1960 screenplay *Inherit the Wind*, responded. In both versions,

---

71. Giuliano, *Thrice-Born*, 19.

72. Wright, *Saints and Sinners*, 76–84. See also Bakker, *I Was Wrong*, 1–5, which records Bakker's conviction for fraudulent appropriation of funds and a prison term of four to five years.

73. Hadden and Shupe, *Televangelism*, 15.

74. McLoughlin, *Modern Revivalism*, 489, 500–503.

the Scopes evolution trial of 1925 was the crystallizing event that its authors, Lawrence and Lee, reenacted and reinterpreted. How the play and the film versions of *Inherit the Wind* answered to the politics of their contemporary situation and at the same time dramatized the epic confrontation at Dayton, Tennessee, is the subject to which I now turn.

CHAPTER 7

TRANSHISTORICAL PARABLE

Jerome Lawrence and Robert E. Lee's *Inherit the Wind*

ACCORDING TO THE theory of Pierre Bourdieu, a literary work's cultural capital ought to diminish in equal degree as it acquires financial capital, since the former is created by a select group of artists whose esteem functions as a kind of compensation.[1] But *Inherit the Wind* confounds these expectations. Despite being lucrative, it has generated an astonishing amount of cultural capital because it possesses the ability to "actively change history" by altering the way people remember the Scopes trial.[2]

As a play (1955) and a film (1960), *Inherit the Wind* reenacts the historic Scopes "monkey" trial of 1925, but as a work of fiction. Nevertheless, its treatment of the subject was so compelling that the play has replaced the trial in America's cultural memory. Effectively, Lawrence and Lee's play both interprets the trial and governs our modern understanding of it. For a number of historians of science, this substitution is regrettable, especially

---

1. Bourdieu, *Cultural Production*, 50–52, 86. On the distinction between "symbolic capital" and "cultural capital," see Randal Johnson, "Introduction: Pierre Bourdieu," 7.
2. Guterman, "Field Tripping," 566–67. I agree with Guterman's argument but do not accept his assessment that the reviews of *Inherit the Wind* fit neatly into a paradigm wherein high-cultural assessments were negative and popular-market reviews positive.

since the trial event was the most memorable public confrontation between modern evolutionary science and fundamentalist Christianity in American history—comparable to Britain's legendary debate between Archbishop Wilberforce and Darwin's "bulldog," Thomas Huxley.

The news that turned a minor law case in Dayton, Tennessee, into an international event was the arrival of two of the nation's most celebrated lawyers, who took opposite sides. Joining the prosecution team was three-time presidential candidate and defender of orthodox Christianity William Jennings Bryan, and for the defense American Civil Liberties Union appointee, the brilliant agnostic Clarence Darrow, whose client, John Scopes, was charged with violating Tennessee's new (1925) Butler Act that prohibited "the teaching of the Evolution Theory in all the Universities, Normals and all other public schools of Tennessee."[3] The momentousness of this confrontation was further enhanced when Bryan accepted Darrow's invitation to serve as an authoritative witness on the Bible while Darrow questioned him. As trial observer Joseph Wood Krutch wrote, despite the "circus day" atmosphere, "the whole question of fundamentalism versus modern scientific skepticism was aired."[4]

The process whereby the play appropriated this historic event and then replaced it in the public mind was extraordinary. After its premiere in Dallas on January 10, 1955, *Inherit the Wind* moved to Broadway and had a run of 806 performances.[5] In addition, the play enjoyed two Broadway revivals, one in 1996 and another in 2007.[6] Along the way, its authors won the Donaldson Award for best new play (1955) and the Variety Critics Poll Award, both in New York (1955) and London (1960). The film, directed and produced in black and white by Stanley Kramer, is based on the play, although the screenplay was written by Nedrick Young and Harold Jacob Smith. It reached ever-larger numbers of viewers after it was nominated for four Academy Awards, including best screenplay based on material from another medium and best actor (Spencer Tracy as Drummond/Darrow), even though it lost in these latter categories to *Elmer Gantry*.[7] *Inherit the Wind* also remained in the public eye during three made-for-television adaptations in 1965, 1988, and 1999.[8] Moreover, in its original film ver-

---

3. Grebstein, *Monkey Trial*, 3.
4. Krutch, "Monkey Trial," 83.
5. Guterman, "Field Tripping," 567, and Lawrence and Lee, "*Inherit the Wind*: Genesis and Exodus," 33.
6. Guterman, "Field Tripping," 567.
7. *Academy Awards Index*, 35, 95, 118, 169.
8. Guterman, "Field Tripping," 567.

sion the work continues to be shown on television channels in schools and private homes.

Particularly in its film version, *Inherit the Wind* has proven to be a crossover work with wide popular appeal and a good measure of critical esteem. For instance, *New York Times* reviewer Bosley Crowther described it as "excellent. . . . One of the most intelligent, respectable and entertaining motion pictures of this year," and *Variety* hailed it as an "outstanding screen achievement."[9] Reviewers fixing on technical matters, such as the film's cinematography, makeup, and Fredric March's overplaying of Bryan's role, were more censorious, as were such middlebrow publications as *Time* and the *Saturday Review*.[10] The *Herald Tribune* combined all these strands when it affirmed that the film "may have its faults but it remains an exceptional film and says a great deal more by inference than its bluff heartiness would lead one to expect."[11]

However, leading historians of evolutionary science Ronald Numbers and Edward Larson fault the play for being in important respects ahistorical and in other respects biased in representing the principal figures at the trial. To be clear, in my view documentary history is not the only valuable kind of historiography. Cultural historicism, as I have argued, supports readers in their attempt to examine another kind of power—the power of social-historical fiction to shape perceptions about evolutionary and scriptural ways of interpreting the world. Furthermore, *Inherit the Wind* also possesses a more traditional kind of power inasmuch as it seeks to dramatize repressive religious and political ideologies in American culture over time. To lay the groundwork for this analysis of Lawrence and Lee's play, I begin by examining the failings that Numbers and Larson discover in it.

I

Ronald Numbers presents a list of observations specifying Lawrence and Lee's faulty historical practice. His critique, alongside that of fellow historian of science Edward Larson, offers the most straightforward way of assessing what counts—and what does not count—as being historical. Numbers's review focuses on the film. It begins by conceding that "the

---

9. Crowther, review of the film *Inherit the Wind*, 249–50, and "Pry," review of *"Inherit the Wind,"* 250.

10. Review of the film *Inherit the Wind*, *Film Facts*, 250–51, and Arthur Knight, review of the film *Inherit the Wind*, 250.

11. Beckley, review of the film *Inherit the Wind*, 251.

moral—the danger of allowing religion to regulate science—is timely" and then pivots to pose the essay's guiding question, "But is the movie good history?"[12] It answers at length in the negative.

Numbers begins by pointing out that the John Scopes character, Bertram Cates (played by Dick York), is shown in jail discussing his case with a young schoolteacher named Rachel, the daughter of the fire-and-brimstone preacher, the Reverend Jeremiah Brown. Neither the jailing of Scopes nor the romantic melodrama that pits the reverend against his own daughter and her fiancé, Cates, is historical. Scopes was a high school sports coach and substitute instructor, not a regular biology teacher, who volunteered to test the new antievolution Butler law. He was never caught teaching evolution in the classroom and never spent time in jail. Larson's colorful prose draws attention to the fictional alterations Lawrence and Lee introduced. In Larson's words, Dayton/Hillsboro "gained a mayor and a fire-breathing fundamentalist preacher," and Scopes "acquired a fiancée," creating "brilliant theater," though "it all but replaced the actual trial in the nation's memory."[13]

Besides objecting to the interpolation of characters who never existed, Numbers inveighs against the misrepresentation of Bryan's views on Genesis, "falsely portraying him as a hidebound biblical literalist," even though he had publicly expressed his view that the "days" of Genesis need not be twenty-four hours in length and could represent geological ages. Numbers even cites from the trial testimony Brady's answer to the question of the earth being made in six days: "Not six days of twenty-four hours.... No, sir." Numbers also charges that in the movie (and the play as well), the playwrights erringly make Brady endorse as "literal fact" Bishop Usher's calculation that "the Lord began the Creation" on October 23, 4004 BC "at 9 AM!" (96).[14] Larson, for his part, argues that Bryan's character has been transformed "into a mindless, reactionary creature of the mob" who "denounces all science as 'Godless'" rather than the science of evolution alone.[15] In support of this latter view, Larson references with approval Numbers's own conclusion that Lawrence and Lee's loose treatment of these issues "dramatically illustrates why so many Americans continue to believe in the mythical war between science and religion."[16]

---

12. Numbers, "Inherit the Wind," 764.
13. Larson, *Summer for the Gods*, 240–41.
14. Lawrence and Lee, *Inherit the Wind*. All citations from *Inherit the Wind* are to this edition and appear in the text.
15. Larson, *Summer for the Gods*, 241–42.
16. Ibid., 242, citing from Numbers, "Inherit the Wind," 764.

In addition, Numbers makes the apt points that the trial did not kill Bryan, nor did he die offering a summative speech on his beliefs; a diabetic, he died in his sleep five days later. Furthermore, Numbers and Larson, following Scopes's autobiography and Krutch, who wrote about the congenial, "circus day" atmosphere of the Dayton trial, take exception to the "sinister" tone of *Inherit the Wind*. In the reckoning of these historians, these liberties may make *Inherit the Wind* dramatic, but the result "sacrifices the far more complex historical reality."[17]

As this review clearly shows, fidelity to "historical reality" is the standard by which Numbers and Larson assess *Inherit the Wind*. This is a conception of history that I associate with Leopold von Ranke's ambition to record the past "as it actually happened" (*wie es eigentlich gewesen*) by being unfailingly impartial and building up facts one datum at a time.[18] Coming from historians of evolution, this factual reality emerges, quite understandably, not from literature but documentary history, which in turn is based on such evidence as trial testimony or, as we have seen, the writings of eyewitnesses or on what are thought to be reliable earlier histories of events.

But this is not the only responsible way historians work. As social and intellectual historian Richard Hofstadter writes,

> History seems most objective, most uncontroversial—most "scientific" if you must—in those monographs in which historians exhaustively explore an extremely narrow segment of reality. . . . The answers to small questions sometimes shed bright but narrow beams of light on the larger problems of human behavior and the social process. . . . But there is no reason to think that the answers to all such questions will add up to a comprehensive view of society or of historical processes.[19]

An example of this more difficult, and perhaps elusive, brand of historical investigation is cultural history. As Jacques Barzan observes, unlike political, diplomatic, or economic facts,

> cultural facts do not unmistakably exist as such. . . . The publication of *The Origin of Species* in 1859 may resemble a political fact in the uproar it provoked, but we know that evolutionary theory and the belief in it do not date from 1859. This imposes on the cultural historian the delicate task of

---

17. Ibid. For "circus day," see Krutch, "Monkey Trial," 83, and the chapter "The Circus Comes to Dayton," in Scopes, *Center of the Storm*, 77–100.
18. Introduction to Ranke, *Ideal of Universal History*, 55, 57.
19. Hofstadter, "History and the Social Sciences," 369.

telling us how and where Evolution existed as a cultural fact for a century before 1859.[20]

In short, some of the most important things historians want to know are not always accessible through the accumulation of data points.

I cite from Hofstadter and Barzan not to diminish the kind of meticulous history Numbers and Larson prize, but to continue to open a space for the cultural historicism practiced in this book, and also to foster a scholarly appreciation of *Inherit the Wind* as a literary work of considerable social-historical significance. Still, I would again underscore the useful overseeing function of Numbers and Larson's analysis. What really irritates them, it certainly appears, is *not* merely that the creators of *Inherit the Wind* play loose with the facts of the Dayton trial, but that the play and film have become the default vehicles through which the history of the trial is purportedly—but erroneously—transmitted to most Americans. That is to say, in their view, the role of *Inherit the Wind* in culture is misplaced. Instead of being received as a literary-historical interpretation of events, it functions as a trustworthy record of the trial itself, which it is not.

There is good ground for this complaint. However, I don't think Lawrence and Lee can be held responsible for what some may regard as a hijacking of history. Certainly the playwrights gave due notice in their preface when they announced, "*Inherit the Wind* is not history." They went on to elucidate what they meant. The events in Dayton, Tennessee, they wrote, "are clearly the genesis of this play. It has, however, an exodus entirely its own." With its elegant suggestion of the choral opening and closing dances of a Greek drama, these lines intimate that whereas the play begins with particulars resembling the Scopes trial, its concluding movement generates a larger set of concerns. These intimations then become explicit. The clash between Bryan and Darrow "was dramatic, but it was not a drama." Moreover, the issues dividing them have since acquired a "new dimension," for "*Inherit the Wind* does not pretend to be journalism. It is not 1925. The stage directions set the time as 'Not too long ago.' It might have been yesterday. It could be tomorrow." So saying, the dramatists present a broader field of vision than the Scopes trial itself.

In a revelatory essay, Lawrence and Lee disclose that they discovered their method years earlier while reading Maxwell Anderson's *Winterset* (1935), a play that echoes the Sacco and Vanzetti case. "We asked for the same liberty," they explained, "that Anderson had availed himself of in

---

20. Barzan, "Cultural History: A Synthesis," 394.

Winterset, to allow the actuality to be the springboard for the larger drama so that the stage could thunder a meaning that wasn't pinned to a given date or a given place."[21] Precisely what this "larger drama" was Tony Randall (the original Hornbeck) explained and a student interviewer corroborated: Lawrence and Lee were troubled by 1950s McCarthyism, and this dark experience, which hit Hollywood hard, found its way into their play.[22]

Given these contexts, the similitude between the 1920s antievolution crusade and the 1950s anticommunist crusade led by Joseph McCarthy rewards closer examination. Unlike those historians whose goal has been to demonstrate that the authors of *Inherit the Wind* allowed the contemporary issue of McCarthyism to color their representation of the historical events in 1925, my goal is to examine straightforwardly the playwrights' thesis that *Inherit the Wind* has acquired "new dimension and meaning" because it identifies a set of cultural tendencies that apply to the 1950s as well as the 1920s. My aim, in short, is not to show that *Inherit the Wind* fails as documentary history, but that it succeeds in illustrating that two distinct periods of American history display a common set of religious, political, and scientific value conflicts. The point of such an endeavor is to reveal these clashing value conflicts as enduring features of America's culture.

II

Inherit the Wind is a thoughtfully crafted, metaphoric play that begins in history and opens outward toward parable. By *parable* I mean that the play is a dramatic fable demonstrating a proverbial moral truth with broad applicability. In keeping with this moral truth, each of the major characters is identified by a salient moral position. For instance, the Clarence Darrow figure, Henry Drummond, comes to Dayton to defend the right of Scopes/Cates to teach evolutionary science in public schools. His social identity is that of an outsider and iconoclast, whom the local spiritual leader, the angry Reverend Brown, further defines by calling Drummond "the agnostic"—"a vicious godless man!" (27). From this solid historical identity, the community then assigns to Drummond a typological, Christian identity as "an agent of darkness" (27). Decried as a "slouching hulk of a man, whose head juts out like an animal's," he is first dehumanized and then demonized as "a creature

---

21. Lawrence and Lee, "*Inherit the Wind*: Genesis and Exodus," 33.
22. These comments pertaining to the playwrights' concerns in *Inherit the Wind* about McCarthyism are recorded in Larson, *Summer for the Gods*, 240.

of the devil, perhaps even the Devil himself!" (28). At the end of the scene, Drummond appears as a hunched, shadowy figure whose symbolic identity is revealed when a young girl cries, "It's the Devil!" (36) and then runs away.[23] This is a model in one of its purest forms of what demonization is and how it functions in culture.

Such demonization, especially of secular humanists, has been a recurring trope among fundamentalists and evangelicals. In fact, large numbers believe in the living reality of Satan, who roams the earth. Stephens and Giberson report,

> A clandestine invisible power, without apparent resources, dedicated armies, or physical structures, working against God, is almost a definition of Satan for many evangelicals. In some of the more extreme views, Satan, and demons in particular, have an overt physical presence, manifested as demon possession . . . or . . . Satan is viewed as a quiet tempter who persuades people in certain directions.[24]

This construction of a dark Satan certainly conforms to the specter of Drummond, the atheist lawyer.

Similarly, Jeremiah Brown may be a fictional fundamentalist preacher, but his antirational jeremiads illustrate the dualism, the binary thinking, and the antirationalism that is deeply anchored in the religious history of more extreme fundamentalists.[25] For instance, in 1925 a fundamentalist minister writing for the Moody Bible Institute urged Christian readers to "rally in prayer . . . to combat this propaganda of the Devil [the theory of evolution] and paid smoke screen of the so-called scientists."[26] Billy Sunday, the most influential evangelist of the 1920s, preached that "the Devil was a formidable foe" who cunningly worked through evil men to thwart God's will.[27] Not surprisingly, Sunday and Bryan himself saw evolution as a manifestation of the Antichrist, "a creature invading hearts and minds, destroying faith, perverting educational institutions, churches, legislatures, and the media, attacking the soul of America."[28] Similarly, in 1960 when John

---

23. I use the term *morality play* sparingly because *Inherit the Wind* is more supple and ironic than a medieval morality play, but for a full-blown interpretation mounted on this premise, see Hye, "Tennessee Morality Play: Notes on *Inherit the Wind*," 17–20.

24. Stephens and Giberson, *Anointed*, 259.

25. Jacoby, *American Unreason*, 44, and Appleby, "Rethinking Fundamentalism," 231.

26. Nelson, "The Real Issue in Tennessee," 199.

27. Martin, *Hero of the Heartland: Billy Sunday*, 88.

28. Bruns, *Preacher: Billy Sunday*, 274.

Scopes returned to Dayton, Tennessee, for the premiere of the film *Inherit the Wind*, he wrote that things had not changed much in thirty-five years. While listening to an "Open Bible" radio program with the Reverend Paul Levengood, Scopes heard himself demonized. "The devil is here in Dayton and is having a heyday," the reverend declared, "in tones that sounded like an echo of 1925."[29]

The larger point, however, is that when the playwrights represent Preacher Brown in his unforgiving anger, they summon the same kind of stereotypical demonization that they elsewhere decry. For audiences of the 1950s, the most widely recognized form of demonization emerged from the real-life investigations of the House Committee on Un-American Activities (HUAC) and, later, by Joseph McCarthy's Senate Subcommittee on Internal Security.[30] HUAC's "Hollywood Ten" hearings were focused on left-leaning actors and writers, who at the risk of being "blacklisted" or cited for contempt of Congress were expected to prove their loyalty by implicating fellow artists as Communists or "pinkoes."[31] By 1950 this chilling state of affairs prompted some courageous writers, producers, and directors to resist by writing plays and producing films whose premise was analogous to contemporary circumstances. Among these, no play became more symbolic of HUAC's and McCarthy's "witch-hunting" activities than Arthur Miller's *The Crucible* (1952), in which the accusers in seventeenth-century Salem, Massachusetts, saved themselves from the magistrates by naming others as devil-possessed. As Miller observed in his description of the Reverend John Hale, the Salem witch-hunter, "At this writing, only England has held back before the temptations of contemporary diabolism."[32] Thus, when Lawrence and Lee introduced Henry Drummond as a "devil" figure, the playwrights were referencing not merely the historical figure of Clarence Darrow, but a recurring socioreligious iconography with transhistorical significance. This point is crucial to the argument I am making, that Lawrence and Lee were striving to depict a more general historical truth about radical fundamentalisms in America.

Several historians and reviewers, perhaps following Scopes's statement that the dramatists "had to invent romance for the balcony set," have responded to the ahistorical subplot as if it were of little consequence.[33]

---

29. Scopes, *Center of the Storm*, 269.
30. On the more extensive, and earlier, work of HUAC, see Morgan, *Reds*, 514–17.
31. Murphy, *Congressional Theatre*, 1–5. On the "pink" decade of the 1930s, see Morgan, *Reds*, 166–83.
32. Arthur Miller, *The Crucible*, 34.
33. Scopes, *Center of the Storm*, 270.

The *New Yorker*, for instance, called the love plot "pat, unlikely, and annoyingly irrelevant."[34] Yet the subplot bears the weight of the proverbial biblical title, "He that troubleth his own house . . . shall inherit the wind" (67). The subplot also illustrates concretely the theme of thinking for oneself, which, as we have seen in *Elmer Gantry*, is part of the ideology of the secular asserting itself. The romance between Cates and Rachel actually enacts a symbolic domestic triangle that drives Reverend Brown's daughter Rachel to choose between her father's zealous authoritarianism and her fiancé's conviction that he has the right to teach scientific ideas. Brown's public damnation of both Cates and Rachel, "though they be blood of my blood, and flesh of my flesh!," illustrates his fanaticism and the stakes for the couple (66).

Overwrought with melodrama and the stereotypical characterization of the preacher, the scene fails to imagine Brown as a human being. That said, Brown effectively represents the vehemence of fundamentalist opposition to evolution in the 1920s.[35] According to historian Norman Furniss, fundamentalist rhetoric was accompanied by "violent language and vituperative personal invective."[36] In this respect, Brown's preaching style is conventional and historically grounded. For example, when scriptural literalist Reuben A. Torrey, who was still evangelizing in the 1920s, delivered his fire-and-brimstone sermon, a reporter described him "with shining beads streaming down his face, which was red as fire with his intense effort, with tight-clenched fists which like sure hammers drove home his fiery darts and in trumpet tones that fall on the vast assemblage like prophetic warnings."[37] In addition, Lawrence and Lee make the substance of Brown's speech a literal reading of the six days of creation as told in Genesis, economically establishing the fundamentalist position against which the defense's argument for Darwinian evolution is later presented.

Brown's sermon also establishes an allied theme: the sheeplike behavior of the crowd. In response to every point Brown makes, it bleats, "We believe" or "Amen" (62–64). Such patterned responses are characteristic of the evangelical tradition. "Sunday's revivals," states one biographer, "were models of controlled mass response. . . . Anyone who did not conform

---

34. Gibbs, "Mixed Bag," 67.

35. During the 1920s, a multitude of fundamentalist organizations sprang up, many marching under an antievolution banner. For an account, see Bruns, *Preacher: Billy Sunday*, 272–73. For Sunday's antievolutionist position, see McLoughlin, *Billy Sunday*, 121, and for evangelist Reuben Torrey's view, see McLoughlin, *Modern Revivalism*, 373.

36. Furniss, *Fundamentalist Controversy*, 37.

37. McLoughlin, *Modern Revivalism*, 372.

to the limited patterns of unified response . . . was summarily whipped back into line."[38] This historical context shows the aptness of the play's thematic contrast between Brown's conformist congregation and more independent individuals who learn to weigh and assess (like the schoolboy Howard), despite the prejudices of those around them. Important in this regard is Rachel, who begins as a dutiful conformist, begging Cates to return to the fold of conventional belief, but gradually learns to act independently of her father's wishes. Reluctantly, she also reads Darwin, but near the play's end expresses the belief that new ideas must come out. As an everyman figure, she is an emblem of ordinary humanity trying to find her way in a changing world.

By contrast, the Reverend Brown, in his implacable anger, becomes the first person to whom the proverbial wisdom of the play's title is applied. That is, because Brown troubles his own house, he will inherit the wind. The person who speaks these cautionary words is William Harrison Brady, who also comforts and redirects Brown. The juxtaposition of the two Christian leaders casts a softer light upon Brady, who gently explains that "zeal" may make one "destroy that which you hope to save" (66–67). Brady's God, the text makes clear, encourages forgiveness of one another. With touching sensitivity, Brady then addresses the townspeople, not as a mass of humanity, but as "good friends" and bids them return to their homes (67). It is one of Brady's finest moments. Thematically, the scene contrasts Brady's evangelical care with Brown's frightening fundamentalist zealotry.

I emphasize this neglected scene because the representation of Brady as the nation's leading spokesman for biblical inerrancy has become a contentious issue. Extravagantly, Larson charges that "the writers transformed Bryan into a mindless, reactionary creature of the mob."[39] But can anyone viewing the rally scene call Bryan "mindless," or, in view of his calming words to the townspeople, "a creature of the mob"? Furthermore, the nuanced depiction of Brady at the rally, in contrast to Brown, shows the latter to be the one cast as a fanatic. Brady's views, it is true, are rigid. He is also vain, pompous, and gluttonous, but the total impression he makes is mixed.[40] Later he is a fallen champion, a humiliated, pathetic, perhaps tragic figure, but he is not a villain. This view comports with the play's ideological lesson: Brady is the worn-out champion of outworn beliefs, but his stature

---

38. McLoughlin, *Billy Sunday*, 127.

39. Larson, *Summer for the Gods*, 241.

40. For accounts of Bryan's personal failings, see Leinwand, *William Jennings Bryan*, 159–64, and Coletta, *William Jennings Bryan*, 3:284–87. In *Center of the Storm*, 86–87, Scopes attests to Bryan's legendary gormandizing with numerous examples.

is sufficient to make him a sincere, credible opponent to Drummond in the struggle of ideas.

Nevertheless, a recurring cluster of critical arguments spins around the idea that Lawrence and Lee depict Brady invidiously. Larson objects that the playwrights make Brady denounce "all science as 'Godless,' rather than the so-called false science of evolution."[41] But this one science ought actually to be referred to as "the evolutionary sciences." Within the historical world of the trial, Scopes allegedly taught evolution from Hunter's *Civic Biology* textbook. Also, Dr. Maynard Metcalf gave testimony for the defense as a zoologist, and expert doctors from the fields of agriculture, anthropology, geology, and Hebrew studies submitted statements for the defense.[42] In respect to human cultural evolution, it would also have been appropriate to call upon classical scholars, historians, and linguists. Thus, even in 1925 the "Godless" science of evolution drew to it multiple scientific and social scientific disciplines. Defense counsel Dudley Malone went so far as to argue that "there is no branch of science which can be taught today without teaching the theory of evolution."[43]

A related view is that Lawrence and Lee's depiction of Bryan is demeaning and misleading because it makes him out to be a "hidebound biblical literalist" when he had actually held more flexible views on evolution before the trial.[44] Besides being a former secretary of state, Bryan had been a progressive Democrat on issues such as women's suffrage and expanding the federal government to promote the welfare of working and middle-class Americans—the Great Commoner.[45] Many of these objections about the play's and screenplay's lack of balance have at their root the political consideration that Bryan's political beliefs are devalued, while those of the modernist Darrow are elevated. However, this view assumes that the playwrights ought to be writing documentary history, a goal, as I have labored to demonstrate, they renounce. Rather, they strive, in keeping with the play as parable, to dramatize the virtue of citizens who, despite social pressure, think for themselves.

The suspicion underlying the charge that Lawrence and Lee portray Brady as a doctrinaire fundamentalist is that the dramatists play fast and

---

41. Larson, *Summer for the Gods*, 241–42.
42. *World's Most Famous Court Trial*, 227–80.
43. Ibid., 115.
44. The quotation is from Numbers, "Inherit the Wind," 764. On the failure to acknowledge Bryan's progressivism, see Menton, "*Inherit the Wind*: A Hollywood History," 3.
45. Michael Kazin, *Godly Hero*, xviii, 67, 157–58, 215–42.

loose with history in order to promote their liberal agenda. But while their liberalism and, let us remember, their secularism, is manifestly undeniable, the evidence does not support a conspiratorial interpretation. The trial record does show Brady/Bryan to be a fundamentalist and, more broadly, a defender of Christianity. On the one hand, Bryan enacted the role of "Defender of the Protestant Faith" during the trial.[46] His testimony shows that he declined to champion one sect over another and avoided Darrow's phrase that he "literally interpreted" the Bible; instead, he took the position that "I accept the Bible absolutely,"[47] which is to say that Bryan was not speaking exclusively for his own personal beliefs, but politically and publicly for the Christian cause—which included scriptural literalists. As Bryan stated in the trial, his personal impression was that the days of Creation "were periods, but I would not attempt to argue against anybody who wanted to believe in literal days."[48] Lawrence and Lee appear to respect this testimony, having Brady try desperately to defend the main point: "We must *not* abandon faith! Faith is the important thing!" (93).

On the other hand, Bryan's broad religious commitment had serious costs. Rather than get pinned down on knotty doctrinal matters, Bryan pretended that he had no opinion about important biblical issues. Constantly evading Darrow's probing questions about the age of the earth and other biblical questions, Bryan sought refuge within a defensive wall until at last he declared that if the God of creation had willed it, the creation could have taken place in "six years or in 6,000,000 or in 600,000,000."[49] In the play, this statement (not verbatim) is given to Drummond, whose triumphant deliverance signals the confutation of Brady's literalist fundamentalism. This alteration opens the play to censure for misrepresenting Bryan's position, which it does in the important sense that Bryan was not personally confounded. Yet the strict position of the literal-reading fundamentalists was neither well defended nor sustained.

Compounding the argument is the allegation of another critic that Bryan's climactic testimony did not include Bishop Usher's opinion on the date of the earth as 4004 BC—and certainly not the precise hour.[50] But while Bryan did not mention the 4004 BC date or the morning hour, both appear in the trial record, as do the repetitions of the 9 AM hour. So the playwrights

---

46. The epithet given to Bryan in this paragraph is an adaptation of the title in Levine, *Defender of the Faith: William Jennings Bryan: The Last Decade, 1915–1925*.
47. *World's Most Famous Court Trial*, 285–86.
48. Ibid., 302.
49. Ibid.
50. Menton, "*Inherit the Wind*: A Hollywood History," 3.

did not invent these details. Furthermore, the trial record clearly establishes Bryan's respect for Usher's calculation (endorsed in the King James Bible, on which Bryan was sworn in), since Bryan repeatedly used the calculation, along with Darrow, to date biblical events.[51]

The crux of the issue, then, is that while Bryan acknowledged his respect for Usher's calculation, he did not in the trial admit that the bishop's view was his own. In the play he does. Poetic license alone should justify this alteration as true to the spirit of the trial. But in the larger sense—and not just dramatically—Lawrence and Lee are true to the idea that the fundamentalist position was not sustained at the trial, and Bryan had to pretend that the date of creation did not matter. Bryan was, after all, a subscriber to the Five Fundamentals and by 1925 was the accepted leader of the fundamentalists.[52] Given this larger context, the charge that Lawrence and Lee invidiously paint Bryan/Brady as a "hidebound literalist" overstates the case without acknowledging the general sense in which Bryan was a champion of the fundamentalist cause. What we are left with is that the playwrights were not picture takers producing a photographic record; what they used was paint, and it was drawn from the paint buckets of the trial and of life.

Reviewing these lines of argument, I think the essence of the issue is not what Bryan's personal beliefs were (biographical history) but rather the cultural fact that in both history and dramatic fiction Bryan/Brady's trial testimony offers little to sustain the biblical literalists. Most historians have assented to this conclusion. Paolo Coletta stated that at the end of the trial, a worn-out Bryan "stood almost alone, for he was considered to be a defector from Fundamentalism."[53] Mid-twentieth-century historian Ray Ginger reported that fundamentalists who attended the trial disapproved of Bryan's concessions on scriptural literalism.[54] Creationist historian Henry Morris, who wrote in the early 1990s, held Bryan directly responsible for his own disappointing testimony, stating, "Probably the most serious mistake made by Bryan on the stand was to insist repeatedly that he had implicit confidence in the infallibility of Scripture, but then to hedge on the geological question, relying on the day/age theory."[55]

---

51. *World's Most Famous Court Trial*, 261, 288–90. Also, White, *Warfare of Science*, 1:9, points out that the 9 AM hour is associated with Bishop Usher through the scholarship of Dr. John Lightfoot.

52. Coletta, *William Jennings Bryan*, 3:203, 213.

53. Coletta, *William Jennings Bryan*, 3:267.

54. Ginger, *Six Days or Forever?*, 174.

55. Morris, *History of Modern Creationism*, 73.

Given this data, I reach the conclusion that in the most important matters, the history of Bryan's performance during the Scopes trial is not essentially different from its fictive reenactment. In both narratives, Bryan's and Brady's image as the defender of the faith were severely impaired, particularly among fundamentalists. Even though *Inherit the Wind* renders Brady's personal humiliation as one and the same with his own compromised fundamentalist position, this intervention seems to me appropriate, for it does what good historical fiction ought to do: it respects in the main the historical features on which the play is based and epitomizes the drama of conflicting ideas in its principal characters.

III

The parable that is *Inherit the Wind* achieves its shape through the moralized conflict of the two principal characters: Drummond, the progressive secularist, stands for independence of thought, skepticism, and a provisional but welcoming attitude toward modern scientific knowledge, while his adversary, Brady, champions the everlasting values of the Bible, the bedrock of the moral order in the home and in the nation. These clashing value systems prepare the way for a diachronic interpretation of *Inherit the Wind*.

Lawrence and Lee make visible their generalized purpose through their dramatization of the meaning of the play's proverbial title, with its tentacle-like applications. Brady, as we have seen, first applies the proverb to the Reverend Brown, who curses his own daughter. Brown has troubled his own house. The application is apt and literal. However, at the end of the play, the proverb is again invoked, this time symbolically, and applied to Brady himself, whose household is the whole nation. Since Brady was a national figure and long-standing crusader against those who opposed his fixed religious and political views, the broader application is again fitting.

The play's proverbial wisdom also invites application in other contexts. For contemporary audiences in 1955, just such a topical context came into view during the hearings conducted by the House on Un-American Activities Committee (1945–1975) and by Joseph McCarthy's Senate subcommittee (1950–1954) investigating subversion in the U.S. government, Hollywood, and academia, where Communist agents and sympathizers allegedly thrived and had to be rooted out.[56] The very phrase *McCarthyism* has

---

56. O'Reilly, *Hoover and the Un-Americans*, 3–12; Leinwand, *William Jennings Bryan*, 169–70, and Kazin, *Godly Hero*, 263.

become synonymous with the troubling of the nation's house. This 1950s context, no less than that of the 1920s, is integral to the play's function as parable.

From the 1920s Furniss cites numerous sources to support his generalization that "in the Fundamentalists' minds modernism, evolution, and communism were complementary agents producing the noxious weed of unbelief," or worse, the scourge of atheism.[57] The quotation is arresting because it embeds 1950s concerns in a 1920s context. Among fundamentalists, one threatening ideology leads to another until American civilization, undermined from within, loses its founding identity and falls. These dire prognostications emerging out of feelings of dispossession and a conspiratorial mentality apply in much the same way to both periods.[58] They are all part of one discursive formation, one endless argument that identifies the ideological commitments of the modernists as part of the same assault on traditional religious values.

Also prominent in both eras was the determination to purge nonconformists. Early in the nineteenth century, conservative Protestant churches established elaborate procedures for detecting "heresy." Likely targets included modernists, theists, and others who strayed from orthodoxy by accepting scientific explanations for issues of faith. Under such a looming charge of heresy, Pearl Buck, a Presbyterian and famous author of *The Good Earth*, resigned from her missionary position in China in 1933.[59] With the example of Buck preceding her, Alice Hobart's 1936 novel, *Yang and Yin*, depicted a young American missionary who is actually expelled from her fundamentalist mission because she believes that "Buddha is Christ for the Chinese."[60] Historically, the most cited case of the period was that of Henry Emerson Fosdick, whose pamphlet, "Shall the Modernists Win?" (1922), led to a protracted investigation that amounted to a judgment of heresy. His modernist sermon questioned literal interpretation of the Virgin Birth and other dogmas seemingly made archaic by modern science and set off a firestorm in his adopted Presbyterian Church (he was ordained a Baptist). Rather than submit to the Confession of Faith, Fosdick resigned.[61]

---

57. Furniss, *Fundamentalist Controversy*, 18.
58. On these matters of hysteria and dispossession, see Hofstadter, *Paranoid Style in American Politics*, 29–36.
59. Wacker, "Waning of the Missionary Impulse," 191–93.
60. Hobart, *Yang and Yin*, 190. See the account of this trial in Tricomi, *Missionary Positions*, 110–11.
61. Marsden, *Fundamentalism*, 171–73, 181; Cole, *History of Fundamentalism*, 102–105; Furniss, *Fundamentalist Controversy*, 131–36.

The 1950s counterpart of this fundamentalist crusade for ideological purity was the right-wing practice of "blacklisting," an informal procedure hindering, often preventing, a person from finding a job for years to come. Although the discovery of Communist infiltrators was their stated purpose, in practice investigators cast a wider net to ensnare their critics and adversaries. Prominent among these critics were proponents of social change, principally leftist-leaning intellectuals, academicians, and artists.[62] In the 1920s and 1950s, common tactics were public humiliation or shaming, denunciation, and exclusion.[63]

The reverse tactic of demanding ideological conformity was even more endemic. Thus, in the 1920s, activist fundamentalists demanded professions of loyalty from clergymen and seminary professors, sought to shame freethinkers, and strove to ban the public school teaching of evolution.[64] Bryan himself expressed the view, with evolution in mind, that "no teacher paid from taxation be hired or retained unless he believed in God."[65] Similarly, during the McCarthy era, public school teachers could be dismissed if they refused to sign a loyalty oath or had affiliations at any time in their lives with a communist organization.[66] To still greater effect, President Truman and, later, President Eisenhower, under pressure from HUAC, instated loyalty oaths as a condition of government employment. Indeed, from 1951 "reasonable doubt" about an employee's loyalty was sufficient to have the person dismissed.[67]

The underlying ideological similarities between the 1920s and 1950s, particularly the enforced allegiance to traditional American values, religious and patriotic, was part of the same conservative determination to curb the advances of secularization. The push-back was especially notable in mass media outlets. For example, in the 1950s, Christian culture was affirmed through the outlets of mainstream novels and film. So, while Miller's intellectual tragedies *The Crucible* (1953) and *A View from the Bridge* (1955) explored the topical issue of individuals struggling to maintain their integrity in the face of oppression, America's mass market movie theaters were celebrating in epic fashion biblical and early-Christian subjects such

---

62. Hofstadter, *Anti-intellectualism in American Life*, 3–4, and Fuller, "Ideology of the 'Red Scare' Movement," 231.

63. On blacklisting in Hollywood, see Murphy, *Congressional Theatre*, 25–34.

64. Bruns, *Preacher: Billy Sunday*, 273.

65. Coletta, *William Jennings Bryan*, 3:200. The opposing idea theorized by Bertrand Russell in 1940 was that professionals and experts in the field, not the people themselves, should determine the curriculum. See Pigliucci, *Denying Evolution*, 84–86.

66. Redish, *Logic of Persecution*, 11–12.

67. Murphy, *Congressional Theatre*, 11.

as *The Robe* (1953), *The Silver Chalice* (1954), *The Ten Commandments* (1956), and *Ben-Hur* (1959).[68] Likewise, the best-selling fiction of the early fifties fed the appetite for such religious subjects as *The Cardinal* (1950), loosely based on the life of Cardinal Spellman of New York; *Moses* (1951); and numbers one- and two-ranked *The Robe* and *The Silver Chalice* (1953). In nonfiction the number-one best-selling book was a new edition of *The Holy Bible* (1952–1954), then *A Man Called Peter* (1952, 1955), *This I Believe* (1953–1954), *The Prayers of Peter Marshall* (1954), and a biography of Jesus called *The Greatest Faith Ever Known* (1953).[69]

These popular expressions of America's Christian identity appeared, we cannot fail to notice, during the same years that HUAC and McCarthy were pressing their assault against the godless Communists and American subversives. Religion was being enshrined in the American flag, and nowhere could this be heard more clearly than in the amending of the pledge of allegiance in 1955. This action consisted of the insertion of a new phrase, "under God," after the words "one nation." With this incisive stroke, the United States not only distinguished itself from the atheistic, Marxist-materialist Soviet Union but also reaffirmed America's historical identity as a religious (many would explicitly say "Christian") nation under God's special protection.[70]

As for the fate of evolution, it used to be thought that most fundamentalists withdrew from the political scene following their humiliation at the Scopes trial. However, Edward Larson, among others, has demonstrated that the antievolution movement continued its activist agenda at the state and local levels until at least 1930.[71] Not much noticed, either, is that a second wave of fundamentalist fervor, stimulated by the anti-Communist crusade along with the issue of prayer in the public schools, emerged in the 1950s.[72] If these groups worked with evangelicals, they reasoned they could be a powerful force in America, perhaps even a majority.[73]

The preacher who strove to unite these groups was Billy Graham. As the inheritor of Billy Sunday's brand of revivalism, Graham initially preached

---

68. *Academy Awards Index*, 466, 472, 483, 499.
69. For both fiction and nonfiction, see Hackett, *60 Years of Best Sellers*, 196, 199, 202, 205, 208, 211.
70. Throughout the paragraph, I draw from Ellis, *To the Flag*, xiii–xiv, 126–32. On the flag as a religious symbol, see Wills, *Under God*, 81, who cites a Christian Pledge of Allegiance that begins, "We pledge allegiance to the Christian flag, and to our Savior, for whom it stands."
71. Larson, *Summer for the Gods*, 229–34.
72. Wilcox, *God's Warriors*, 9–10, and Hunter, *Evangelicalism*, 121.
73. Watt, *Transforming Faith*, 43.

sermons on the terrors of hell, spurned the higher criticism, and rejected the theory of evolution. But in the early 1950s, he moved quietly toward the center of American Protestantism, calling himself an "evangelical."[74] Joseph McCarthy, in his turn, approved of the anti-Communist contributions of the fundamentalist clergy and the International Council of Christian Churches, which he described as a "militant anti-Communist Protestant group" who were "serving the interests of America and God."[75] Although Graham never publicly endorsed McCarthy or his methods, he made his position quite clear when he wrote, "If you would be a loyal American, then become a loyal Christian."[76] In this manner, the crusade of the 1920s to preserve religious orthodoxy by suppressing alien beliefs found its way into the discourse of the 1950s, where the pressure to conform in religious and political matters became intense.

IV

The film *Inherit the Wind*, much more than the play, is a commentary on the repressive political and religious environment of the 1950s. It also directs more attention to the threats posed to Cady, the teacher of evolution, with the result that its 1950s concerns are superimposed on those of the 1920s so that the film becomes a layered cultural document invoking both periods. This orientation is evident in the opening scene, silent but for vocalist Leslie Uggams solemnly singing "Give Me That Old Time Religion." An ominous tension builds as the mayor consults his watch; resolutely walks across the street; joins two well-dressed townsmen, a cleric, and finally a photographer, all of whom enter Bertram Cates's biology classroom in the Hillsboro Consolidated School; hear him teaching evolution; and promptly place him under arrest. The dark tonality of Kramer's realization of *Inherit the Wind* departs radically from the play and from history as well, for there was no intrusion into Scopes's classroom, no pretrial curtailment of academic freedom, no public arrest, no prison, no sensational news account of his arrest, and no tone of menace.

These features in Kramer's film bespeak a McCarthy-inspired atmosphere of repression that replaces the charming opening of the 1955 play, in which two children dispute in their imperfect way the phenomenon of

---

74. Throughout the paragraph, quotations from Graham's writings are from McLoughlin, *Modern Revivalism*, 500.
75. Gasper, *Fundamentalist Movement*, 64–65. See also Hunter, *Evangelicalism*, 123.
76. McLoughlin, *Modern Revivalism*, 511.

evolution. The organ-grinder with his monkey and a Bible-touting hillbilly from the original play are preserved, but the humor they provide has acquired a satiric edge. The town, which the original states should be *"visible always, . . . as much on trial as the individual defendant"* (3), in effect presides over its citizens, who march as one behind banners for the Bible and for Brady. Their solidarity exemplifies the reflexive mass behavior, or "group-think," of the crowd. In a night scene following the evening Bible rally, the imprisoned Cates is besieged by an ugly mob, experiences a rock thrown through his prison window, and sees a hostile crowd carrying banners denouncing Cates and Drummond while it chants, "We'll hang Bert Cates to a sour apple tree!" After the fashion of the Ku Klux Klan, who ardently supported both Bryan and the antievolution crusade, a whitesheeted effigy appeared of Cates himself—in the process of being consumed by fire.[77]

In contrast to the crowd-turned-mob, Rachel struggles for autonomy and intellectual independence. Following her forced testimony at the trial, Rachel walks to Brady's room and announces to Mrs. Brady that her husband is a fake. Following Mrs. Brady's challenging rejoinder that he is a man who believes in something, and "What do you stand for?," a weary Brady appears and paternalistically calls Rachel "my child." Rachel's retort answers both husband and wife. Refusing to be infantilized, she declares, "I'm not your child any longer, Mr. Brady, or anybody else's."

There is nothing like this in the original. But the ideological point, which is effectively made on behalf of democratic individualism, soon succumbs to a binary presentation. Between the traditionalists, who march and think as one, and the individualistic, science-supporting progressivists, the film delineates two antipathetic cultures, two value systems.[78] Drummond not only points to this yawning divide from his intellectual perch, but he becomes an active agent in producing it, as when he exclaims, "I'm trying to stop you bigots and ignoramuses from controlling the education of the United States!" (98), or in the film, when he announces, "This community is an insult to the world." Yet in both play and film Drummond is an idealist. In the film, and only in the film, Drummond delivers a peroration on freedom of speech, which Darrow himself delivered during the Scopes trial. Bringing together three convergent themes—the teaching of evolution, the place of religion in American civilization, and the freedom to think—it reads,

---

77. Leinwand, *William Jennings Bryan*, 136–37.
78. On individual and collective consciousness, see Pecora, *Secularization*, 118.

> Can't you understand that if you take a law like evolution and you make it a crime to teach it in the public schools, tomorrow you may make it a crime to teach it in the private schools, and tomorrow you can make it a crime to read about it, and soon you may ban books and newspapers, and then you may turn Catholic against Protestant, and Protestant against Protestant, and try to foist your own religion upon the mind of man. If you can do one, you can do the other, because fanaticism and ignorance is forever busy and needs feeding.

When all this comes to pass, he concludes, then "we'll be marching backward, backward, through the glorious ages of that sixteenth century when bigots burned the man who dared to bring enlightenment and intelligence to the human mind."[79]

If ever there were a single speech embodying the ideology of secularism, this would be the exemplary text. Yet it is at bottom frustratingly problematic since its foundation rests on a crude binarism that reifies and essentializes religion as barbaric, fanatical, and irrational, whereas the secular stands at the opposite pole. As Taylor might characterize the speech, Drummond's response to the specter of religious fanaticism leading to civil war is to substitute the rationality of the secular.[80] Secularism does, of course, seek to distinguish itself from the superstition and irrationalism of earlier eras, but the speech overreaches since rationality itself, we recognize, can also lead to fanaticism and can serve barbaric ends.[81] There is also rhetorical excess in Drummond's vision of fanaticism and heretic-burning, which he contends will drag civilization backwards, for in the extremity of his imagining, he summons a vision of the end of days that begins to resemble the apocalypse of certain fundamentalist preachers.

This melodramatic element notwithstanding, Lawrence and Lee build their drama on the common threats posed to a free society by 1950s McCarthyism and the antievolution crusade of the 1920s. The substantive parallels between the two eras hold a mirror up to American civilization in one of its recurring dimensions. Seen from this vantage, *Inherit the Wind* functions as a transhistorical parable. It strives to reveal a truth more philosophical than documentary drama, and on that ground makes an important contribution to American letters.

---

79. The quotation is from the film. For Darrow's court speech, on which the quotation is based, see *World's Most Famous Court Trial*, 87.
80. Taylor, "Western Secularity," 35, 49.
81. Calhoun, "Secularism," 77, and Taylor, "Western Secularity," 38.

But when *Inherit the Wind* reaches beyond parable to prophecy, it overreaches. In both play and film, the concluding bit of stage business shows Drummond weighing the Bible and Darwin's *Origin of Species* in his hands, and then packing both in his briefcase. This is an iconic moment. Although the unfolding logic of events could easily have justified Drummond's taking Darwin's book with him while leaving the Bible behind, the play and film celebrate accommodation. Instead of dramatizing the supersession of modern scientific discovery over the Bible, at least as literal truth, the playwrights endorse a *reformed* manner of reading it. Thus, Spencer Tracy as Drummond/Darrow flashes a grin of satisfaction as he departs carrying both books. It is a self-congratulatory gesture that anticipates the incorporation of scientific thinking into religious belief. Conservative Christians will keep their traditions and their faith, the play implies, but when it comes to biblical interpretation, they will, in accord with the spirit of progress and reason, henceforth be modernists.

This reconciliation, we recognize, is achieved on unequal (and unacknowledged) terms, since the result would appear to be an enduring victory for progressive science over dogmatic forms of faith—a liberal synthesis, as it were. As far back as 1925, a reporter for the *Christian Century* articulated the implications of this new birth of knowledge, reminding readers,

> No theory is final. New facts will amplify or limit it. But back to yesterday's conceptions of nature and the Bible we shall never go. And the men who are best prepared to comprehend the new truth as it breaks out from nature and the word of God in every generation are those who have made most adequate use of the emerging truths of their own time.[82]

These are high-sounding thoughts, except that the prediction has proven to be full of hubris. Far from marking a new beginning, *Inherit the Wind* ironically marks the beginning of the end of a period of unusual confidence, at least among progressives, in the power of science to penetrate—and alter—dogmatic religious faith. As it has eventuated, many forms of conservative Christianity today, including large numbers of fundamentalists and evangelicals, do not accept modern science, nor do many members of these churches wish to be absorbed into the broad mainstream of the American culture they deplore. Viewed from these perspectives, the would-be liberal synthesis has proven illusory.

---

82. "Amateur Dramatics at Dayton," 198. With greater caution, Wyatt's 1955 review of the play *Inherit the Wind* argues that reason and faith need one another and that reason without faith begets Marx (226).

PART 3

A POSTSECULAR AGE?

CHAPTER 8

CONTEMPORARY PERSPECTIVES

James Scott Bell's *The Darwin Conspiracy*
and the Soul of America

WHEREAS PART 1 of this work showed how the early novels (from the 1880s to 1916) treated the challenges to faith posed by evolution, the higher criticism, and new academic disciplines, Part 2 examined works in several genres celebrating what appeared to be an enduring victory of science and the secular over a discredited fundamentalism. But Part 3, "A Postsecular Age?," examines the resurgence of a hard-line fundamentalism that for a very long time now has bitterly resented its marginalization in the public sphere.[1] In response it has fashioned a faith-based challenge to secular science in the forms of creation science and intelligent design (ID). The chapter also examines the clashing cultural forces that appear to have brought about the cessation after 1960 of nationally recognized novels that treat contemporary or historical subjects on the relationships between science and religion.

This development has meant that the period in which novels celebrated the advance of science and secularization, which we saw in Part 2, seems clearly to have passed. Instead, the sole novel we have on the clash between science and religion is Bell's *The Darwin Conspiracy*—a Christian

---

1. Appleby, "Rethinking Fundamentalism," 230.

fundamentalist creation, principally written for a like-minded target audience. *The Darwin Conspiracy* is a concrete illustration of a remarkably altered cultural environment in the United States. So much have the relative cultural positions of science and religious conservatives changed in the last twenty years that some call the present era no longer *secular*, but *postsecular*. In *Rethinking Secularism*, Calhoun, Juergensmeyer, and VanAntwerpen describe the origin of this term as issuing from the thorough "separation of religion from politics" in America to the point that for some this separation "has become all but definitive of the modern for some."[2] Concerns about the relegation of religion to the margins of a secular society have thus prompted discussions among some theorists of religion about the utility of positing an alternative, a postsecular age. A very different conception of the postsecular, one more useful in explaining current developments, posits the arrival of a new religious age. From this latter standpoint, the postsecular proceeds not just from intellectual discussion, but from the rise of radical religious movements, particularly radical fundamentalism, which is actively resisting its marginalization.[3]

The implied significance of these remarkable developments furnishes the subject for this chapter, which I have divided into three sections. The first presents several contributory reasons for the virtual absence of nationally recognized novels on the clash between religion and science. It then links this phenomenon to the development of a fundamentalist counterculture that challenges mainstream science and science education in a programmatic way through creation science and intelligent design. The second examines James Scott Bell's *The Darwin Conspiracy* as a didactic example of creation science in action. The third and concluding section examines the prospects for warding off the advent of a postsecular, neofundamentalist age. In particular, it attempts to weigh the degree of threat posed to the general public by science-denying people of faith, and also to gauge the prospects for a recommencement of high-quality, nationally acclaimed novels on science and faith that were formerly part of the American scene.

---

2. Calhoun, Juergensmeyer, and VanAntwerpen, introduction to *Rethinking Secularism*, 18; Calhoun, "Secularism," 78.

3. For a discussion of the loosely defined term *postsecularism*, and the debate over whether it refers to a period "which comes *after* 'the secular,'" or to an "interpretative *perspective*," see Mączyńska, "Postsecular Literary Criticism," 73–74. For the view that postsecularism is an ideological intervention to "resist any master narrative" of secularization, see Kaufmann, "Locating the Postsecular," 68. Helpfully, Pecora, *Secularism*, 6, 14, references the rise of fundamentalist religions around the globe, a development that corresponds to the growth of Christian fundamentalism in America as a reaction to secularism over the last twenty years.

I

Why, we ask, have there been no contemporary novels on the place of spirituality in a scientific age, for instance, or on the impact of science teaching on an evangelical or fundamentalist community? And why has the social-historical novel about science, faith, and doubt virtually disappeared? The most obvious explanation is that the triumphalism of novelists and secularists celebrating the relegation of religion to the margins of public debate succeeded all too well. That very triumphalism may have been substantially responsible for driving out evangelical conservatives and fundamentalists from the public square of national debate into more welcoming sectarian venues. Among the general public, the subject of the relationship between faith and evolution and higher learning no longer seems to be as urgent or as controversial as it had been a century ago. In fact, many moderate and even conservative Christians have discovered ways of accommodating science to faith. If this assessment is correct, then the field of debate is left open to those alienated groups that want to do battle with modern science and secularism.

To judge from the plenitude of information sources now available to the public, Americans have turned away from the kind of novel this study has examined—that is, away from a genre known to be exploratory, especially in treating subjective states of being, detailed, and usually complex in point of view—and toward more easily consumable forms of nonfictional discourse, including formats featuring tendentious iterations of social and political ideology. Then, too, insofar as novels on science, faith, and religious doubt often feature nuanced, subjective assessments of controversial ethical issues, this mode of information gathering seems to be out of step with contemporary preferences for more partisan, overtly ideological, information outlets.

The paucity of novels treating major issues of science and faith also appears to be an effect of the fracturing of a national readership that had formerly provided novelists with a ready means to explore the interdependency of scientific knowledge and religious faith on a national stage. Instead, there has appeared a proliferation of media outlets for specialized audiences. The result has been less fiction writing that explores issues and more overtly ideological, nonfictional forms of presentation. Theoretically, the multiplication of cable TV channels, blogs, and interactive Internet sites ought to be a welcome development in a democratic republic, but the end result has been that audiences do not have to contend any longer with the conflicting beliefs of other groups. Like communicates with like so that individuals become more and more like the groups they already prefer.

But it does not follow that socially and ethically alienated persons of faith have willingly abandoned the domain of the secular, including science education, to the secularists. The evidence is that few scriptural literalists are content with the status quo. In fact, large numbers of fundamentalists, including some evangelicals, have felt driven to develop their own counterculture with its own counterdiscourse.[4] But they don't want to be marginalized. Beleaguered, they fight on every front—the political, the social, and especially the representational—to create an ideological space for themselves. In R. Scott Appleby's psychological analysis, the fundamentalist sensibility chooses those "elements most resistant to relativism, pluralism, and other concomitants of secular modernity that work to reduce the autonomy and hegemony of the religious. Hence fundamentalists embrace *absolutism* and *dualism*." Furthermore, fundamentalists across cultures underscore the "transrational" nature of their faith by attempting "to protect the holy book or hallowed tradition from the depredations of historical, literary, and scientific criticism."[5] According to Stephens and Giberson, fundamentalism by its nature is not only antimodernist but "aggressive and polemical."[6] Bell's novel is the product of this heritage, although it is only one manifestation of a robust counterculture still unfolding.

In matters pertaining to science, the evidence for this polarization is strong. In the 1987 case *Edwards v. Aguillard*, the Supreme Court struck down the teaching of "creation science" (that is, Bible-based science, predicated on the belief that the earth is young, no more than ten thousand years old) in public schools on the ground that the "science" illicitly promoted a religious viewpoint.[7] Subsequent attempts to refashion creationism as intelligent design (ID)—the doctrine that a Divine hand must be posited as guiding the course of natural selection—were also struck down in the now-famous decision in Dover, Pennsylvania (2005), which led the Public Broadcasting Corporation to produce the widely viewed documentary *Judgment Day: Intelligent Design on Trial*.[8] The ruling, however, has not prevented proponents of ID from framing their claims as a First Amendment right to free speech.

---

4. Stephens and Giberson, *Anointed*, 7.

5. Throughout the paragraph, I cite from Appleby, "Rethinking Fundamentalism," 231.

6. Stephens and Giberson, *Anointed*, 49.

7. Forrest and Gross, *Creationism's Trojan Horse*, 205. These authors also show how proponents of creationism used the 1987 Supreme Court decision to develop their case for ID. On the failed ID tactic of "teaching the controversy," see Humes, *Monkey Girl*, 350.

8. *Judgment Day: Intelligent Design on Trial*, directed by Johnstone and McMaster.

As the frequency of these decisions suggests, the Supreme Court has been unable to resolve the struggle for cultural authority between purely physical explanations of events and those rooted in miracle and fortified by dogma and scripture. This long-term struggle between advocates of science and those committed to scriptural literalism now manifests itself in surprisingly novel contexts. Consider the renowned natural history museums of the United States and, particularly, the Museum of Natural History in New York City, with its permanent exhibition of approximately one hundred fossil dinosaurs, the largest in the world, including a horned specimen called Triceratops who roamed the earth 65 million years ago. Young children learn about this ancient history of plant and animal life as a matter of course as they come to comprehend the earth's almost unimaginable antiquity. Nevertheless, America's creationist counterculture has built or claims it is planning to build an imposing set of creation science museums, over twenty in number, located in numerous states as well as Canada.[9] A striking example of its method appears in the Creation-Education Ministry website, which, aimed at young people, features Bible-centered questions and answers that purport to correct the untrue assertion of evolutionists that dinosaurs and humans did not live at the same time. For support, it presents illustrations that claim dinosaurs and people coexisted in Peru two thousand years ago.[10] Lending legitimacy to this latter view is the evangelical Creation Evidence Museum in Glen Rose, Texas, which displays the results of what it claims to have discovered: a hundred fossilized human footprints alongside almost 500 dinosaur footprints. However, when outside researchers examined the evidence, they found dinosaur tracks only.[11]

Such creationist museums and Web sites cannot be called *scientific* in any normative sense. Self-evidently, the motivation for constructing such creation-science museums and websites is not the discovery and dissemination of scientific findings that have been vetted and corroborated by the scientific community, but the validation of doctrines of faith. So alienated from modern life and scientific epistemology are the creators of these museums that they are impelled to fashion what I would describe as an alternate material reality that includes an alternative natural history of the earth, based on biblical authority. This alternate reality also expresses itself in the creationist production of documentaries put out by the entertainment industry. In this cultural competition, ID proponents now produce DVD

---

9. See http://www.nwcreation.net/museum.html.
10. See http://www.projectcreation.org/ark_museum.php.
11. Randy Moore, "Creation Evidence Museum," 34–35.

documentaries to counter mainstream documentaries on evolution. Many of these have production values of fair quality and are available on Netflix streaming. One notable series strains to illustrate the impossibility of evolution being able to account for the existence of certain animals. Boastfully but genially, its producers call the documentary *Incredible Creatures That Defy Evolution*.[12] These productions often sport catchy titles such as *Flock of Dodos: The Evolution and Intelligent Design Circus*, and they feature well-known leaders in the ID movement such as Michael Behe.[13] If any of these faith-based documentaries were to be placed beside, say, an IMAX production of *Dinosaurs: Giants of Patagonia*, with its paleontologist consultant, viewers would discover the vast distance separating the alleged facts of evolution presented by ID proponents and mainstream scientists.[14] But from a cultural standpoint, these developments demonstrate the intensive energy and the considerable extent to which a creation science of opposition is being developed and marketed at the state and national levels.

II

The alternate reality propounded by opponents of the modern sciences has a concrete literary application in the field of science fiction. For some decades now, science fiction has become one of the most popular genres in which conservative Christians like to work. The authors find in science fiction ample opportunities to present creatures from the spirit world participating in human activities. The genre also comfortably accommodates the depiction of miraculous events and the intervention of such spiritual agents as angels and devils and their minions. Still, this subgenre is worthy of notice for the attitudes it cultivates.

Frank Peretti's *This Present Darkness* (2003) is a good example of Christian science-fiction writing, in which ordinary reality–the naturalistic kind that obeys the laws of physics—is in tension with a surprising spiritual reality. This niche writing clearly commands the attention of a broad segment of America's religious conservatives. Peretti's engagement with science is

---

12. *Incredible Creatures that Defy Evolution*, directed by Greisen.

13. *Flock of Dodos: The Evolution and Intelligent Design Circus*, directed by Olson. Behe was the principal ID scientist who testified in the *Kitzmiller v. Dover Area School District* decision (2005) and is the author of *Darwin's Black Box*. See also *Expelled: No Intelligence Allowed*, directed by Frankowski, which treats the subject of ID scholars being chastised, fired, or denied tenure by evolutionists.

14. *Dinosaurs: Giants of Patagonia*, directed and written by Fafard.

motivated by the author's desire to show its total inadequacy as a vehicle to explain human experience, which is fair enough. However, the fiction in the representation of science soon takes over, for Peretti makes no effort to really engage the findings of science with faith. But it does target what it depicts as America's deplorable college educational system, singling out the godless discipline of psychology for special opprobrium. The novel goes so far as to depict a female psychology professor as a witch. These novels typically present a Christian fundamentalist outlook and depict characters dichotomously, either as of the devil or as followers of Christ. Most of the characters are crudely drawn types, treated either with approbation or disapproval and thus hardly appropriate to the cultivation of understanding. But for readers wanting faith-based judgments, lively incident, and swift-paced narrative, these novels are exhilarating page-turners.

More notable because it actively confronts scientific ideas is James Scott Bell's novel *The Darwin Conspiracy*. Published by Broadman and Holman, whose list features Christian Standard Bibles, the novel, which repeatedly employs the term *fundamentalist* to describe the brand of biblical inerrancy Bell defends, won the Christy Award for Excellence in Christian fiction.[15] Significant because it illustrates the ID movement extending itself into Christian fiction, the novel treats the theory of evolution as it affects Christians today and, consequently, makes relentless arguments denying the verifiability of Darwinism. As an admonitory work, it seeks to undermine the authority of Darwinism—one of the most mind-altering theories ever developed—by treating it as a fad. In so doing, it imaginatively constructs the same sort of wished-for alternate reality that appears in other forms of fundamentalist writing, such as science fiction.

In Bell's novel, Darwin's theory of the evolution of species is so pernicious, so God-denying, that its advocates are accused of being possessed by a demonic force that aspires to be like Lucifer himself. Accordingly, the novel's hate-filled antagonist is Sir Max Busby, the dark light, who in hopes of destroying faith everywhere, and particularly in America, goads an intellectually unimpressive Darwin into publishing *The Origin of Species* so that Busby himself can disseminate it. The content of Sir Max's secret manuscript, "discovered" by James Scott Bell, is a confession of a "Darwin Conspiracy" against God. The manuscript's existence is what enables Bell to describe Darwinism as diabolic. But by the novel's end, Sir Max's repentance completes a homiletic process of reaffirmation of Christian faith.

---

15. James Scott Bell, *Darwin Conspiracy*, 264. Page numbers from this book follow quotations and appear in the text.

In between these framing events is a narrative that vilifies Darwinian evolution. Thus, the character of the author, Bell as himself, reveals that despite his initial interest in evolution, he found the evidence for Darwinism science to be "virtually non-existent" (2). The publisher's statement that the author "once believed in evolution; he went to public schools" captures Bell's hostility to the secularism of public education (264). Bell himself states that his public education "hoodwinked" him (2). These words make Bell's education a trick, a hoax, that conforms to Richard Hofstadter's famous insight that fundamentalists and others on the American right exhibit a characteristic paranoia that comes from their feelings of alienation and dispossession after having lost much of their former influence.[16] Conspiracy is thus everywhere.

The novel's ridicule of Darwinism takes several forms. One of these has less to do with invalidating evolution than with identifying its unacceptable theological consequences. The reason that a literal, young-earth understanding of biblical creation is non-negotiable is that it provides the foundation of the Lord's plan for man. If one believes in evolution, there are no objective moral values and no objective moral order. Consequently, one is likely to be an atheist, and atheists who belong to the "intellectual elite" have "their own religion"—self-love (196). Bell's example is serial killer Charles Manson, whose malevolence is a "perfect consequence of evolutionary philosophy" (197). How this should be is not made clear.

The explanation Bell provides for the rise of new species according to Darwinian theory is not badly handled. Urged on by Sir Max, the young Darwin of the novel excitedly explains that new species arise from naturally occurring variations within a species. Nature, operating by blind chance, then selects for survival those most "favorable variations"—a principle that, operating over many thousands of years, creates a new species (66). Unfortunately, the explanation introduces without clarification the anachronous, post-Darwinian term *mutation* (12, 103). Furthermore, the novel claims that the crucial "empirical flaw" of evolution is the "absence of transitional forms in the fossil record" (95). This blanket assertion about the content of the fossil record—quite the opposite of the complex reality scientists have reported—is tantamount to a science-fiction conspiracy all its own.[17]

To defend this extreme position, Bell marshals the apparatuses of authority, "Editor's Notes" and "End-Notes," both apparently created by the author. An example of the former is the unsupported assertion that

---

16. Hofstadter, *Paranoid Style in American Politics*, 3–40.
17. Kenneth R. Miller, *Only a Theory*, 92–95.

modern man appeared suddenly and was a great leap ahead of everything preceding. The assertion that humankind emerged suddenly as a species, unlike any other, shows no familiarity with Neanderthal man who, paleontologists have discovered, coexisted and competed with modern man as recently as 35,000 years ago, perhaps only 24,000, or even fewer.[18] These claims also swim feebly against the swift currents of new discoveries since the publication of Bell's novel in 2002. Most notably, in October 2004, the still-controversial announcement was made that skeletal evidence points to a new species, *Homo floresiensis*, familiarly called hobbit people because of their diminutive stature, who became extinct only recently—between 17,000 and 14,000 years ago.[19]

A striking example of Bell's treatment of an endnote is the entry on "Archaeopteryx," the bird-reptile that is one of the best examples of just the kind of transitional form that Bell denies exists. Bell, however, asserts that it is a forgery, and only then argues that it cannot be transitional because no fossils lead to it or follow from it.[20] Similarly, Bell repeatedly employs the tactic of invoking famous hoaxes to dismiss the evolutionary position in its entirety. In this spirit, Bell dramatizes the notorious Piltdown Man hoax in the 1950s after the original hoax in 1912. He does this by having Sir Max say that he—the prime promoter of the false theory of evolution—was responsible for the hoax, since fraud was "the only way evolution could be 'proven a fact'" (98)![21] These particulars lead to Sir Max's hyperbolic conclusion that "the odds against Darwinism" are "incalculable" (233).

Frequently Bell also declares there to be an equivalence between what he describes as religious and scientific faith. Darwinism is a faith, he contends, as "zealously guarded as any form of Fundamentalism" (16). But there is a great deal of difference between faith based on belief in what one cannot know and commitment to a methodology. The falsity of the equivalence is further demonstrated by the consideration that the scientist holds convictions provisionally based on further investigation, whereas the literal-reading

---

18. For a full discussion of the range of dates before the extinction of the Neanderthals, see Jordan, *Neanderthal*, 212–14. On confidence in carbon isotope dating for this group, see Sarmiento, Sawyer, and Milner, *Last Human*, 215. See also Ruse, *Evolution Wars*, 187.

19. Falk, *Fossil Chronicles*, 93–94, 167, 207n2. For an extended argument that floresiensis is not a new species, see Henneberg, Eckhardt, and Schofield, *Hobbit Trap*.

20. Ruse, *Evolution Wars*, 267–68, contextualizes the "Creationist/Intelligent Design" argument that historically has focused on "Archaeopteryx" and gives a temperate assessment of the philosophical position laid out by its most talented advocates.

21. The Piltdown Hoax created a sensation. For the facts, see Ruse, *Evolution Wars*, 179–81.

Christian holds *a priori* biblical beliefs about what is geologically or astronomically true. These major differences notwithstanding, Bell has Sir Max wittily and malevolently harness Herbert Spencer's memorable phrase, the "survival of the fittest," to the social Darwinist's belief that the fittest in society will outlast the weak (130). Of course, neither the novelist nor Sir Max has any interest in removing the concealed ambiguity of this argument, which is that scientists may accept fitness as a functional principle—a statement about how nature operates—without having to embrace or believe in it as a social philosophy or a way of directing one's life.

Beneath these skewed accounts of how evolution functions lurks the anxiety that Darwinism is really a rival religion. So powerful is this apprehension that it prompts Bell to borrow from the history of science one of its most sensational episodes: the burning of heretics for their scientific beliefs. It then appropriates this history for the martyrs to intelligent design. In this fashion, Bell claims that institutional Darwinists burn heretics "at the scholastic stake" (137). This metaphor presents an implicit argument that exalts to the point of martyrdom the penalty imposed on an ID faculty member who was removed from his teaching duties in biology in 1993. That is to say, Bell constructs an equivalence between modern academic administrators who behave like inquisitors of yore and who, for example, took Renaissance cosmological theorist Giordano Bruno to the stake and burned him to ashes, as A. D. White recorded in *A History of the Warfare of Science with Theology in Christendom*.[22] All this reveals an astonishing lack of proportion, not to say insensitivity to metaphor.

Bell's afterword to *The Darwin Conspiracy* candidly states that he draws inspiration from ID philosopher of science Phillip Johnson, author of *Darwinism on Trial* and a trenchant critic of mainstream Darwinism today (252). Yet whereas Johnson makes measured statements denying the *fact* of Darwinian evolution while emphasizing its precarious theoretical status, Bell describes the case for Darwinian evolutionary theory as "sheer puffery" (248).[23] Bell, moreover, gloats that "Darwinists were outraged" when his novel was used by "secular" high school students for book reports (247). If these recollections are intended as humor, their content appears in heated earnest. Furthermore, the anecdote shows that for fundamentalists of Bell's stamp, religious convictions alone determine what counts for scientific truth. More revealing still, Johnson lends his celebrity in the ID community

---

22. White, *Warfare of Science*, 1:57.
23. Phillip E. Johnson, *Darwin on Trial*, 63–72. Johnson focuses on the need to formulate Darwin's hypothesis of descent with modification so that the hypothesis can be confirmed or falsified.

to the marketing of Bell's novel, declaring on the back cover, "Darwinists will be outraged." This use of the very phrase that Bell employs reveals Johnson to be less interested in the scientific content of Bell's novel than in gloating with Bell over the outrage that *The Darwin Conspiracy* will elicit among mainstream scientists.

III

According to Elizabeth Fenton, in the first half of the nineteenth century, most Americans viewed Catholicism as the embodiment of authoritarianism and superstition in the United States. As such, it became a foil for liberal democratic ideals, providing the American nation with "the impetus for continual renewal."[24] Among nineteenth-century American historians of science, the truth of this insight is borne out in John Draper's *History of the Conflict between Religion and Science* (1874). His book identified the authoritarianism of the Catholic Church as the natural opponent of science, while championing a generic Protestantism as the natural ally of scientific inquiry, since freedom of thought in a democracy and "the right of private interpretation of the Scriptures" work together to encourage new knowledge.[25] A generation later, in 1896, Andrew D. White's *A History of the Warfare of Science with Theology in Christendom* renewed the argument against the Roman Church but added a triumphalist, destinarian element, arguing that in the ceaseless war between the sciences and the superstition and ignorance enforced by Christian theologians, scientific thinking has prevailed.[26]

But by 1927, the target of scientific anxiety in America had shifted. An insurgent group of conservative Protestants, who had come to be called fundamentalists, emerged as the most feared opponent of scientific inquiry. The year 1927 was the date that Maynard Shipley's *The War on Modern Science* was published, and it identified the fundamentalist movement as the focal point of opposition to the teaching of evolution. Impressively, the work documented on a state-by-state basis how scientific teaching of

---

24. Fenton, *Religious Liberties*, 5.
25. Draper, *History of the Conflict between Religion and Science*, 363.
26. White typically follows a programmatic pattern for each scientific issue treated. See, for example, *Warfare of Science*, 2:256–63, for White's rendering of the stages whereby a scientific attitude toward "the Dead Sea legends" emerged following vigorous disputation by Christian theologians. See also Simpson's *Landmarks in the Struggle between Science and Religion* (1925), who followed Draper and White even as he softened their more polemical arguments.

evolution was being curtailed, and in places outlawed by these activist fundamentalists.[27] Later in the century, fundamentalist opposition to the teaching of evolution in the public schools reemerged with fresh vigor, and now in this twenty-first century, a much more extensive challenge to the methods and findings of science has been marshaled.

In view of these developments, I would like to consider whether Elizabeth Fenton's hypothesis, that opposition to Catholicism became a goading stimulus to liberal democratic ideas, can be applied to modern fundamentalism. That is to say, could it be that in our present century the fundamentalist challenge to the teaching of science is thought to be sufficiently threatening to our democratic institutions that it could galvanize mainstream opposition? To respond to this question, it is necessary to gauge the degree of threat to the core values that fundamentalists themselves feel, and I will use Bell's novel as a starting point. I then propose to do the same in reverse: measure the degree of threat that supporters of modern science feel from the creation science and ID movements.

The Darwin Conspiracy opens a window on the degree of fundamentalist alienation from America's secular culture. Again, James Scott Bell's central character, Sir Max Busby, provides a striking illustration, as he comes to the stark insight that there is just one "inevitable conclusion: this is all a battle for the soul" (245). Not a clash, not a struggle over disagreements about knowledge, but a battle, as it were, for the soul of everyman. John Caputo explains the psychology of this beleaguered religious group, stating that "faced with a new Babylon, or a new Sodom, the fundamentalists clench their fists around the Word of God, which seems to them the one constant in a world gone mad."[28] Caputo concludes that "fundamentalists have gone public and changed the face . . . of American politics."[29] Bell's fundamentalism is a product of this inheritance, and for that reason the intensity of his metaphors is not surprising.

Astonishingly, however, two twenty-first-century historians of science employ exactly the same terminology and metaphor to describe their struggle to uphold the teaching of scientific evolution. Brown University professor Kenneth Miller and journalist Edward Humes both write about the landmark trial case of *Kitzmiller v. Dover*, 2005, and each bears the same subtitle: Miller's book is called *Only a Theory: The Battle for America's Soul* and Humes's is *Monkey Girl: The Battle for America's Soul*.

---

27. Shipley, *War on Modern Science*, 21–43.
28. Caputo, *On Religion*, 102.
29. Ibid., 103.

The arresting qualities about these metaphors are, first, that the imagery of battle is employed on both sides, and, second, that this battle imagery is employed to describe what is really an internal state. Both sides recognize that they are locked in a contest for America's *soul*—one side locating that soul in the reality of a promised eternal life, the other in a scientific education based on unfettered empirical inquiry and assessment. Bell's stated purpose of changing minds to save souls is not surprising, but the fact that two modernist historians appropriate the same imagery of a battle for souls surely is. Together they point to a bitter inner as well as outer struggle for allegiance and hegemony.

In a democratic society, the idea of a battle for the soul of America also signifies urgency. According to Miller and to Forrest Gross, both the conception and practice of science are at risk, as is the effective functioning of government, which requires informed decisions. Each warns that the ID movement poses a strategic challenge to science itself, for it seeks not just to secure a place for creationism in the public schools but, far more boldly, to achieve the long-term goal of overthrowing the methodology and institutionalization of the natural sciences, replacing them with a dogmatic Christian science.[30] Were proponents of ID ever to succeed in colonizing the teaching of science, they would engender a scientific and cultural revolution all their own. Given its ample funding, skillful planning, and step-by-step strategy to gain mainstream respectability before finally battling for dominance,[31] the ID movement has come to be regarded as a formidable opponent of scientific investigation. If current standards for what constitutes science were to give way to a new episteme based on fundamentalist methods, then there would be irresistible evidence that we have, indeed, entered a postsecular era.

Even without this fundamentalist alternative to America's existing educational institutions, there is the dismal state of our national legislative institutions. Although in practice, the separation of church and state clearly privileges secular voices and tends to marginalize religious ones, many fundamentalist and conservative evangelical voices in the U.S. Congress and the Senate are not only speaking out in the public marketplace. This is good,

---

30. Forrest and Gross, *Creationism's Trojan Horse*, 30–31. In *Only a Theory*, 40–43, Kenneth R. Miller, a scientific witness in the *Kitzmiller v. Dover* case and a frequent debater of ID advocates, contends that the quarrel of ID proponents is at bottom not just with Darwin but with the methods of physics, geology, astronomy, and biology—in short, science itself.

31. For a comprehensive analysis, not of creationism per se, but of the insemination of religion into virtually every aspect of American life, see Gilbert, *Redeeming Culture*.

but they are making policy decisions at the national level on scientific issues with little or no scientific foundation. The U.S. Congress has become, arguably, the most visible institution in which resistance to the methods and findings of science has already had a major impact on the decision-making process. There, numerous members of both houses, especially Republican Party members, with their substantial base of very conservative evangelicals, are hostile to government and to theoretical (as opposed to practical) science. Consequently, they have routinely derided evidence of acid rain, the linkage between fatty foods and obesity, climate change traced to human activity, and evolution itself. One striking example is the statement of Georgia Republican representative Paul Broun, who in 2013 sat on the House Committee on Science, Space and Technology, and flatly asserted on videotape, "All that stuff I was taught about evolution and embryology and Big Bang theory, all that is lies straight from the pit of hell."[32] This dismissive junking of sound science has become so endemic to a faltering political process that investigative journalist Chris Mooney entitled his best-selling book *The Republican War on Science*.[33] The very extent of this resistance to scientific evidence demonstrates that the secular has by no means succeeded in crowding out the religious from public discourse.

The intractability of the problem can hardly be underappreciated. No less a person than the late paleontologist Stephen Jay Gould mapped out a methodological argument for the compatibility of science and religion. He did so by affirming the separateness of the material and spiritual realms, claiming that religion and science are *nonoverlapping magisteria*—that is, they operate in separate domains. Creationism, Gould argued, does not conflict with science because it "does not raise any unsettled issues about the nature of biology or the history of life." In the Catholic and Judaic traditions, he observed, the Bible is interpreted by the appropriate authorities, while only a "fringe" set of Protestants that Gould described as a "local and parochial movement" read the Bible literally. Setting aside the disparaging, now out-of-date depiction of literal-reading evangelicals and fundamentalists as merely "local" (they have become, as we have seen, a major national force on local, state, and national policy issues), Gould's hypothesis of nonoverlapping magisteria simply does not work when applied to the beliefs of biblical literalists. When, for instance, literalist readers claim that Noah's ark spared from the Flood a pair of each kind of creature, and, furthermore, that

---

32. Tucker, "'Republicans' Rabid Right is Leading Party to Ruin," 10A.

33. Mooney, *Republican War on Science*, 6, 65–76. On climate change, acid rain, and the fatty foods–obesity link, see, respectively, 78–101, 41–43, 124–27; on antievolution positions, 36–39.

the age of the earth as derived from the Bible is approximately 6,000 years, then religion and science do obviously compete with one another.[34]

Furthermore, Gould's argument is a separatist one because it, in effect, reproduces a "separate but equal" situation, wherein the magisteria of religion are, once again, relegated to the domain of the private while proponents of science are accorded the domain of public speech in respect to issues of education and politics.

Gould's argument may also be contrasted with that of atheistic scientist Richard Dawkins, who reasons that when biblical literalists make dogmatic claims about material reality, confrontation becomes unavoidable because religion cannot be divorced from the physical world. To illustrate, he relates that one of Gould's students, Kurt Wise, went through his Bible cutting out every verse that did not accord with scientific truth, and in the end he had very little of the book left.[35] Such is the extent of the contested ground.

Nevertheless, I would argue that a situation in which interested parties are at loggerheads is preferable to a well-meaning argument that has the effect of cutting off communication between religious voices and everyone else. No long-enduring condition of alienation and noncommunication can be good for the nation, conceived as an assemblage of interests. There are, however, concrete indications that point to increasing alienation among Christians. Stephens and Giberson report that fundamentalist attitudes of the kind just described are spreading among the evangelical community to the extent that about one hundred million evangelicals embrace the idea of living in a "parallel culture."[36] Mary Worthen calls the situation among evangelicals one of a crisis of authority.[37] The need for responsible leadership among evangelicals is especially strong if further alienation and radicalization are to be blunted.

Ironically, it seems intuitively true that if this crisis of authority grows more acute and if climate change denial becomes more widespread, then the likelihood that novelists and other creative writers will address the dimensions of this cultural conflict increases. Another possibility is that fundamentalist allegiance to ID, with its alternative science agenda, will display even greater potency and thus provoke effective mainstream countermeasures. But to wish for this kind of future is, indeed, to invite a postsecular inauguration after all.

---

34. Throughout the paragraph I cite from Gould, "Nonoverlapping Magisteria," 19, 16, and 18, respectively.
    35. Richard Dawkins, *God Delusion*, 321–23.
    36. Stephens and Giberson, *Anointed*, 7.
    37. Worthen, *Apostles of Reason*, 19.

But the cultural landscape is not totally bleak. There are at least some signs of a more productive national conversation that overcomes binary thinking. In this scenario, the role of more moderate religious groups may be crucial. After all, even many conservative Christians are not militant, and numerous Christian churches, including those of evangelicals, Pentecostals, fundamentalists, and Catholics, have shown themselves eager to explore ways of reconciling, or even harmonizing, scientific findings with established Christian doctrine.[38] This synthesizing impulse of Calvin College professor Howard J. Van Till prompts him to propose a model of conservative Christianity in which believers take seriously both the Bible and the cosmos. This model emphatically denies the "assumption that natural processes somehow compete with or constitute an alternative to divine action."[39] Similarly, Christian chemistry professor Clarence Menninga draws a sharp distinction between creationist practices and his conservative Protestantism, which holds that the scientific attempt to know God's world is not incompatible with faith. Thus, in *If the Truth be Known*, Menninga seeks to redress creationist omissions and distortions of the scientific record by pointing out that whereas many creationists claim support for their theological commitments by citing scientific sources, sometimes the data presented "are not the same as the data reported in the original scientific publication, that is, the data from the scientific source are not reported faithfully."[40]

Prominent among those seeking accommodation have been professors of religious studies and philosophers of religion. For instance, philosophy of religion professor Willem B. Drees acknowledges that scientific investigations into the laws and properties of nature have yielded "an increasingly integrated and unified understanding of reality, resulting in precise predictions which correspond to empirical results."[41] In view of science's extraordinary achievements, Drees holds that there is no evidence of, and therefore no room for, a dualistic philosophy that includes the supernatural along with natural causation. A philosophical reconciler, Drees counsels

---

38. This impulse to find common ground has driven the projects of revisionist historians James Moore and David Livingstone, who contend that most conservative Christians neither were nor are the rabid, uncompromising antievolutionists that mainstream historians have made them out to be. Both claim that until the formation of modern-day fundamentalism, most leading evangelicals and other conservative Christians took pains to try to harmonize the discoveries of science with the precepts of their faith. See James R. Moore, *Post-Darwinian Controversies*, 101–22, and Livingstone, *Darwin's Forgotten Defenders*, 145.

39. Van Till, *Fourth Day*, 223.

40. Menninga, *If the Truth be Known*, 4.

41. Drees, "Religious Naturalism and Science," 109.

that instead of attempting to disprove naturalistic causation, theologians may find it more fruitful "to explore religious options within the context of naturalism, which may turn out to be more hospitable to religious motives than antagonists suggest."[42] Such a pathway holds out the prospect of dialogue, not "warfare," between the proponents of these two worldviews.

Perhaps there are enough progressive, moderate, and even conservative voices who may yet regain the common ground that diverse readers of literature once shared. So long as this integrative impulse remains strong, the likelihood of our entering a postsecular epoch diminishes. This agenda of reconciliation notwithstanding, it must be conceded that the positions just described are not ones that those committed to a literal interpretation of scripture can—or want—to adopt. It must also be conceded that the position of militant creationists and ID proponents has generated far greater cultural energy than that of those supporting moderate positions.[43]

And there is this sobering consideration as well: although many moderate Christian fundamentalists and evangelicals seek to accommodate their faith to the findings of modern science, these religious groups have produced no novel or play over the last fifty years that has influenced the national debate in any notable way. Indeed, over much of this period, the cultural and political initiative has belonged principally to the militant fundamentalists, in great part because they have proven themselves resourceful enough to alter, or at least threaten, the normative practice of science in American classrooms in our K–12 public schools.

Moreover, if we are to have once again nationally recognized novels treating the roles of science and religion in our time, the specific subject must be one that truly matters to the public. In our present circumstances, the teaching of evolution in the schools would appear to qualify, but thus far the subject has produced competing documentaries, not art—and certainly not the probing perspectives characteristic of good novels and plays. A precondition for the production of such literature is that America regain the national readership it once had, rather than the divided, deeply polarized one we have today. If it could do so, the country would experience a national renewal and, odds are, a literary one as well.

Whether such a set of inviting cultural conditions is currently available is doubtful. If this is, in fact, the case, so then is the prospect of the rebirth of quality novels on faith, science, and doubt. The discouraging reality of our

---

42. Ibid., 108.
43. Stephens and Giberson, *Anointed*, 47–50, with emphasis on Ken Ham's leadership in the ID movement.

time is that schism, polarization, and noncommunication have now been with us for several decades. While it is surely too early to tell whether the United States is about to enter a postsecular age driven by fundamentalist precepts,[44] the prospects for such a transformation begin, like an unfamiliar horizon, to ease into view.

---

44. See Calhoun, "Secularism," 78–79, for a working discussion of the term *postsecular age*.

BIBLIOGRAPHY

Abbott, Lyman. "A Summary of Conclusions." In *The Theology of an Evolutionist*, 176–91. Boston and New York: Houghton Mifflin, 1897. Reprinted in *Darwinism and Theology in America: 1850–1930: Science and Religion*, vol. 3, edited by Frank X. Ryan, 153–59. Bristol: Theommes, 2002.

The Academy Awards Index: The Complete Categorical and Chronological Record. Compiled by Richard Shale. Westport, CT: Greenwood Press, 1993.

Adams, Henry. *The Education of Henry Adams.* Edited by Ira B. Nadel. [1907.] Reprint. Oxford: Oxford University Press, 1999.

———. *Esther: A Novel.* 1884. Reprint. New York: Scholars' Facsimiles and Reprints, 1938.

———. *Mont-Saint-Michel and Chartres.* [1904.] Reprint. New York: Penguin, 1986.

Adkins, Nelson F. Introduction to *Paine: Common Sense and Other Political Writings*, xi–xlix. New York: Macmillan, 1953.

Agassiz, Louis. "Professor Agassiz on *The Origin of Species.*" From *American Journal of Science and Arts*, 2nd series, 30 (1860): 142–54. In *Darwinism and the American Intellectual: An Anthology*, edited by R. Jackson Wilson, 10–17. 2nd ed. Chicago: Dorsey Press, 1989.

Allen, James Lane. "Realism and Romance." *New York Evening Post*, July 31, 1886. Reprinted in *The Heritage of American Literature*, vol. 2, edited by Lyon N. Richardson, George H. Orians, and Herbert R. Brown. Boston: Ginn and Company, 1951.

———. *The Reign of Law: A Tale of the Kentucky Hemp Fields.* New York: Macmillan, 1900. Reprint. U.S.A.: Kessinger Publishing, n.d.

———. *The Reign of Law: A Tale of the Kentucky Hemp Fields.* Freeport, NY: Books for Libraries Press, 1971.

———. *The Reign of Law: A Tale of the Kentucky Hemp Fields.* New York; London: Macmillan, 1982.

———. *The Reign of Law: A Tale of the Kentucky Hemp Fields*. No c.: Create Space Publishing, 2014.

"Amateur Dramatics at Dayton." *Christian Century*, July 30, 1925. Reprinted in *Monkey Trial: The State of Tennessee vs. John Thomas Scopes*, edited by Sheldon Norman Grebstein, 195–98. Boston: Houghton Mifflin, 1960.

Anderson, David D. *Robert Ingersoll*. New York: Twayne Publishers, 1972.

Angoff, Charles. *H. L. Mencken: A Portrait from Memory*. New York: Thomas Yoseloff, 1956.

Appleby, R. Scott. "Rethinking Fundamentalism in a Secular Age." In *Rethinking Secularism*, edited by Craig Calhoun, Mark Juergensmeyer, and Jonathan VanAntwerpen, 225–47. New York: Oxford University Press, 2011.

Asad, Talal. *Formations of the Secular: Christianity, Islam, Modernity*. Stanford: Stanford University Press, 2003.

Ashton, Rosemary. *The German Idea: Four English Writers and the Reception of German Thought 1800–1860*. Cambridge: Cambridge University Press, 1980.

———. Introduction to *Robert Elsmere*, vii–xxiv. Edited by Rosemary Ashton. Oxford and New York: Oxford University Press, 1987.

Bakker, Jim, with Ken Abraham. *I Was Wrong*. Nashville: Thomas Nelson, 1996.

Barzan, Jacques. "Cultural History: A Synthesis." In *The Varieties of History: From Voltaire to the Present*, introduced and edited by Fritz Stern, 387–402. New York: Random House, 1973.

Bayly, Ada Ellen [Edna Lyall, pseud.]. *Donovan, a Novel*. 3 vols. London: Hurst and Blackett, 1882. Reprint. New York and London: Garland Publishing, 1976.

Beckley, Paul V. Review of *Elmer Gantry*. Based on the novel by Sinclair Lewis. *New York Herald Tribune*. Reprinted in *Film Facts* 3, no. 27 (August 5, 1960): 161.

———. Review of *Inherit the Wind*. Based on the play by Jerome Lawrence and Robert E. Lee. *New York Herald Tribune*, October 13, 1960. Reprinted in *Film Facts* 3, no. 41 (November 11, 1960): 251.

Behe, Michael J. *Darwin's Black Box: The Biochemical Challenge to Evolution*. New York: Simon and Schuster, 1996.

Bell, James Scott. *The Darwin Conspiracy: The Confessions of Sir Max Busby: A Novel*. [1995.] Nashville: Broadman and Holman, 2002.

Bell, Millicent. "Adams' *Esther*: The Morality of Taste." *New England Quarterly* 35, no. 2 (June 1962): 147–61.

Bennett, Bridget. *The Damnation of Harold Frederic: His Lives and Works*. Syracuse: Syracuse University Press, 1997.

Bergmann, Harriet F. "Henry Adams's *Esther:* No Faith in the Patriarchy" 10 (Summer 1981): 63–67.

Billman, Carol. "McGuffey's Readers and Alger's Fiction: The Gospel Of Virtue According to Popular Children's Literature." *Journal of Popular Culture* 11 (1977): 614–19.

Birkhead, L. M. *Is Elmer Gantry True?* Girard, KS: Haldeman-Julius, 1928.

Bishop, Ferman. *Henry Adams*. Boston: Twayne Publishers, 1979.

Blair, Emily Newell. "Treasure Trove." *Good Housekeeping* (June 1927): 92, 240.

Bortolotti, Lisa. *Delusions and Other Irrational Beliefs*. Oxford: Oxford University Press, 2010.

Bottorff, William K. *James Lane Allen*. New York: Twayne, 1964.

Bourdieu, Pierre. *The Field of Cultural Production: Essays on Art and Literature*. Edited by Randal Johnson. New York: Columbia University Press, 1993.

Boynton, H. W. "Some Outstanding Novels of the Year." *The Nation* 103, no. 2683 (November 30, 1916): 507–8.

Branch, Lori. *Rituals of Spontaneity: Sentiment and Secularism from Free Prayer to Wordsworth*. Waco, TX: Baylor University Press, 2006.

Brannigan, John. *New Historicism and Cultural Materialism*. New York: St. Martin's Press, 1998.

Briggs, Austin Jr. *The Novels of Harold Frederic*. Ithaca and London: Cornell University Press, 1969.

Bronowski, J. *The Common Sense of Science*. Cambridge, MA: Harvard University Press, 1978.

Brown, Jerry Wayne. *The Rise of Biblical Criticism in America, 1800–1870: The New England Scholars*. Middletown, CT: Wesleyan University Press, 1969.

Brumm, Ursula Uhlig. "The Religious Crisis of the 19th Century in *Robert Elsmere* and *The Damnation of Theron Ware*." *Die Amerikanische Literatur in die Weltliteratur: Themen und Aspkte* (1982): 159–75.

Bruns, Roger A. *Preacher: Billy Sunday and Big-Time American Evangelism*. New York and London: W. W. Norton, 1992.

Buckle, Henry Thomas. *History of Civilization in England*. New York: 1866. Excerpted in *The Varieties of History: From Voltaire to the Present*, edited by Fritz Stern, 121–35. New York: Random House, 1973.

Butler, Jon. *Awash in a Sea of Faith: Christianizing the American People*. Cambridge, MA: Harvard University Press, 1990.

Butterfield, Herbert. *The Origins of Modern Science, 1300–1800*. New York: Macmillan, 1960.

Cady, Edwin H. *The Realist at War: The Mature Years, 1885–1920, of William Dean Howells*. Syracuse: Syracuse University Press, 1958.

Calhoun, Craig. "Secularism, Citizenship, and the Public Sphere." In *Rethinking Secularism*, edited by Craig Calhoun, Mark Juergensmeyer and Jonathan VanAntwerpen, 75–91. New York: Oxford University Press, 2011.

Calhoun, Craig, Mark Juergensmeyer, and Jonathan VanAntwerpen. Introduction to *Rethinking Secularism*, 3–30. Edited by Craig Calhoun, Mark Juergensmeyer and Jonathan VanAntwerpen. New York: Oxford University Press, 2011.

Cambridge Dictionary of American Biography. Edited by John H. Bowman. Cambridge: Cambridge University Press, 1995.

Cameron, Nigel M. de S. *Biblical Higher Criticism and the Defense of Infallibilism in 19th Century Britain*. Lewiston/Queenston: Edwin Mellen Press, 1987.

Canby, Henry Seidel. "Fighting Success." *Saturday Review of Literature* 1 (March 7, 1925): 575. Reprinted in *Twentieth Century Interpretations of Arrowsmith: A Collection of*

Critical Essays, edited by Robert J. Griffin, 110–12. Englewood Cliffs, NJ: Prentice-Hall, 1968.

Caputo, John D. *On Religion*. London and New York: Routledge, 2002.

Carter, Everett. *Howells and the Age of Realism*. Philadelphia and New York: J. B. Lippincott, 1954.

———, ed. Introduction to *The Damnation of Theron Ware*, by Harold Frederic, vii–xxiv. Cambridge: Belknap Press of Harvard University Press, 1960.

Carus, Paul. "Science a Religious Revelation." 1893. In *The Dawn of a New Religious Era and Other Essays*, 22–40. Chicago and London: Open Court, 1916. Reprinted in *Darwinism and Theology in America: 1850–1930: Science, Humanism and the Scopes Trial*, vol. 4, edited by Frank X. Ryan, 75–85. Bristol: Theommes, 2002.

Cary, Richard. *Sarah Orne Jewett*. New York: Twayne Publishers, 1962.

Casanova, José. "The Secular, Secularizations, and Secularisms." In *Rethinking Secularism*, edited by Craig Calhoun, Mark Juergensmeyer and Jonathan VanAntwerpen, 54–74. New York: Oxford University Press, 2011.

[Chambers, Robert]. *Vestiges of the Natural History of Creation*. [1844.] 10th ed. 1853. Reprint. Bristoll, England, and Sterling, VA: Thoemmes Press, 2000.

Charles, Elizabeth. *The Bertram Family*. 1876. Reprint. New York and London: Garland Publishing, 1975.

Colacurcio, Michael. "'Democracy' and 'Esther'; Henry Adams' Flirtation with Pragmatism." *American Quarterly* 19, no. 1 (Spring 1967): 53–70.

Cole, Stewart G. *The History of Fundamentalism*. New York: Richard R. Smith, 1931.

Coletta, Paolo E. *William Jennings Bryan*. 3 vols. Lincoln: University of Nebraska Press, 1969.

Commager, Henry Steele. Foreword to *McGuffey's Fifth Eclectic Readers, 1879 Edition*, v–xiv. New York: New American Library, 1962.

———. *Jefferson, Nationalism, and the Enlightenment*. New York: George Braziller, 1975.

Conroy, Stephen S. "Sinclair Lewis's Sociological Imagination." *American Literature* 43, no. 3 (November 1970): 348–62.

Corelli, Marie. *Ardath, The Story of a Dead Self*. New York: Hurst, [1890].

Creation Museum and Dinosaur Park. http://www.projectcreation.org/arkmuseum.php. January 14, 2016.

Creation Science Museums and Learning Centers. http://www.nwcreation.net/museums.html. January 14, 2016.

Crowley, John W. "The Nude and the Madonna in *The Damnation of Theron Ware*." *American Literature* 45, no. 3 (1973): 379–89.

Crowther, Bosley. Review of *Inherit the Wind*. Based on the play by Jerome Lawrence and Robert E. Lee. *New York Times*, October 13 and October 16, 1960. Reprinted in *Film Facts* 3, no. 41 (November 11, 1960): 249–50.

Curti, Merle. *The Growth of American Thought*. 3rd ed. New York, Evanston, and London: Harper and Row, 1964.

Cuvier, Georges. *Essay on the Theory of the Earth*. Translated by Robert Kerr. Edinburgh, 1813. Reprint. Farnborough, England: Gregg, 1971.

———. *Recherches sur les ossemens fossiles de quadrupedès, où l'on rétablit les caractères de plusieurs espèces d'animaux que les révolutions du globe paroissent avoir détruites*. 4 vols. Paris, 1812.

Daniel, Douglass K. *Tough as Nails: The Life and Films of Richard Brooks*. Madison: University of Wisconsin Press, 2011.

Darwin, Charles. *The Descent of Man*. [1872.] [2nd ed.] Amherst, NY: Prometheus Books, 1998.

———. *The Origin of Species by Means of Natural Selection, or the Preservation of Favoured Races in the Struggle for Life*. 1st ed. 1859. Reprint. London: Penguin, 1987.

Davenport, Frederick Morgan. *Primitive Traits in Religious Revivals: A Study in Mental and Social Evolution*. 1905. Reprint. New York: Negro Universities Press, 1968.

Davidson, Edward H., and William J. Scheick. *Paine, Scripture, and Authority: "The Age of Reason" as Religious and Political Idea*. Bethlehem: Lehigh University Press; London and Toronto: Associated University Presses, 1994.

Davies, Horton. *A Mirror of the Ministry in Modern Novels*. New York: Oxford University Press, 1959.

Davies, Wallace Evan. "Religious Issues in Late Nineteenth-Century American Novels." *John Rylands Library Bulletin* 41 (1959): 328–59.

Dawkins, Richard. *The God Delusion*. Boston and New York: Houghton Mifflin, 2006.

de Kruif, Paul. *Microbe Hunters*. 1926. Edited by F. Gonzalez-Crussi. Reprint. San Diego, New York, and London: Harcourt Brace, 1996.

Deneen, Patrick J. "Mont-Saint-Michel and Chartres: From Unity to Multiplicity." In *A Political Companion to Henry Adams*, edited by Natalie Fuehrer Taylor, 171–89. Lexington: University Press of Kentucky, 2010.

Derrida, Jacques. "Faith and Knowledge: The Two Sources of 'Religion' at the Limits of Reason Alone." In *Religion*, edited by Jacques Derrida and Gianni Vattimo, 1–78. Stanford: Stanford University Press, 1998.

Dinosaurs: Giants of Patagonia. Produced by Carl Samson. Directed and written by Marc Fafard. Imax Corp., 2007. DVD.

Disraeli, Benjamin. *Tancred; or, the New Crusade*. 1847. Reprint. [London:] Lane, [1927].

Doctorow, E. L. Afterword to *Arrowsmith*, by Sinclair Lewis, 451–56. 1925. New York: New American Library, 1998.

Donaldson, Scott. Introduction to *The Damnation of Theron Ware, Or Illumination*, by Harold Frederic, vii–xxx. New York: Penguin, 1986.

———. "The Seduction of Theron Ware." *Nineteenth-Century Fiction* 29, no. 4 (March 1975): 441–52.

Donoghue, Denis. "Henry Adams' Novels." *Nineteenth-Century Fiction* 39, no. 2 (September, 1984): 186–201.

Donovan, Josephine. *Sarah Orne Jewett*. New York: Frederick Ungar, 1980.

Dooley, D. J. *The Art of Sinclair Lewis*. Lincoln: University of Nebraska Press, 1967.

Draper, John William. *History of the Conflict between Religion and Science*. New York and London: D. Appleton, 1874.

———. *History of the Intellectual Development of Europe*. 2 vols. New York: Harper and Brothers, 1876.

Drees, Willem B. "Religious Naturalism and Science." In *The Oxford Handbook of Religion and Science*, edited by Philip Clayton and Zachary Simpson, 108–23. Oxford: Oxford University Press, 2006.

Dreisbach, Daniel L., Mark David Hall, and Jeffry H. Morrison, ed. Preface to *The Forgotten Founders on Religion and Public Life*, xiii–xxi. Notre Dame, IN: University of Notre Dame Press, 2009.

Eggleston, Edward. *The Faith Doctor, a Story of New York*. New York: D. Appleton, 1891.

Ellis, Richard J. *To the Flag: The Unlikely History of the Pledge of Allegiance*. Lawrence: University Press of Kansas, 2005.

Elmer Gantry. Produced by Bernard Smith. Directed and written by Richard Brooks. United Artists, 1960.

Emerson, Haven. "A Doctor Looks at Arrowsmith." *Survey* 54 (May 1, 1925): 180. Reprinted in *Twentieth Century Interpretations of Arrowsmith: A Collection of Critical Essays*, edited by Robert J. Griffin, 107–8. Englewood Cliffs, NJ: Prentice-Hall, 1968.

Epicurus. *The Essential Epicurus: Letters Principal Doctrines, Vatican Sayings and Fragments*. Translated by Eugene O'Connor. Buffalo, NY: Prometheus Books, 1993.

———. "Letter to Pythocles." In *The Essential Epicurus: Letters, Principal Doctrines, Vatican Sayings and Fragments*, translated by Eugene O'Connor, 43–60. Buffalo, NY: Prometheus Books, 1993.

Evans, Rod L., and Irwin M. Berent. *Fundamentalism: Hazards and Heartbreaks*. La Salle, IL: Open Court, 1988.

Expelled: No Intelligence Allowed. Directed by Nathan Frankowski. Premise Media Corporation, 2008. DVD.

Falk, Dean. *The Fossil Chronicles: How Two Controversial Discoveries Changed Our View of Human Evolution*. Berkeley, Los Angeles, London: University of California Press, 2011.

Fangerau, Heiner M. "The Novel *Arrowsmith*, Paul de Kruif (1890–1971) and Jacques Loeb (1859–1924): A Literary Portrait of 'Medical Science.'" *Medical Humanities* 32 (2006): 82–87.

Fara, Patricia. *Sex, Botany and Empire: The Story of Carl Linnaeus and Joseph Banks*. Cambridge: Icon, 2003.

Feigenoff, Charles. "Sexuality in the Leatherwood God." *Studies in the Novel* 12 (1980): 183–91.

Fenton, Elizabeth. *Religious Liberties: Anti-Catholicism and Liberal Democracy in Nineteenth-Century U.S. Literature and Culture*. New York: Oxford University Press, 2011.

Fiske, John. *Through Nature to God*. Boston and New York: Houghton Mifflin, 1900.

Flock of Dodos: The Evolution and Intelligent Design Circus. Directed by Randy Olson. Produced by Steven Miller. Talking Evolutions Productions, 2006. DVD.

Follett, Helen Thomas, and Wilson Follett. "Contemporary Novelists: William Dean Howells." *Atlantic Monthly* 119 (March 1917): 362–72. In *Critical Essays on W. D. Howells, 1866–1920*, compiled by Edwin H. Cady and Norma W. Cady, 246–59. Boston: G. K. Hall, 1983.

Forrest, Barbara, and Paul R. Gross. *Creationism's Trojan Horse: The Wedge of Intelligent Design*. New York: Oxford University Press, 2004.

Foucault, Michel. *The Order of Things: An Archaeology of the Human Sciences*. Translated from the French by Sheridan Smith. New York: Vintage, 1973.

———. *Power/Knowledge: Selected Interviews and Other Writings, 1972–1977*. Edited by Colin Gordon. Translated by Colin Gordon, Leo Marshall, John Mepham, and Kate Soper. New York: Pantheon Books, 1980.

"Four New Novels." Review of *The Damnation of Theron Ware*, by Harold Frederic. *Atlantic Monthly* 78 (August 1896): 270–72.

Frederic, Harold. *Correspondence*. Edited by George E. Fortenberry, Stanton Garner, and Robert H. Woodward. Fort Worth: Texas Christian University Press, 1977.

———. *The Damnation of Theron Ware or Illumination*. Edited by Charlyne Dodge. Lincoln and London: University of Nebraska Press, 1985.

Frei, Hans W. *The Eclipse of Biblical Narrative: A Study in Eighteenth and Nineteenth Century Hermeneutics*. New Haven and London: Yale University Press, 1974.

Froude, J[ames] A. *The Nemesis of Faith*. 1849. Reprint. New York and London: Garland Publishing, 1975.

Fruchtman, Jack Jr. *Thomas Paine and the Religion of Nature*. Baltimore and London: The Johns Hopkins University Press, 1995.

Fuller, Linda K. "The Ideology of the 'Red Scare' Movement: McCarthyism in the Movies." In *Beyond the Stars*, edited by Paul Loukides and Linda K. Fuller, 229–47. Bowling Green, OH: Bowling Green University Popular Press, 1990.

Furniss, Norman F. *The Fundamentalist Controversy, 1918–1931*. Hamden, CT: Archon Books, 1963.

Gaines, Clarence H. "Some Modern Novels." Review of *Arrowsmith*, by Sinclair Lewis. *North American Review* 222 (March 15, 1925): 163–70.

Garner, Stanton. *Harold Frederic*. Minneapolis: University of Minnesota Press, 1969.

———. "History of the Text." In *Harold Frederic: The Damnation of Theron Ware or Illumination*, 353–415. Lincoln and London: University of Nebraska Press, 1985.

Gasper, Louis. *The Fundamentalist Movement*. The Hague: Mouton, 1963.

Gassner, John. Introduction to *Four Great Plays by Ibsen*, vii–xv. New York: E. P. Dutton, 1976.

Gay, Peter. *The Enlightenment, An Interpretation: The Science of Freedom*. New York and London: Norton, 1969.

Gibbs, Wolcott. "Mixed Bag." Review of *Inherit the Wind*. Based on the play by Jerome Lawrence and Robert E. Lee. *New Yorker* 31, no. 11 (April 30, 1955): 67.

Gilbert, James. *Redeeming Culture: American Religion in an Age of Science*. Chicago and London: University of Chicago Press, 1997.

Gilleen, James, and Anthony S. David. "The Cognitive Neuropsychiatry of Delusions: From Psychopathology to Neuropsychology and Back Again." *Psychological Medicine* 35, no. 1 (2005): 5–12.

Gillispie, Charles Coulston. *Genesis and Geology: A Study in the Relations of Scientific Thought, Natural Theology, and Social Opinion in Great Britain, 1790–1850*. New York: Harper and Row, 1959.

Gilman, Dorothy F. "A Pulpiteer of the Middle West." Review of *Elmer Gantry*, by Sinclair Lewis. *Boston Evening Transcript* (March 12, 1927): 4.

Giltner, Leigh G. "James Lane Allen—A Study." *Modern Culture* 12 (December 1900): 347–52.

Ginger, Ray. *Six Days or Forever? Tennessee v. John Thomas Scopes*. Boston: Beacon Press, 1958.

Giuliano, Michael J. *Thrice-Born: The Rhetorical Comeback of Jimmy Swaggart*. Macon, GA: Mercer University Press, 1999.

Godwin, John. *Lucretius*. London: Bristol Classical Press, 2004.

Gonzalez-Crussi, F. Introduction to *Microbe Hunters*, by Paul de Kruif, edited by F. Gonzalez-Crussi, vii–xiv. 1926. Reprint. San Diego, New York and London: Harcourt, Brace, 1996.

Goodman, Susan, and Carl Dawson. *William Dean Howells: A Writer's Life*. Berkeley, Los Angeles, and London: University of California Press, 2005.

Gould, Stephen Jay. "Nonoverlapping Magisteria." *Natural History* 106, no. 2 (March 1997): 16–22, 60–62.

———. *The Structure of Evolutionary Theory*. Cambridge, MA, and London: Belnap Press of Harvard University Press, 2002.

Gray, Asa. *Darwiniana: Essays and Reviews Pertaining to Darwinism*. New York: D. Appleton, 1876.

———. *Natural Science and Religion*. New York: Charles Scribner's Sons, 1880.

Grebstein, Sheldon Norman, ed. *Monkey Trial: The State of Tennessee vs. John Thomas Scopes*. Boston: Houghton Mifflin, 1960.

———. *Sinclair Lewis*. Boston: Twayne, 1962.

Greenblatt, Stephen. *Shakespearean Negotiations: The Circulation of Social Energy in Renaissance England*. Berkeley and Los Angeles: University of California Press, 1988.

Greene, John C. *American Science in the Age of Jefferson*. Ames, IA: Iowa State University Press, 1984.

Greene, William Chase. *Moira: Fate, Good, and Evil in Greek Thought*. 1944. New York and Evanston: Harper and Row, 1963.

Guillory, John. *Cultural Capital: The Problem of Literary Canon Formation*. Chicago and London: University of Chicago Press, 1993.

Guterman, Gad. "Field Tripping: The Power of *Inherit the Wind*." *Theatre Journal* 60, no. 4 (December 2008): 563–83.

Guthrie, William Norman. "Fiske's 'Through Nature to God.'" *Sewanee Review* 8, no. 1 (January 1900): 12–25.

Hackett, Alice Payne. *60 Years of Best Sellers, 1895–1955*. New York: R. R. Bowker, 1956.

Hadden, Jeffrey K., and Anson Shupe. *Televangelism: Power and Politics on God's Frontier*. New York: Henry Holt, 1988.

Hamner, Everett. "Damning Fundamentalism: Sinclair Lewis and the Trials of Fiction," *Modern Fiction Studies* 55, no. 2 (Summer 2009): 265–92.

Hawthorne, Nathaniel. *The Scarlet Letter: An Authoritative Text, Essays in Criticism and Scholarship*. Edited by Seymour Gross, Sculley Bradley, Richmond C. Beatty, and E. Hudson Long. 3rd ed. New York and London: W. W. Norton, 1988.

Hazard, Lucy L. "The Frontier in *Arrowsmith*." In *The Frontier in American Literature*, edited by Philip Durham and Everett L. Jones, 283–85. New York: Thomas Y. Crowell, 1927. Reprinted in *Twentieth Century Interpretations of Arrowsmith: A Collection of Critical Essays*, edited by Robert J. Griffin, 113–14. Englewood Cliffs, NJ: Prentice-Hall, 1968.

Henkin, Leo J. *Darwinism in the English Novel: 1860–1910: The Impact of Evolution on Victorian Fiction*. New York: Corporate Press, 1940.

Henneberg, Maciej, Robert B. Eckhardt, and John Schofield. *The Hobbit Trap: How New Species Are Invented*. 2nd ed. Walnut Creek, CA: Left Coast Press, 2011.

Hobart, Alice Tisdale. *Yang and Yin: A Novel of an American Doctor in China*. Indianapolis and New York: Bobbs-Merrill, 1936.

Hocking, Joseph. *Jabez Easterbrook, a Religious Novel*. London: Ward, Lock, and Co., [1890].

Hofstadter, Richard. *Anti-intellectualism in American Life*. New York: Alfred A. Knopf, 1963.

———. "History and the Social Sciences." In *The Varieties of History: From Voltaire to the Present*, introduced and edited by Fritz Stern, 359–70. New York: Random House, 1973.

———. *The Paranoid Style in American Politics and Other Essays*. New York: Alfred A. Knopf, 1966.

Hollenweger, W. J. *The Pentecostals: The Charismatic Movement in the Churches*. Minneapolis: Augsburg Publishing, 1972.

Howells, William Dean. *The Leatherwood God*. Edited by Eugene Pattison. Bloomington and London: Indiana University Press, 1976.

———. *The Leatherwood God*. Bloomington: Indiana University Press, 1976.

———. *The Leatherwood God*. New York: AMS Press, 1970.

———. *The Leatherwood God*. No c.: Barnes and Noble Digital Library, 2011.

———. "My Favorite Novelist and His Best Book." *Munsey's Magazine* 17 (April 1897): 18–25.

———. *A Modern Instance*. 1882. New York: Penguin, 1988.

———. *Selected Letters, Volume 6: 1912–1920*. Ed. William M. Gibson and Christoph K. Lohmann. Boston: Twayne Publishers, 1983.

Humes, Edward. *Monkey Girl: Evolution, Education, Religion, and the Battle for America's Soul*. New York: Harper Collins, 2007.

Hungerford, Amy. *Postmodern Belief: American Literature and Religion since 1960*. Princeton: Princeton University Press, 2010.

Hunter, James Davison. *Evangelicalism: The Coming Generation*. Chicago and London: University of Chicago Press, 1987.

Hutchisson, James M. "*Arrowsmith* and the Political Economy of Medicine." In *Sinclair Lewis: New Essays in Criticism*, edited by James M. Hutchisson, 110–24. Troy, NY: Whitson Publishing, 1997.

———. "Sinclair Lewis, Paul De Kruif, and the Composition of *Arrowsmith*." *Studies in the Novel* 24, no. 1 (Spring 1992): 48–66.

Hutton, Laurence. "Literary Notes," *Harper's* 93 (September 1896): supplement, 3–4.

Huxley, Thomas Henry. *Lay Sermons, Addresses, and Reviews*. New York, 1871.

Hye, Allen E. "A Tennessee Morality Play: Notes on *Inherit the Wind*." *Markham Review* 9 (1979): 17–20.

Hyland, Jack. *Evangelism's First Modern Media Star: The Life of Reverend Bill Stidger*. New York: Cooper Square Press, 2002.

"The Increasing Purpose." Review of *The Reign of Law*, by James Lane Allen. *Athenaeum* no. 3794 (July 14, 1900): 53.

"The Increasing Vogue of the American Novel and Play in London." Review of *The Reign of Law*, by James Lane Allen. *Literary Digest* 21 (November 3, 1900): 524.

Incredible Creatures that Defy Evolution. 2 vols. Directed by Steven Greisen. Exploration Films, 2000. DVD.

Ingersoll, Robert G. *Superstition and Other Essays*. New York: Prometheus Books, 2004.

"Is Mr. Allen's 'Reign of Law' an Infidel Work?" *Literary Digest* (February 16, 1901): 198–99.

Jacoby, Susan. *The Age of American Unreason*. New York: Pantheon Books, 2008.

"James Lane Allen, An Inquiry." *Academy* 59 (July 14, 1900): 35–36.

"James Lane Allen's New Novel, *The Reign of Law. A Tale of the Kentucky Hemp Fields*." *New York Times*, June 30, 1900.

James, William. *Pragmatism, a New Name for Some Old Ways of Thinking [1907]; The Meaning of Truth, a Sequel to Pragmatism*. Cambridge, MA: Harvard University Press, 1978.

———. *Some Problems of Philosophy*. [1911.] Cambridge, MA, and London: Harvard University Press, 1979.

Jewett, Sarah Orne. *A Country Doctor*. 1884. Reprint. Introduction by Paula Blanchard. New York: Bantam, 1999.

Johnson, George W. "Harold Frederic's Young Goodman Ware: The Ambiguities of a Realistic Romance." *Modern Fiction Studies* 28 (1962–63): 361–74.

Johnson, Phillip E. *Darwin on Trial*. Washington, DC: Regnery Gateway; Lanham, MD: National Book Network, 1991.

Johnson, Randal. "Introduction: Pierre Bourdieu on Art, Literature and Culture." In *The Field of Cultural Production: Essays on Art and Literature*, by Pierre Bourdieu, edited by Randal Johnson, 1–25. New York: Columbia University Press, 1993.

Jones, Howard. *The Epicurean Tradition*. London and New York: Routledge, 1989.

Jones, Joel. "Howells's *The Leatherwood God*: The Model in Method For the American Historical Novel." *Explicator* 51, no. 2 (Winter 1993): 96–103.

Jordan, Paul. *Neanderthal: Neanderthal Man and the Story of Human Origins*. Stroud, Gloustershire: Sutton Publishing, 1999.

Judgment Day: Intelligent Design on Trial. Produced by Joseph McMaster, Gary Johnstone, and Vanessa Tovell. Directed by Gary Johnstone and Joseph McMaster. Written by Joseph McMaster. Corporation for Public Broadcasting, 2007. DVD.

Kaufmann, Michael W. "Locating the Postsecular." *Religion and Literature* 41, no. 3 (Autumn 2009): 68–73.

———. "The Religious, the Secular, and Literary Studies: Rethinking the Secularization Narrative in Histories of the Profession." *New Literary History* 38, no. 4 (Autumn 2007): 607–27.

Kaye, Harvey J. *Thomas Paine and the Promise of America*. New York: Hill and Wang, 2005.

Kazin, Michael. *A Godly Hero: The Life of William Jennings Bryan*. New York: Alfred A. Knopf, 2006.

Kelner, L. *Alexander von Humboldt*, London: Oxford University Press, 1963.

Kitto, H. D. F. *The Greeks*. 1901. Reprint. Baltimore: Penguin, 1960.

Knight, Arthur. Review of *Elmer Gantry*. Based on the novel by Sinclair Lewis. *Saturday Review*, May 25, 1960. Reprinted in *Film Facts* 3, no. 27 (August 5, 1960): 159–60.

———. Review of *Inherit the Wind*. Based on the play by Jerome Lawrence and Robert E. Lee. *Saturday Review*, October 8, 1960. Reprinted in *Film Facts* 3, no. 41 (November 11, 1960): 250.

Knight, Grant C. *James Lane Allen and the Genteel Tradition*. Chapel Hill: University of North Carolina Press, 1935.

Krutch, Joseph Wood. "The Monkey Trial." *Commentary* (May 1967): 83–84.

———. "Mr. Babbitt's Spiritual Guide." *Nation* 124 (January–June 1927): 291–92.

Kuhn, Thomas S. *The Structure of Scientific Revolutions*. 2nd ed. Chicago: University of Chicago Press, 1970.

Kuklick, Bruce, ed. *Thomas Paine: Political Writings*. Cambridge, New York, Port Chester, Melbourne, Sydney: Cambridge University Press, 1989.

Kummer, George. Introduction to *The Leatherwood God (1869–70): A Source of William Dean Howells's Novel of the Same Name in Two Versions*, vii–xv. Gainesville, FL: Scholars' Facsimiles and Reprints, 1966.

Laing, S. *Human Origins*. London: Chapman and Hall, 1894.

Larson, Edward J. *Evolution: The Remarkable History of a Scientific Theory*. New York: Modern Library, 2004.

———. *Summer for the Gods: The Scopes Trial and America's Continuing Debate over Science and Religion*. Cambridge, MA, and London: Harvard University Press, 1997.

Lawrence, Jerome, and Robert E. Lee. *Inherit the Wind*. New York: Ballantine Books, 1955.

———. "*Inherit the Wind*: Genesis and Exodus." *Theatre Arts* (August 1957): 33, 94.

Le Blanc, Thomas J. "Scientific Books." Review of *Arrowsmith*, by Sinclair Lewis. *Science* 61 (June 19, 1925): 632–34.

LeConte, Joseph. *Evolution: Its Nature, Its Evidences, and Its Relation to Religious Thought*. 1888. 2nd ed. New York and London: D. Appleton, 1891.

———. "The General Relation of Theology to Science." In *Religion and Science: A Series of Sunday Lectures on the Relation of Natural and Revealed Religion*, 227–49. New York: 1874. Reprinted in *Darwinism and Theology in America: 1850–1930: Science and Religion*, vol. 3, edited by Frank X. Ryan, 110–22. Bristol: Theommes, 2002.

Leinwand, Gerald. *William Jennings Bryan: An Uncertain Trumpet.* Lanham, MD: Rowman and Littlefield, 2007.

Lemert, Charles C., and Garth Gillan. *Michel Foucault: Social Theory as Transgression.* New York: Columbian University Press, 1982.

Levine, Lawrence W. *Defender of the Faith: William Jennings Bryan: The Last Decade, 1915–1925.* New York: Oxford University Press, 1965.

Lewis, Sinclair. *Arrowsmith.* 1st ed. New York: Harcourt, Brace, 1925.

———. *Arrowsmith.* 1925. Reprint. New York: New American Library, 1998.

———. *Elmer Gantry.* 1927. Reprint. New York: New American Library, 1967.

———. *Elmer Gantry.* New York: Harcourt, Brace, 1927.

———. *From Main Street to Stockholm: Letters, 1919–1930.* Edited by Harrison Smith. New York: Harcourt, Brace, 1952.

———. *Main Street.* 1920. New York: Barnes and Noble, 2003.

Lingeman, Richard. *Sinclair Lewis: Rebel from Main Street.* New York: Random House, 2002.

Linton, Eliza Lynn. *The Autobiography of Christopher Kirkland.* 3 vols. 1885. Reprint. New York and London: Garland Publishing, 1976.

Lippmann, Walter. "Sinclair Lewis." In *Sinclair Lewis: A Collection of Critical Essays*, edited by Mark Schorer, 84–94. 1927. Reprint. Englewood Cliffs, NJ: Prentice-Hall, 1962.

"Literature." Review of *The Damnation of Theron Ware*, by Harold Frederic. *Critic* 25 (May 2, 1896): 309–10.

Livingstone, David N. *Darwin's Forgotten Defenders: The Encounter between Evangelical Theology and Evolutionary Thought.* Grand Rapids, MI: William B. Eerdmans, 1987.

Lovett, Robert Morss. "An Interpreter of American Life." Review of *Arrowsmith. Dial* 78 (June 1925): 515–18.

Lubbock, John. *Ants, Bees, and Wasps: A Record of Observations on the Habits of the Social Hymenoptera.* 17th ed. London: Kegan Paul, Trench, Trübner, 1906.

Lucas, John. Introduction to *The New Republic: Culture, Faith and Philosophy in an English Country House*, by W[illiam] H[urrell] Mallock, 7–34. 1878. Reprint. Leicester: Leicester University Press, 1975.

Luedtke, Luther S. "Harold Frederic's Satanic Soulsby: Interpretation and Sources." *Nineteenth Century Fiction* 30, no. 1 (June 1975): 82–104.

Lyell, Charles. *Principles of Geology.* Vol. 1. 1830. Chicago and London: University of Chicago Press, 1990.

Lyons, John O. "Hebraism, Hellenism, and Harold Frederic's *Theron Ware*." *Arnoldian* 6, no. 2 (Winter 1979): 7–15.

Mączyńska, Magdalena. "Toward a Postsecular Literary Criticism: Examining Ritual Gestures in Zadie Smith's *Autograph Man*." *Religion and Literature* 41, no. 3 (Autumn 2009), 73–82.

Maison, Margaret M. *The Victorian Vision: Studies in the Religious Novel.* New York: Sheed and Ward, 1961.

Mallock, W[illiam] H[urrell]. *The New Republic: Culture, Faith and Philosophy in an English Country House*. Introduction by John Lucas. 1878. Reprint. Leicester: Leicester University Press, 1975.

Marsden, George M. *Fundamentalism and American Culture*. 2nd ed. New York and Oxford: Oxford University Press, 2006.

Martin, Robert Francis. *Hero of the Heartland: Billy Sunday and the Transformation of American Society, 1862–1935*. Bloomington: Indiana University Press, 2002.

Maurice, Arthur Bartlett. "The History of Their Books: Sinclair Lewis" 69 *Bookman* (March 1929): 52–53.

———. "James Lane Allen's Country." *Bookman* 12 (October 1900): 154–62.

May, Henry F. *The Enlightenment in America*. New York: Oxford University Press, 1976.

Mayr, Ernst. *One Long Argument: Charles Darwin and the Genesis of Modern Evolutionary Thought*. Cambridge, MA: Harvard University Press, 1991.

McLoughlin, William G. Jr. *Billy Sunday Was His Real Name*. Chicago: University of Chicago Press, 1955.

———. *Modern Revivalism: Charles Grandison Finney to Billy Graham*. New York: Ronald Press, 1959.

Menand, Louis *The Metaphysical Club*. New York: Farrar, Straus and Giroux, 2001.

Mencken, H. L. "*Arrowsmith*." *American Mercury* 4 (April 1925): 507–9. Reprinted in *Twentieth Century Interpretations of Arrowsmith: A Collection of Critical Essays*, edited by Robert J. Griffin, 100–102. Englewood Cliffs, NJ: Prentice-Hall, 1968.

———. "At the Mercy of the Mob." Review of *Civilization*, by Clive Bell. New York, 1928. In *American Mercury* (January 1929): 123–24. Reprinted in *A Second Mencken Chrestomathy: Selected, Revised, and Annotated by the Author*, edited by Terry Teachout, 125–27. New York: Alfred A. Knopf, 1995.

———. "The Dean." From *A Mencken Chrestomathy*. New York: Knopf, 1947. In *Critical Essays on W. D. Howells, 1866–1920*, edited by Edwin H. Cady and Norma W. Cady, 259–62. Boston: G. K. Hall, 1983.

———. *Prejudices, Fifth Series*. 1926. New York: Octagon Books, 1977.

Menninga, Clarence. *If the Truth Be Known*. N. p.: Clarence Menninga, 2013.

Menton, David N. "*Inherit the Wind*: A Hollywood History of the Scopes Trial." *Contrast* 4, no. 1 (January–February 1985): 1–4.

Meyer, D. H. "The Uniqueness of the American Enlightenment." *American Quarterly* 28, no. 2 (Summer 1976): 165–86.

Miller, Arthur. *The Crucible: Text and Criticism*. Edited by Gerald Weales. 1952. New York: Penguin, 1996.

Miller, Kenneth R. *Only a Theory: Evolution and the Battle for America's Soul*. New York: Viking, 2008.

Miller, Steven P. *Billy Graham and the Rise of the Republican South*. Philadelphia: University of Pennsylvania Press, 2009.

Minnich, Harvey C. *William Holmes McGuffey and His Readers*. 1936. Reprint. Detroit: Gale Research Company, 1975.

"Miss Jewett's First Novel." Review of *A Country Doctor*, by Sarah Orne Jewett. *Literary World* (June 28, 1884): 13, 15.

Modern, John Lardas. *Secularism in Antebellum America*. Chicago and London: University of Chicago Press, 2011.

Mooney, Chris. *The Republican War on Science*. New York: Basic Books, 2005.

Moore, James R. *The Post-Darwinian Controversies: A Study of the Protestant Struggle to Come to Terms with Darwin in Great Britain and America, 1870–1900*. Cambridge, London, New York, and Melbourne: Cambridge University Press, 1971.

Moore, Randy. "Creation Evidence Museum." *Reports of the National Center for Science Education* 25, no. 5 (September–October 2009): 34–35.

Morgan, Ted. *Reds: McCarthyism in Twentieth-Century America*. New York: Random House, 2003.

Morris, Henry M. *History of Modern Creationism*. 2nd ed. Santee, CA: Institute for Creation Research, 1993.

Muir, Edwin. Review of *Elmer Gantry*, by Sinclair Lewis. *Nation and Athenaeum* 41 (April 23, 1927): 85.

Murphy, Brenda. *Congressional Theatre: Dramatizing McCarthyism on Stage, Film, and Television*. Cambridge: Cambridge University Press, 1999.

Myers, Robert M. *Reluctant Expatriate: The Life of Harold Frederic*. Westport, CT: Greenwood Press, 1995.

Nelson, Craig. *Thomas Paine: Enlightenment, Revolution, and the Birth of Modern Nations*. New York: Viking, 2006.

Nelson, Thomas H. "The Real Issue in Tennessee." *Moody Bible Institute Monthly*. Chicago, September 1925. Reprinted in *Monkey Trial: The State of Tennessee vs. John Thomas Scopes*, edited by Sheldon Norman Grebstein, 198–200. Boston: Houghton Mifflin, 1960.

"Notes." Review of *The Damnation of Theron Ware*, by Harold Frederic. *The Critic* 25 (April 2, 1896): 302.

Numbers, Ronald L. *Darwinism Comes to America*. Cambridge: Harvard University Press, 1998.

———. "Inherit the Wind." *Isis* 84, no. 4 (1993): 763–64.

O'Connor, Leo F. *The Protestant Sensibility in the American Novel: An Annotated Bibliography*. New York: Garland Publishing, 1992.

O'Donnell, Thomas F., and Hoyt C. Franchere. *Harold Frederic*. New York: Twayne, 1961.

O'Donnell, Thomas F., Stanton Garner, and Robert H. Woodward, ed. *A Bibliography By and About Harold Frederic*. Boston: G. K. Hall, 1975.

O'Reilly, Kenneth. *Hoover and the Un-Americans: The FBI, HUAC, and the Red Menace*. Philadelphia: Temple University Press, 1983.

Pagliucci, Massimo. *Denying Evolution: Creationism, Scientism, and the Nature of Science*. Sunderland, MA: Sinauer Associates, 2002.

Paine, Thomas. *The Age of Reason: Being an Investigation of True and of Fabulous Theology: Part First (1794)*. In *Thomas Paine, Political Writings*, edited by Bruce Kuklick, 209–57. Cambridge: Cambridge University Press, 1989.

———. *Common Sense (1776)*. In *Thomas Paine, Political Writings*, edited by Bruce Kuklick, 2–38. Cambridge: Cambridge University Press, 1989.

Paley, William. *Natural Theology: or, Evidences of the Existence and Attributes of the Deity, Collected from the Appearances of Nature*. Philadelphia, 1814.

———. *Natural Theology, with Illustrative Notes, &c.* 2 vols. [1802.] New York: Harper and Brothers, 1840.

Pattee, Fred Lewis. *A History of American Literature Since 1870*. New York: Century, 1915.

Payne, William Morton. "Recent Fiction." Review of *The Damnation of Theron Ware*, by Harold Frederic. *Dial* 20 (June 1, 1896): 336.

———. "Recent Fiction." Review of *The Reign of Law*, by James Lane Allen. *The Dial* 29, no. 337 (July 1, 1900): 21–22.

———. Review of *The Faith Doctor*, by Edward Eggleston. *Dial* 12 (December 1891): 278.

Peck, H[arry] T[hurton]. "*The Damnation of Theron Ware*." *Bookman* (New York) 3 (June 1896): 351–52.

Pecora, Vincent P. *Secularization and Cultural Criticism: Religion, Nation, and Modernity*. Chicago: University Press, 2006.

Peirce, Charles Sanders. *Pragmatism as a Principle and Method of Right Thinking, The 1903 Harvard Lectures on Pragmatism*. Edited by Patricia Ann Turrisi. Albany: State University of New York, 1997.

Pigliucci, Massimo. *Denying Evolution: Creationism, Scientism, and the Nature of Science*. Sunderland, MA: Sinauer, 2002.

Polk, Noel. *The Literary Manuscripts of Harold Frederic: A Catalogue*. New York and London: Garland, 1979.

"Pry." Review of *Elmer Gantry*. Based on the novel by Sinclair Lewis. *Variety*, May 29, 1960. In *Film Facts* 3, no. 27 (August 5, 1960): 161.

———. Review of *Inherit the Wind*. Based on the play by Jerome Lawrence and Robert E. Lee. *Variety* (July 6, 1960). Reprinted in *Film Facts* 3, no. 41 (November 11, 1960): 250.

Ragozin, Zénaide A. *The Story of Chaldea From the Earliest Times to the Rise of the Assyrians*. New York and London: G. P. Putnam's Sons, 1886.

Raleigh, John Henry. "*The Damnation of Theron Ware*." *American Literature* 30, no. 2 (May 1958): 210–27.

Randel, William Peirce. *Edward Eggleston*. New York: Twayne Publishers, 1963.

———. *Edward Eggleston*. New York: King's Crown Press, 1946.

Ranke, Leopold von. *The Ideal of Universal History*. In *The Varieties of History: From Voltaire to the Present*, introduced and edited by Fritz Stern, 54–62. New York: Random House, 1973.

Reade, Winwood. *The Outcast*. New York: Peter Eckler, [1875].

"Recent Novels." Review of *The Damnation of Theron Ware*, by Harold Frederic. *London Morning Post*, April 18, 1896, 4.

Redish, Martin H. *The Logic of Persecution: Free Expression and the McCarthy Era*. Stanford: Stanford University Press, 2005.

Renan, Ernest. *The Life of Jesus*. Translated from the French by Charles Edwin Wilbour. New York: Carleton, 1864.

———. *Recollections of My Youth*. Translated from the French by C. B. Pitman. 1876. Boston and New York: Houghton Mifflin, 1929.

Review of *A Country Doctor*, by Sarah Orne Jewett. *Atlantic Monthly* 54 (September 1884): 418–20.

Review of *The Damnation of Theron Ware*, by Harold Frederic. *London Daily News*, April 29, 1896, 8.

Review of *The Damnation of Theron Ware*, by Harold Frederic. *Manchester Guardian*, May 14, 1896, 10.

Review of *The Faith Doctor*, by Edward Eggleston. *Critic* 17 (January 2, 1892): 6–7.

Review of *The Faith Doctor*, by Edward Eggleston. *Literary World* 22 (October 24, 1891): 373.

Review of *Inherit the Wind*. Based on the play by Jerome Lawrence and Robert E. Lee. *Time*, October 17, 1960. Reprinted in *Film Facts* 3, no. 41 (November 11, 1960): 250–51.

Review of *The Leatherwood God*, by William Dean Howells. *Athenaeum* 4612 (December 1916): 596.

Review of *The Leatherwood God*, by William Dean Howells. *Catholic World* 104 (1916/17): 397.

Review of *The Leatherwood God*, by William Dean Howells. *New York Times Book Review*, April 30, 1916, 184, and October 29, 1916, 453, 460.

Review of *The Leatherwood God*, by William Dean Howells. *Times Literary Supplement*, November 16, 1916, 548.

Richardson, Lyon N. "*Arrowsmith*: Genesis, Development, Versions." *American Literature* 27, no. 2 (May 1955): 225–44.

Rosenberg, Alex. *The Philosophy of Science: A Contemporary Introduction*. 3rd ed. Oxford: Routledge, 2012.

Rosenberg, Charles E. "Martin Arrowsmith: The Scientist as Hero." *American Quarterly* 15 (1963): 447–58.

Rovelli, Carlo. *The First Scientist: Anaximander and his Legacy*. Yardley, PA: Westholme, 2007.

Rudwick, Martin J. S. *Georges Cuvier, Fossil Bones, and Geological Catastrophes*. Chicago and London: University of Chicago Press, 1997.

Ruse, Michael. *The Evolution-Creation Struggle*. Cambridge, MA, and London: Harvard University Press, 2005.

———. *The Evolution Wars: A Guide to the Debates*. Santa Barbara, CA: ABC-Clio, 2000.

Russett, Cynthia Eagle. *Darwin in America: The Intellectual Response, 1865–1912*. San Francisco: W. H. Freeman, 1976.

Sagan, Carl. *The Demon-Haunted World: Science as a Candle in the Dark*. New York: Random House, 1995.

Samuels, Ernest. *Henry Adams: The Middle Years*. Cambridge, MA: Belnap Press, 1958.

Samuelson, Richard. "The Politics of Scientific History." In *A Political Companion to Henry Adams*, edited by Natalie Fuehrer Taylor, 153–70. Lexington: University Press of Kentucky, 2010.

Sandeen, Ernest R. *The Origins of Fundamentalism: Toward a Historical Interpretation*. Philadelphia: Fortress Press, 1968.

Sarmiento, Estaban, G. J. Sawyer, and Richard Milner. *The Last Human: A Guide to Twenty-Two Species of Extinct Humans*. New Haven, CT: Yale University Press, 2007.

Sayce, A. H. *A Primer of Assyriology*. New York and Chicago: Fleming H. Revell, 1894.

Schorer, Mark. Afterword to *Arrowsmith*, by Sinclair Lewis, 431–38. New York: New American Library, 1961.

———. *Sinclair Lewis, An American Life*. New York, Toronto, and London: McGraw-Hill, 1961.

———. "Sinclair Lewis and the Method of Half-Truths." In *Sinclair Lewis: A Collection of Critical Essays*, edited by Mark Schorer, 46–61. Englewood Cliffs, NJ: Prentice-Hall, 1962.

Scopes, John T., and James Presley. *Center of the Storm: Memoirs of John T. Scopes*. New York, Chicago, and San Francisco: Holt, Rinehart and Winston, 1967.

Scott, Milton R. *Henry Elwood, a Theological Novel*. Newark, OH: Newark American, 1892.

Sherman, Stuart Pratt. "A Way Out: Sinclair Lewis Discovers a Hero." *The New York Herald Tribune: Books*, March 8, 1925, 1–2.

Shipley, Maynard. *The War on Modern Science: A Short History of the Fundamentalist Attacks on Evolution and Modernism*. New York and London: Alfred A. Knopf, 1927.

Simpson, J. Y. *Landmarks in the Struggle between Science and Religion*. 1925. Port Washington, NY, and London: Kennikat Press, 1971.

Smith, W[illiam] Robertson. *Answer to the Form of Libel Now Before the Free Church Presbytery of Aberdeen*. Edinburgh, 1878.

———. *The Old Testament in the Jewish Church: Twelve Lectures on Biblical Criticism*. Edinburgh, 1881.

Spiller, Robert E. *The Cycle of American Literature: An Essay in Historical Criticism*. New York: Macmillan, 1956.

———. Introduction to *Esther: A Novel*, by Henry Adams, iii–xxii. 1884. Reprint. New York: Scholars' Facsimiles and Reprints, 1938.

Springer, Haskell S. "The Leatherwood God: From Narrative to Novel." *Ohio History* 74 (1965): 191–202.

Starr, Paul. *The Social Transformation of American Medicine*. New York: Harper Collins, 1982.

Stephens, Randall J., and Karl W. Giberson. *The Anointed: Evangelical Truth in a Secular Age*. Cambridge, MA: Belnap Press, 2011.

Stevick, Philip. *The Theory of the Novel*. New York: Free Press, 1967.

Straton, John Roach. "'Elmer Gantry' Is Bunk, Vanity and Vulgarity." *New York Evening Post, Literary Review*, March 12, 1927, 1, 10.

Strauss, David Friedrich. *The Life of Jesus, Critically Examined*. 2 vols. Translated from the German by Marian Evans. 1835. 4th ed. New York, 1860.

Strodach, George K. *The Philosophy of Epicurus: Letters, Doctrines, and Parallel Passages from Lucretius*. Translated by George K. Strodach. Evanston, IL: Northwestern University Press, 1963.

Suderman, Elmer F. "*The Damnation of Theron Ware* as a Criticism of American Religious Thought." *Huntington Library Quarterly* 33, no. 1 (November 1969): 61–75.

Sweet, William Warren. *Revivalism in America: Its Origin, Growth and Decline*. Gloucester, MA: Peter Smith, 1965.

Taneyhill, Richard H. *The Leatherwood God (1869–70): A Source of William Dean Howells's Novel of the Same Name in Two Versions*. Gainesville, FL: Scholars' Facsimiles and Reprints, 1966.

Taylor, Charles. *A Secular Age*. Cambridge: Belnap Press, 2007.

———. "Western Secularity." In *Rethinking Secularism*, edited by Craig Calhoun, Mark Juergensmeyer, and Jonathan VanAntwerpen, 31–53. New York: Oxford University Press, 2011.

Thomas, George M. *Revivalism and Cultural Change: Christianity, Nation Building, and the Market in the Nineteenth-Century United States*. Chicago and London: University of Chicago Press, 1989.

Tricomi, Albert H. *Missionary Positions: Evangelicalism and Empire in American Fiction*. Gainesville: University Press of Florida, 2011.

———. *Reading Tudor-Stuart Texts Through Cultural Historicism*. Gainesville: University Press of Florida, 1996.

Tucker, Cynthia. "'Republicans' Rabid Right is Leading Party to Ruin." *Binghamton Press and Sun Bulletin*, February 5, 2013, 10A.

Tyler, Joseph Z. "The Historical Background of Allen's *Reign of Law*." *Modern Culture* 12 (December 1900): 352–54.

Vanderbeets, Richard. "The Ending of *The Damnation of Theron Ware*." *American Literature* 64, no. 3 (November 1964): 358–59.

Van Doren, Carl. "Sinclair Lewis and the Revolt from the Village." From *The American Novel, 1789–1939*. Rev. ed. New York: Macmillan, 1940. In *Twentieth Century Interpretations of Arrowsmith: A Collection of Critical Essays*, edited by Robert J. Griffin, 83–92. Englewood Cliffs, NJ: Prentice-Hall, 1968.

———. "Vicious Ignorance." *Saturday Review* 3 (March 12, 1927): 637, 640.

Van Till, Howard J. *The Fourth Day: What the Bible and the Heavens Are Telling Us about the Creation*. Grand Rapids, MI: William B. Eerdmans, 1986.

Verhave, Jan Peter. "*Arrowsmith*: The People Behind the Characters." *Sinclair Lewis Newsletter* 19, no. 2 (Spring 2011): 1, 9–17.

Veysey, Laurence R. *The Emergence of the American University*. Chicago and London: University of Chicago Press, 1970.

Wacker, Grant. "The Waning of the Missionary Impulse: The Case of Pearl S. Buck." In *The Foreign Missionary Enterprise at Home: Explorations in North American Cultural*

History, edited by Daniel H. Bays and Grant Wacker, 191–205. Tuscaloosa and London: University of Alabama Press, 2003.

Ward, Mary Augusta (Mrs. Humphry Ward). *Robert Elsmere.* Edited by Rosemary Ashton. Oxford and New York: Oxford University Press, 1987.

Wasser, Henry, "Science and Religion in Henry Adams's *Esther.*" *Markham Review* 2, no. 3 (May 1970): 4–6.

Watt, David Harrington. *A Transforming Faith: Explorations of Twentieth-Century American Evangelicalism.* New Brunswick, NJ: Rutgers University Press, 1991.

Waugh, Arthur. "London Letter." *The Critic* 25 (May 2, 1896): 316.

Webb, George E. *The Evolution Controversy in America.* Lexington: University Press of Kentucky, 1994.

Weber, Timothy P. "Premillennialism and the Branches of Evangelicalism." In *The Variety of American Evangelicalism,* edited by Donald W. Dayton and Robert K. Johnston, 5–21. Knoxville: University of Tennessee Press, 1991.

Weiler, A. H. Review of *Elmer Gantry.* Based on the novel by Sinclair Lewis. *New York Times,* July 8, 1960. In *The New York Times Guide to the Best 1,000 Movies Ever Made: Vincent Canby, Janet Maslin, and the Film Critics of the New York Times,* edited by Peter M. Nichols, 257–58. New York: Times Books, 1999.

Weiner, Jonathan. *Time, Love, and Memory: A Great Biologist and His Quest for the Origins of Behavior.* New York: Alfred A. Knopf, 1999.

Weinstein, Allen, and David Rubel. *The Story of America: Freedom and Crisis from Settlement to Superpower.* New York: Agincourt, 2002.

West, Rebecca. "Sinclair Lewis Introduces Elmer Gantry." From *The Strange Necessity,* 1927. In *Sinclair Lewis: A Collection of Critical Essays,* edited by Mark Schorer, 39–45. Englewood Cliffs, NJ: Prentice-Hall, 1962.

White, Andrew D. *A History of the Warfare of Science with Theology in Christendom.* 2 vols. 1896. Reprint. Buffalo: Prometheus Books, 1993.

Wilcox, Clyde. *God's Warriors: The Christian Right in Twentieth-Century America.* Baltimore and London: Johns Hopkins University Press, 1992.

Willey, Basil. "How *Robert Elsmere* Struck Some Contemporaries." *Essays and Studies* 10 (1957): 53–68.

Williams, Raymond *Marxism and Literature.* New York: Oxford University Press, 1977.

———. *Problems in Materialism and Culture: Selected Essays.* London: Verso, 1980.

Wills, Garry. *Under God: Religion and American Politics.* New York: Simon and Schuster, 1990.

Wilson, Edmund. *The Devils and Canon Barham: Ten Essays on Poets, Novelists and Monsters.* New York: Farrar, Straus and Giroux, 1973.

Wilson, Jerome D., and William F. Ricketson. *Thomas Paine: Updated Edition.* Boston: Twayne, 1989.

Wolff, Robert Lee. *Gains and Losses: Novels of Faith and Doubt in Victorian England.* New York and London: Garland, 1977.

Woodward, Robert H. "Some Sources for Harold Frederic's *The Damnation of Theron Ware*." *American Literature* 33, no. 1 (March 1961): 46–51.

Woodward, W. E. "'Elmer Gantry' Is Truth as a Study in Hypocrisy." *New York Evening Post, Literary Review*, March 12, 1927, 1, 10.

The World's Most Famous Court Trial: Tennessee Court Case. 3rd ed. Cincinnati: National Book Company, 1925. Rpt. as *The Scopes Trial*. Birmingham, AL: Notable Trials Library, Division of Gryphon Editions, c. 1990.

Worthen, Molly. *Apostles of Reason: The Crisis of Authority in American Evangelicalism*. New York: Oxford University Press, 2014.

Wright, Lawrence. *Saints and Sinners: Walker Railey, Jimmy Swaggart, Madalyn Murray O'Hair, Anton LaVey, Will Campbell, Matthew Fox*. New York: Alfred A. Knopf, 1993.

Wyatt, Euphemia Van Rensselaer. "Inherit the Wind." *Catholic World* 181 (1955): 225–26.

Young, David. *The Discovery of Evolution*. 2nd ed. Cambridge and New York: Cambridge University Press, 2007.

Zamora, Lois Parkinson. *The Usable Past: The Imagination of History in Recent Fiction of the Americas*. Cambridge: Cambridge University Press, 1997.

Zimmer, Carl. *Evolution: The Triumph of an Idea*. New York: Harper Collins, 2001.

Zinn, Howard. *A People's History of the United States, 1492–Present*. Revised, updated edition. New York: Harper Collins, 1995.

INDEX

Abbott, Lyman, 86
absolutism, in Allen's *Reign of Law*, 76–79
Adams, Henry: acclaim of, 25; *The Education of Henry Adams*, 47–48; *Esther*, 6, 47–52; limitations of, 48n31; *Mont-Saint-Michel and Chartres*, 47–48; on unproven assumptions of science, 50
aestheticism in Frederic's *Damnation of Theron Ware*, 54–55
Agassiz, Louis, 16
The Age of Reason (Paine), 97–98, 105
Agnostic (Eggleston), 37
Allen, James Lane: *The Choir Invisible*, 72; *A Kentucky Cardinal*, 72; "Realism and Romance," 82n17. See also *The Reign of Law*
American Scientific Affiliation, 2–3
Anderson, Maxwell, 161–62
Appleby, R. Scott, 78, 150, 184
Archaeopteryx, 189
Arrowsmith (Lewis): binary oppositions and, 6; comparisons to, 135, 140; critical observations and reception, 128–34; de Kruif and, 7, 117, 118, 126–27; Dr. Pickerbaugh as public health official, 120–22; film version of, 132; Gottlieb and science as religion in, 117–19, 123–25; interpretive issues, 116–17; objectives of, 115–16; Pulitzer prize, Lewis's rejection of, 130–31; resistance to Arrowsmith, 119–22; scientific and historical accuracy in, 7, 125–28; the scientist's prayer, 123; stature of, 25; synopsis, 116
Asad, Talal, 5, 96n13, 106
atheism: in *Arrowsmith*, 119; in *Damnation of Theron Ware*, 54, 63, 64; in *Darwin Conspiracy*, 188; Darwinism and, 16–17, 24, 86, 188; Dawkins and, 195; in *Elmer Gantry*, 25, 137–38, 143, 145, 149–50, 152; in *Esther*, 51; Furniss on Fundamentalists and, 171; Ingersoll and, 23, 86, 143; in *Inherit the Wind*, 163; Lewis and, 131; McCarthyism and, 173; in *Reign of Law*, 88–89; "secularist" as alternative term, 96n13
The Autobiography of Christopher Kirkland (Linton), 18–19

Babbitt (Lewis), 148
Bacon, Francis, 12
Bakker, Jim, 154
Baptists, 76, 141n14. See also *Elmer Gantry*
Barzan, Jacques, 160–61

"battle for the soul" of America, 192–93
Bayly, Ada Ellen, 21n68
Beecher, Henry Ward, 14
Behe, Michael, 186
belief-knowledge binary, 1–3
Bell, James Scott, 24, 181–82, 187–91
Benzer, Seymour, 133–34
The Bertram Family (Charles), 20
Bible: "Bible-based belief," 3; comparative-historical criticism, 52; higher (new) criticism, 19–20, 60–61, 137; literalism, 3, 137–38, 159, 167–69, 184, 185, 194–95
binary oppositions: American novels and, 6–7; *A Country Doctor* and, 32, 36; *Damnation of Theron Ware* and, 64; *Esther* and, 47, 50; *Faith Doctor* and, 37, 39; *Henry Elwood* and, 43, 46–47; *Inherit the Wind* and, 163, 176; knowledge-belief, 1–3; national conversation beyond, 196; *Reign of Law* and, 88; science-religion, 4–5, 32, 194–95; secular-religious, 5, 88, 154
Birkhead, L. M., 144, 146–47
Blair, Emily, 144
Bottorff, William, 85–87
Bourdieu, Pierre, 9n15, 9n17, 156
Branch, Lori, 5, 78n13, 143, 150
Brannigan, John, 94
Briggs, Austin, Jr., 68n40
Brooks, Richard, 151–53
Bruno, Giordano, 80, 190
Bryan, William Jennings, 141, 157, 159–60, 166–70, 172. See also *Inherit the Wind*
Buck, Pearl, 171
Buckle, T. H., 35, 35n9

Calhoun, Craig, 11n23, 182
Canby, Henry, 129
Caputo, John, 192
Carter, Everett, 64n31
Carus, Paul, 86
Casanova, José, 11, 121
Catholicism: authoritarianism and, 13, 131, 191; Bible interpretation in, 194; in *Damnation of Theron Ware*, 54, 61, 67, 70; *Elmer Gantry* film and, 151–52;
Irish American, 61, 70; *Leatherwood God* and, 110; Protestantism and, 61, 70, 191; Renan and, 63n29
Chambers, Robert, 18–19
Charles, Elizabeth, 20
The Choir Invisible (Allen), 72
Christian Science, 37–42, 68
Church of England, 22
Church of Jesus Christ of the Latter Day Saints (Mormonism), 109
Civil War, 73, 84
Cochrane, Jacob, 110
Coe, George A., 140
Common Sense (Paine), 96–97
"common sense," 58, 94, 96–98
comparative-historical criticism, 52
Compton, Francis Snow. See Adams, Henry
consilience, 15
conversion novels, English, 20n68
A Country Doctor (Jewett), 32–36, 115
Crane, Stephen, 55
creation science, 3, 181, 184–86, 194
creation science museums, 185
Crowther, Bosley, 158
The Crucible (Miller), 164, 172
cultural capital, 9, 156
cultural historicism, 8–11
Cuvier, Georges, 11, 79–80, 79n14, 80n15

The Damnation of Theron Ware (Frederic): Brother Pierce and Methodist Episcopal Church in, 57–59; Celia and aestheticism, 54–55, 66–68; comparisons to, 80, 93, 119; conclusion of, 69–71; Dr. Ledsmar, Darwinism, and diabolical symbolism, 54, 62–66; Father Forbes and new biblical criticism, 54, 59–62; Frederic's notes on, 54n2; ironic method in, 55, 61–62; as "problem novel," 62; reception of, 25, 56–57; *Robert Elsmere* and, 23, 53; on secularizing modernity, 24; Sister Soulsby and philosophical pragmatism, 54, 68–69; typological representation in, 53–55
Darrow, Clarence, 131, 136, 157, 162, 164, 168. See also *Inherit the Wind*

INDEX

Darwin, Charles: burial in Westminster Abbey, 22; expansion of scientific methods by, 15–16; *Henry Elwood* and, 45; *Origin of Species*, 15–16, 20, 160–61, 177; *Reign of Law* and, 79; science-religion binary and, 14

The Darwin Conspiracy (Bell), 24, 181–82, 187–91

Darwinian evolution: *Damnation of Theron Ware* and, 63–65; defined, 17; fundamentalists after the Scopes trial and, 173; Scopes "monkey" trial, 89, 136, 137, 155, 156–57; Wilberforce-Huxley debate, 58–59, 157

Darwinism: atheistic reputation of, 86; change of scientific paradigm through, 15–16, 66; defined, 17; denunciations of, 16–17; as faith or rival religion, 189–90; intellectuals and loss of belief through, 85; intelligent design and, 187–88, 190–91; social, 73–74, 83–85, 190. *See also* specific works

Darwinism in the English Novel (Henkin), 17

Darwinism on Trial (Johnson), 190–91

Davenport, Frederick, 106, 140

Dawkins, Richard, 195

deism, 93, 97n19

de Kruif, Paul, 7, 117, 118, 126–27, 132

demonization and diabolical symbolism, 64–66, 102, 119, 162–64, 187

Descartes, René, 49

Disraeli, Benjamin, 18

A Doll's House (Ibsen), 47

Donaldson, Scott, 69

Donoghue, Denis, 48n31

Donovan: A Novel (Bayly), 21n68

Dooley, D. J., 118n6, 125, 128

Dowie, Alexander, 110

Draper, John, 191

Drees, William B., 196–97

Dreisbach, Daniel L., 103n33

Eddy, Mary Baker, 39, 68, 110

education, fundamentalist, in *Elmer Gantry*, 137–42

The Education of Henry Adams (Adams), 47–48

Edwards v. Aguillard, 184

Eggleston, Edward: acclaim of, 25; *Agnostic*, 37; career of, 36–37; *The Faith Doctor*, 6, 36–42, 115, 148

Eliot, George, 13

Elmer Gantry (film), 150–54

Elmer Gantry (Lewis): Brooks screenplay of, 150–54; circumstances around publication of, 146; comparisons to, 93, 135, 140, 148, 165; Elmer as type, 101, 142–47; film version of, 25–26; Frank Shallard as liberal preacher, 149–50; on fundamentalist education, 137–42; ideology, charge of, 4; nonconformist characters, 25; reception and debate over, 136; Sharon Falconer as evangelist, 147–48

empiricism: battle for America's soul and, 193; Darwin's expansion beyond, 15; *Elmer Gantry* and, 138; *Faith Doctor* and, 38, 39; *Leatherwood God* and, 93, 94, 97–100, 100n28; Paine and, 93, 97–98; William James and, 99

English Victorian novels, 17–22

Enlightenment, 5, 13–14, 93, 96–100

Epicurus, 61

Episcopalianism, 44, 48, 52, 76, 84

epistemes: Adams's *Education* and, 48; *Arrowsmith* and, 121–22; *Esther* and, 31–32; in *Faith Doctor*, 41–42; Foucault on, 32n1, 48; *Henry Elwood* and, 48; intelligent design and, 193; Kuhn's paradigms and, 32n1

Esther (Adams), 6, 47–52

evolution, Darwinian. *See* Darwinian evolution

faith and religious knowing, 2–3

The Faith Doctor (Eggleston), 6, 36–42, 115, 148

Fangerau, Heiner, 127–28

Fenton, Elizabeth, 191, 192

Finney, Charles, 101

Fiske, John, 86

Fosdick, Harry Emerson, 149, 171

Foucault, Michel: on epistemes, 31, 32n1, 48; on ideology, 4; *The Order of Things*, 32n1, 41nn19–20, 48; *Power/Knowledge*, 4, 32n1, 41n19
founding fathers, religion of, 102–3
Frazer, James, 140
Frederic, Harold, 53–54. See also *The Damnation of Theron Ware*
Froude, James, 19–20
fundamentalism: in 1920s and 1950s contexts, 171–74; alienation and, 192–95; Appleby on, 78; Bible Colleges in *Elmer Gantry*, 137–42; counterculture and counterdiscourse, 184; creation science and intelligent design, 184–86; emergence of, 3, 191–92; "fundamentalisms," 78n13, 150, 164; *The Fundamentals* pamphlets, 14, 16; *Inherit the Wind* and, 165–70; in *Reign of Law*, 77–78; Scopes trial and, 89; Stephens and Giberson on, 58. See also *Elmer Gantry*; postsecularism and neo-fundamentalism
Furniss, Norman, 165

Gaines, Clarence, 129
Gains and Losses (Wolff), 17
Galileo Galilei, 80
Gay, Peter, 13
germ theory, 36
Giberson, Karl W., 16, 58, 163, 184, 195
Gilder, Richard Watson, 37
Gladstone, William, 21
Gould, Stephen Jay, 194–95
Graham, Billy, 153, 154, 173–74
Gray, Asa, 14, 23
Great Awakening and Second Great Awakening, 101
"Greek theology," 66–67
Greenblatt, Stephen, 9
Greene, John, 12n28
Gross, Forrest, 193
Guillory, John, 9n17
Guterman, Gad, 156n2

Habermas, Jürgen, 11n23
Hadden, Jeffrey K., 153

Hall, Mark David, 103n33
Harnack, Adolph, 140
Hawthorne, Nathaniel, 65, 83, 119
The Healer (Herrick), 115
hemp life cycle in Allen's *Reign of Law*, 74–75
Henkin, Leo, 17
Henry Adams (Samuels), 49n34
Henry Elwood (Scott), 23, 42–47
"heresy," 171
Herrick, Robert, 115
higher (new) biblical criticism, 19–20, 60–61, 137
historical novels, 95
History of Civilization (Buckle), 35n9
History of the Conflict between Religion and Science (Draper), 191
History of the Warfare of Science with Theology (White), 75, 140, 190, 191
Hobart, Alice, 171
Hofstadter, Richard, 160, 188
House Committee on Un-American Activities (HUAC), 164, 170, 172, 173
Howells, William Dean, 23, 55, 56–57, 99, 109. See also *The Leatherwood God*
Hughes, Rupert, 136
Humes, Edward, 192
Hungerford, Amy, 87, 90
Huxley, Thomas H., 21, 45, 58–59, 157

Ibsen, Henrik, 47, 62
ideology, 4, 93–94, 106
The Increasing Purpose (Allen). See *The Reign of Law*
Incredible Creatures That Defy Evolution (documentary), 186
Ingersoll, Robert, 23, 88, 137, 143, 148
Inherit the Wind (play, Lawrence and Lee; film, Kramer): about, 156–58; awards and adaptations, 26; binary oppositions and, 6; Brady as representation of Bryan, 166–70; Brown's preaching style, 165–66; comparisons to, 165; context of, 154–55; criticized as ahistorical, 158–62; cultural capital in, 156; Drummond and demonization

in, 162–64; Drummond/Darrow peroration on freedom of speech, 175–76; film as commentary on 1950s repression, 174–76; ideological similarities of 1920s and 1950s and, 170–74; McCarthyism and, 170–74; non-conformist characters, 25; as parable, proverbial wisdom, or prophecy, 170, 176–77; romance subplot, 164–65; science, level of, 7; title of, 170

intelligent design (ID), 3, 181, 184–86, 193

James, Henry, 99
James, William, 54, 99–100, 140
Jefferson, Thomas, 93
Jewett, Sara Orne: acclaim of, 25; *A Country Doctor*, 32–36, 115; father and, 33; transcendentalism of, 35n9
Jewett, Theodore Herman, 33
Johnson, George, 70
Johnson, Phillip, 190–91
Jones, Joel, 95
Jones, Sam, 101
Juergensmeyer, Mark, 182

A Kentucky Cardinal (Allen), 72
Knight, Grant C., 85n20, 90
knowledge-belief binary, 1–3
Kramer, Stanley, 157, 174
Krutch, Joseph Wood, 142, 144, 157, 160
Kuhn, Thomas, 32n1

Larson, Edward, 93, 158–61, 166, 173
law, scientific, 79–81
Lawrence, Jerome. See *Inherit the Wind*
The Leatherwood God (Howells): binary oppositions and, 6; Braile's empiricism in, 100n28; comparisons to, 93; conclusion of, 108–9; Dylks's ministry and miracles vs. skepticism, 100–105; Enlightenment rationality and, 11; non-conformist characters, 25; Paine's Enlightenment thought in, 11, 95–100; reception of, 92, 110–11; revivalism and, 101, 106, 108–9; secularizing orientation and Enlightenment approach in, 92–94; sociology and psychology of Dylks's followers, 105–7; stature of, 25; Taneyhill's *Leatherwood God* as source, 94–95

The Leatherwood God (Taneyhill), 94–95
LeConte, Joseph, 85–86
Lee, Robert E. See *Inherit the Wind*
Levengood, Paul, 164
Lewis, Sinclair: *Babbitt*, 148; *It Can't Happen Here*, 150; Pulitzer prize, rejection of, 130–31. See also *Arrowsmith*; *Elmer Gantry*
Life of Jesus (Renan), 45, 140
Life of Jesus, Critically Examined (Strauss), 13
Lincoln, Abraham, 97n19
Linnaeus, Carl, 94
Linton, Eliza Lynn, 18–19
Lippmann, Walter, 124, 144
literalism: in *Elmer Gantry*, 137–38; Gould and, 194–95; in *Inherit the Wind*, 159, 167–69; museums and, 185; postsecularism and, 184; truth claims and, 3
Livingston, David, 16, 196n38
Lovett, Robert Morss, 129
Lucretius, 61
Lyell, Charles: about, 79n14; in Linton's *Autobiography of Christopher Kirkland*, 18; *Principles of Geology*, 20, 77; in Reade's *Outcast*, 20; *Reign of Law* and, 77, 79–80; science-religion binary and, 14

MacPherson, Aimee Semple, 147
magnetic theory of energy, 40
Maison, Margaret, 21
Mallock, W. H., 20
Malthus, Thomas Robert, 15, 20
mania, religious. See *The Leatherwood God* (Howells)
McCarthy, Joseph, 154, 162, 164, 170–74
McGarvey, John W., 73, 88–89
McGuffey, William Holmes, 143
McPherson, Aimee Semple, 106
medical science: *Arrowsmith*, 115; *A Country Doctor*, 32–36; *Faith Doctor*, 36–42; germ theory, 36; *Henry Elwood*, 44–45; social transformation of, 34

Menand, Louis, 23
Mencken, H. L., 92, 131, 136, 141, 150
Menninga, Clarence, 196
Methodism, 23, 36–37, 53–60, 68, 76, 95, 101, 141n14
Methodist Episcopal (M. E.) Church, 57–59
Miller, Arthur, 164, 172
Miller, Kenneth, 192–93
miracles, 100–105, 129, 137
Modern, John Lardas, 52n43
A Modern Instance (Howells), 23
"monkey debate," 58–59
Mont-Saint-Michel and Chartres (Adams), 47–48
Moody Bible Institute, 147, 163
Moore, James, 196n38
Mormonism (Church of Jesus Christ of the Latter Day Saints), 109
Morris, Henry, 16, 169
Morrison, Jeffry H., 103n33
Muir, Edwin, 142
museums, 185

natural history and natural theology, 12–17
natural history museums, 185
naturalism, 13–14, 60, 197
natural laws, 82, 98
Natural Theology (Paley), 12, 43n22, 59
Nelson, Craig, 97n19
The Nemesis of Faith (Froude), 19–20
new (higher) biblical criticism, 19–20, 60–61, 137
new historicism, 8n14
The New Republic (Mallock), 20
nonoverlapping magisteria hypothesis, 194–95
novel as genre: cultural historicism and, 8–11; historical novels, 95; ideology and, 93–94; science fiction, 186
Numbers, Ronald J., 85n19, 158–61

O'Connor, Leo, 24
The Order of Things (Foucault), 32n1, 41nn19–20, 48

The Origin of Species (Darwin), 15–16, 20, 160–61, 177
The Outcast (Reade), 20

Paine, Thomas: *Age of Reason*, 97–98, 105; *Common Sense*, 96–97; French Enlightenment and, 93; *Leatherwood God* and, 11, 95–100, 103, 105
paleontology, 58
Paley, William, 12, 43, 43n22, 59
Pascal, Blaise, 51
Payne, William Morton, 56
Peck, Harry Thurston, 56
Peirce, Charles, 54
Peretti, Frank, 186–87
Perry, Thomas S., 109
philosophes, 93
Piltdown Man hoax, 189
postsecularism and neo-fundamentalism: absence of contemporary novels on religion- science binary, 183; alienation of fundamentalists and, 192–95; Catholicism and, 191, 192; creation science and intelligence design, 184–86; *The Darwin Conspiracy*, 181–82, 187–91; Peretti's *This Present Darkness*, 186–87; postsecular, as term, 182; science fiction subgenre and, 186; separationism and noncommunication vs. conversation and accommodation, 194–99
Power/Knowledge (Foucault), 4, 32n1, 41n19
pragmatism, philosophic, 54
prayer, scientist's (*Arrowsmith*), 123
Presbyterianism, 15, 23, 31, 42–47, 44, 57, 76, 141n14, 143, 171
A Primer on Assyriology (Sayce), 13–14, 52n41
Primitive Traits in Religious Revivals (Davenport), 106
Principles of Geology (Lyell), 20, 77
Protestantism: Birkhead on, 146; Bryan as "Defender of the Faith," 168; Catholicism and, 61, 70, 191; denominations, conflict among, 76, 78–79, 109; German new criticism and, 19; heresy and, 171; individual freedom

of interpretation in, 149; rifts within, 14–15; "true," 14. *See also* fundamentalism; specific denominations

Ranke, Leopold von, 160
rationalism, German, 19, 23, 45
Reade, Winwood, 20
Recollections of my Youth (Renan), 62–63
The Reign of Law (Allen): absolutist pastor scene and dogmatism, 76–79; closing peroration, 87; comparisons to, 93; Darwinian/evolutionary worldview in, 11, 79–80, 86; doubt in, 82; evolutionary view of social change in, 73–74; Gabriella as archangel and parable of American social transformation, 83–85; hemp life cycle in, 74–75; ice storm and "law of the storm," 81–82; internalized clash in, 4; new law of life in, 79–80; reception of, 72–73, 85–90; reign of law, notion of, 75–76, 84–85; secular-religious binary and, 88; stature of, 25; transformation and expulsion of David, 80–81
Renan, Ernest, 45, 62–63, 140
research, scientific: in *Arrowsmith*, 115–17, 119, 123, 125–29, 133–34; biographical films on, 132–33; in *A Country Doctor*, 191; in *Damnation of Theron Ware*, 55, 63–66; in *Elmer Gantry*, 141
"Rethinking Fundamentalism in a Secular Age" (Appleby), 78
revivalism: Davenport on, 106; Graham (Billy), 153, 154, 173–74; history of, 101, 108; *Leatherwood God* and, 101, 106, 108–9; televangelism, 153–54. *See also Elmer Gantry*
Richardson, Lyon, 131–32
Richardson, Samuel, 42
Robert Elsmere (Ward), 21, 23, 42, 53
Roberts, Oral, 154
Rudwick, Martin J. S., 79n14
Russell, Bertrand, 141n15, 172n65

saints, scientific, 118–19
salvation: in *Arrowsmith*, 121, 125; in *Damnation of Theron Ware*, 59; in *Elmer Gantry*, 138; in *Leatherwood God*, 100, 102, 108; in *Reign of Law*, 83
Samuels, Ernest, 49n34, 50
Satan, 64–66, 102, 163–64, 187
Sayce, A. H., 13–14, 52n41
The Scarlet Letter (Hawthorne), 65, 83, 119
Schmidt, Nathaniel, 140
science: alliance between natural theology and natural science, 12–13; changing conceptions of, 11–17; Gould on compatibility of religion and, 194–95; ID movement as threat to, 193; "New Science," 79–81; science-faith binary, 64; science-religion binary, 4–5, 32. *See also* Darwinism; medical science; specific works
science fiction, 186
"scientific," 38
scientific knowledge, concept of, 1–2
Scopes, John, 157, 159, 163–64
Scopes "monkey" trial, 89, 136, 137, 155, 156–57. See also *Inherit the Wind*
Scott, Milton, 23, 42–47
secularism: *Arrowsmith* and, 124; atheist label and, 96n13; fundamentalist reactivity to, 78, 182n3; Henry Elwood and, 47; as ideology, 106, 124; *Inherit the Wind* and, 176; *Leatherwood God* and, 92–93, 106; modernist vs. communitarian education and, 140–41, 188; *Reign of Law* and, 78; secular-religious binary, 5, 88, 154. *See also* postsecularism and neo-fundamentalism
Shaw, George Bernard, 62
Shipley, Maynard, 141n16, 191–92
Shupe, Anson, 153
Simpson, James, 16
skepticism: *Arrowsmith* and, 118; Civil War and, 73; *A Country Doctor* and, 35; *Damnation of Theron Ware* and, 70–71; *Elmer Gantry* and, 140, 152; *Esther* and, 48; *Faith Doctor* and, 37, 38; Henry Elwood and, 46; *Inherit the Wind* and, 157, 170; *Leatherwood God* and, 25, 92–93, 96, 100–105; new biblical criticism and, 19; *Robert Elsmere* and, 21; science and, 13
Sloan, Hans, 94

Smith, Harold Jacob, 157
Smith, Joseph, 109
Smith, William Robertson, 14
social Darwinism, 73–74, 83–85, 190
Some Problems of Philosophy (James, William), 99–100
Spencer, Herbert, 45, 190
Spiller, Robert E., 50n36
spiritualism: in *Esther*, 6, 32, 52; in *Faith Doctor*, 40, 41; *Henry Elwood* and, 52; magnetic theory of energy and, 40
Starr, Paul, 34
Stephens, Randall J., 16, 58, 163, 184, 195
Stevick, Philip, 10
Straton, John Roach, 136
Strauss, Friedrich, 13
Sunday, Billy, 101, 106, 120, 148, 163
superstition: in *Autobiography of Christopher Kirkland* (Linton), 19; Catholicism and, 191; in *Elmer Gantry*, 137; in *Faith Doctor*, 37; in *Henry Elwood*, 46; in *Inherit the Wind*, 176; knowledge or science vs., 5, 13, 14; in *Leatherwood God*, 101–2, 109
Supreme Court, 184–85
symbolic capital, 9

Tancred (Disraeli), 18
Taneyhill, Richard H., 94–95
Taylor, Charles, 5, 59, 124–25, 128, 134, 143, 176
televangelism, 153–54
Terry, Edward, 61
theology, evolving concepts of, 11–17
The Theology of an Evolutionist (Abbott), 86
This Present Darkness (Peretti), 186–87
Torrey, Reuben, 101, 165
transcendentalism, 35n9

University of Kentucky Bible College, 72, 73, 75, 76, 88–89
usable pasts, 9

VanAntwerpen, Jonathan, 182
Van Doren, Carl, 142, 145
Van Till, Howard J., 196
Vestiges of the Natural History of Creation (Chambers), 18–19
Veysey, Laurence, 125
Victorian novels, 17–22
A View from the Bridge (Miller), 172
Voltaire, 13, 76–77

Ward, Mary Augusta, 21, 22, 23, 42, 53
War on Modern Science (Shipley), 141n16
The War on Modern Science (Shipley), 191–92
Wasser, Henry, 50n38
Waugh, Arthur, 56
The Web of Life (Herrick), 115
Weiler, A. H., 151
Weiner, Jonathan, 133
Wesley, Charles, 101
Wesley, John, 101
West, Rebecca, 142
White, Andrew D., 14, 75, 140, 190, 191
Whitefield, George, 101
Wilberforce, Samuel, 58–59, 157
Williams, Raymond, 94
Wilson, Edmund, 70
Winterset (Anderson), 161–62
Wise, Kurt, 195
Wolff, Robert, 17
Woodrow, James, 15
Woodward, W. E., 136, 145, 150–51
Wormwood, R. F., 110
Worthen, Mary, 195
Wright, George Frederick, 14

Yang and Yin (Hobart), 171
Young, Nedrick, 157

Zamora, Lois, 9
Zola, Emile, 93n4

www.ingramcontent.com/pod-product-compliance
Lightning Source LLC
Chambersburg PA
CBHW030135240426
43672CB00005B/140